A CHORUS OF WITNESSES

Dwayne Bagley

A Chorus of Witnesses

Model Sermons for Today's Preacher

Edited by

Thomas G. Long and Cornelius Plantinga, Jr.

WILLIAM B. EERDMANS PUBLISHING COMPANY
GRAND RAPIDS, MICHIGAN

Copyright © 1994 by Wm. B. Eerdmans Publishing Co.
255 Jefferson Ave. S.E., Grand Rapids, Michigan 49503

Printed in the United States of America

00 99 98 97 96 95 94   7 6 5 4 3 2 1

Library of Congress Cataloging-in-Publication Data

A Chorus of Witnesses: model sermons for today's preacher /
    edited by Thomas G. Long and Cornelius Plantinga, Jr.
        p.   cm.
    Includes bibliographical references.
    ISBN 0-8028-0132-3
    1. Sermons, English. I. Long, Thomas G., 1946- .
II. Plantinga, Cornelius, 1946- .
BV4241.C49 1994
252 — dc20   94-10494
                                              CIP

For all the gospel preachers everywhere. Especially, for all the gospel preachers who, drawing the short straw, were summoned to preach in our earshot in Michigan and Georgia in the seasons of our youth, and who, despite our adolescent smirks and our hard hearing, managed to get through our dullness with the grace of God.

Thomas G. Long   *Cornelius Plantinga, Jr.*

Contents

THE OCCASIONS OF THE SERMON   235

Editors' Preface

We have chosen, arranged, and introduced the sermons of this volume in the hope that people will ponder, inspect, disassemble, praise, criticize, and, generally, learn from them. (Some of these sermons pack enough of a spiritual wallop that they will also edify readers.)

Our hope rises from the conviction that just as aspiring composers study Haydn symphonies and Bartok string quartets, just as serious chess players learn the great games of Tarrasch and Capablanca, just as army generals master the battle plans of strategic and tactical experts from Alexander the Great to Douglas MacArthur, so students of preaching must study great sermons, learn their moves, and master some of their aims and forms. No seminary ought to launch new preachers who are still cheerfully ignorant of Buechner and the Buttricks and Barbara Brown Taylor and Gardner C. Taylor and other experts. The primary intended use of this volume is therefore to accompany homiletics texts in seminary preaching courses.

But we also have others in view. Shouldn't most established preachers spend a week a year tuning their ears and untethering their imaginations by reading and pondering some crackerjack sermons? And how about mere Christians who want to love God with their whole minds and hearts, and who are always looking for writers to help them do it?

This volume is for such folk and, accordingly, for us.

We want to thank Scott Black Johnston and David M. Rylaarsdam, who have assisted us at every stage of this project.

Introduction

A Chorus of Witnesses presents thirty-six sermons that display an array of excellences in form, style, and content. All but one (Schleiermacher's "Sermon at Nathanael's Grave") are by twentieth-century preachers, many of them our contemporaries. Some are by regular church ministers, some by theologians, some by chaplains, and several, not surprisingly, by homileticians. One is by an Oxford literature professor who became famous as a religious writer. The preachers of these sermons are Christian men and women, Europeans, South Africans, Americans, Canadians, and African-Americans. They are Lutheran, Reformed, Catholic, Methodist, Baptist, and Anglican Christians of particular religious ethos and habits of heart.

Accordingly, the sermons vary in lots of ways, including in their theological and hermeneutical commitments and in their attachment to texts. But each offers features of particular interest to preachers, aspiring preachers, and general Christian readers.

We have assembled the anthology to capture these features and have sectioned it to display them. In the four sections readers will find sermons that make artful use of their sources, that pursue classic aims, that exhibit particular homiletic forms and dynamics, and that fit special occasions.

We know that a number of the sermons in the anthology could just as well have appeared in some other section than the one we chose. For instance, though we have placed Barbara Brown Taylor's sermon in the "Sources" section to illustrate an intelligent following of a biblical trajectory, we might have used it as a section three ("Forms and Dynamics") sermon for its fine use of imagery and of a central waiting-in-line analogy. Similarly, John Claypool's "Life Is a Gift" appears in the "Aims" section, because it is a sermon that attempts to deliver pastoral care. But it is also a father's expression of grief, and it might therefore have appeared with the three funeral sermons (no apology for the piling up of riches here) under the heading of "Occasions."

So the sermons in the anthology may model virtues besides the ones we have chosen to highlight. They may also model vices we have chosen not to highlight. Readers are likely to judge that a given piece serves as a model in some respects and as an anti-model in others. For instance, readers may reject the theology of a sermon whose form they admire. Or they may approve a sermon's aim but not its means of achieving it. Or they may wince at the way a sermon handles its text but find their hearts strangely warmed by the sermon itself. Perhaps homiletic discernment, like general spiritual discernment, is a gift of the Spirit. In any case, serious study of widely varying sermons is likely to sharpen it — and this is so whether such discernment is sheerly given, or acquired by hard work, or, like so much else that is excellent and of good report, by some combination of these means.

Of course, a written sermon is not a preached sermon. Reading a sermon is an importantly different experience from hearing one, and both differ from actually seeing a preacher aim and fire. So, understandably, some written sermons do not do their authors full justice. Lewis Smedes's "The Power of Promises" shivers the bones in its taped version not only because of Smedes's Olympic level of thought and diction but also because of wonderful things he does with crescendos and accelerandos and sforzandos and shadings of timbre. Predictably, the written version preserves the former virtues but not the latter. That is the simple limitation of the genre.

On the other hand, as anyone knows who has heard a tape of Winston Churchill's great World War II speeches, it is quite possible to utter something of nearly final magnificence with a slightly slurred matter-of-factness. Some sermons are better to read than to hear because in the preaching of them their own authors manage to diminish or even to sabotage the sermon by a bland or foolish or otherwise distracting delivery.

Reading a fine sermon is like reading the score of some musical masterpiece. Whether reading a piece is better or worse than hearing it depends in part on the quality of the performance. In any case, reading allows you to stop the machinery so that you can inspect it.

A word on the biblical texts that appear at the heads of most sermons: we have not supplied or inferred any texts, but we have taken the liberty of printing out a number of texts (in RSV, except where otherwise noted) that sermon authors had merely cited. Naturally, we have republished texts that originally appeared in full quotation. Those, too, are all RSV unless otherwise noted.

THE SOURCES
OF THE SERMON

Every sermon at least extends and amplifies its source; many sermons do much more. They imaginatively embellish a text, for example, or explain it, or do the second by doing the first. They publicly ponder the text, turning it this way and that, questioning it, conversing with it. They may juxtapose one text with another, letting the two cross-fertilize each other. Some sermons completely reset a source's context. They change all the drapes and upholstery around a text in such a way that, like an old piano in a newly remodeled room, the text suddenly sounds different to us.

One of the sermons in this section seemingly ignores its biblical text until the sermon is nearly done. Then, late in the day, the text speaks with special poignance.

The sermons of this first section show various apt ways of approaching, developing, and presenting texts and genres of texts. Several of these sermons grow from their text so freshly and naturally that the ripe sermon looks both new and inevitable.

FREDERICK BUECHNER

The Magnificent Defeat

Of all the virtuosities in Frederick Buechner's sermons, one of the most impressive, and least imitable, is the mastery of imaginative narrative retelling. A biblical story under Buechner's care retains its own stalk and shape, but it also begins to bloom with strange and wonderful things we had never noticed before.

"The Magnificent Defeat" retells the story of Jacob and Isaac, and of Jacob and Esau, and of Jacob and God. The retelling is candid, angular, sometimes astonishing. A shifty Jacob one-ups his hairy brother and prospers from this move in discomfiting ways. That's the Bible for you, says Buechner, but that's also the world — a world that is so full of Jacobs and Esaus and Isaacs that it needs the appearance of a stranger, one whose face is "more terrible than the face of death."

The Magnificent Defeat

The same night he arose and took his two wives, his two maids, and his eleven children, and crossed the ford of the Jabbok. He took them and sent them across the stream, and likewise everything that he had. And Jacob was left alone; and a man wrestled with him until the breaking of the day. When the man saw that he did not prevail against Jacob, he touched the hollow of his thigh; and Jacob's thigh was put out of joint as he wrestled with him. Then he said, "Let me go, for the day is breaking." But Jacob said, "I will not let you go, unless you bless me." And he said to him, "What is your name?" And he said, "Jacob." Then he said, "Your name shall no more be called Jacob, but Israel, for you have striven with God and with men, and have prevailed." Then Jacob asked him, "Tell me, I pray, your name." But he said, "Why is it that you ask my name?" And there he blessed him. So Jacob called the name of the place Peniel, saying, "For I have seen God face to face, and yet my life is preserved." The sun rose upon him as he passed Penuel, limping because of his thigh.

Genesis 32:22-31

When a minister reads out of the Bible, I am sure that at least nine times out of ten the people who happen to be listening at all hear not what is really being read but only what they expect to hear read. And I think that what most people expect to hear read from the Bible is an edifying story, an uplifting thought, a moral lesson — something elevating, obvious, and boring. So that is exactly what very often they do hear. Only that is too bad, because if you really listen — and maybe you have to forget that it is the Bible being read and a minister who is reading it — there is no telling what you might hear.

The story of Jacob at the river Jabbok, for instance. This stranger leaping out of the night to do terrible battle for God knows what reason. Jacob crying out to know his name but getting no answer. Jacob crippled, defeated, but clinging on like a drowning man and choking out the words, "I will not let you go, unless you bless me." Then the stranger trying to break away before the sun rises. A ghost, a demon? The faith of Israel goes back some five thousand years to the time of Abraham, but there are elements in this story that were already old before Abraham was born, almost as old as man himself. It is an ancient, jagged-edged story, dangerous and crude as a stone knife. If it means anything, what does it mean? And let us not assume that it means anything very neat or very edifying. Maybe there is more terror in it or glory in it than edification. But in any event, the place where you have to start is Jacob: Jacob the son of Isaac, the beloved of Rachel and Leah, the despair of Esau, his brother. Jacob, the father of the twelve tribes of Israel. Who and what was he?

An old man sits alone in his tent. Outside, the day is coming to a close so that the light in the tent is poor, but that is of no concern to the old man because he is virtually blind, and all he can make out is a brightness where the curtain of the tent is open to the sky. He is looking that way now, his head trembling under the weight of his great age, his eyes cobwebbed around with many wrinkles, the ancient, sightless eyes. A fly buzzes through the still air, then lands somewhere.

For the old man there is no longer much difference between life and death, but for the sake of his family and his family's destiny there are things that he has to do before the last day comes, the loose ends of a whole long life to gather together and somehow tie up. And one of these in particular will not let him sleep until he has done it: to call his eldest son to him and give him his blessing. But not a blessing in our sense of the word — a pious formality, a vague expression of goodwill that we might use when someone is going on a journey and we say, "God bless you." For the old man, a blessing is the speaking of a word of great power; it is the conveying of something of the very energy and vitality of his soul to the one he blesses; and this final blessing of his firstborn son is to be the most powerful of all, so much so that once it is given it can never be taken back. And here even for us something of this remains true: we also know that words spoken in deep love or deep hate set things in motion within the human heart that can never be reversed.

So the old man is waiting now for his eldest son, Esau, to appear, and after a while he hears someone enter and say, "My father." But in the dark one voice sounds much like another, and the old man, who lives now only in the dark, asks, "Who are you, my son?" The boy lies and says that he is Esau. He says it boldly, and disguised as he is in Esau's clothes, and imitating Esau's voice — the flat, blunt tones of his brother — one can imagine that he is almost convinced himself that what he says is true. But the silence that follows his words is too silent, or a shadow falls between them — something — and the old man reaches forward as if to touch the face he cannot see and asks again, "Are you really my son, Esau?" The boy lies a second time, only perhaps not boldly now, perhaps in a whisper, perhaps not even bothering to disguise his voice in the half hope that his father will see through the deception. It is hard to know what the blind see and what they do not see; and maybe it was hard for the old man to distinguish clearly between what he believed and what he wanted to believe. But anyway, in the silence of his black goatskin tent, the old man stretches out both of his arms and says, "Come near and kiss me, my son." So the boy comes near and kisses him, and the old man smells the smell of his garments and gives him the blessing, saying, "See, the smell of my son is the smell of a field which the Lord has blessed." The boy who thus by the most calculating stealth stole the blessing was of course Jacob, whose very name in Hebrew may mean "he who supplants," or, more colloquially translated, "the go-getter."

It is not, I am afraid, a very edifying story. And if you consider the aftermath, it becomes a great deal less edifying still. What I mean is that if Jacob, as the result of duping his blind old father, had fallen on evil times, if he had been ostracized by his family and friends and sent off into the wilderness somewhere to suffer the pangs of a guilty conscience and to repent his evil ways, then of course the moralists would have a comparatively easy time of it. As a man sows, so shall he reap. Honesty is the best policy. But this is just not the way that things fell out at all.

On the contrary. Once his dishonesty is exposed and the truth emerges, there is really surprisingly little fuss. Old Isaac seemed to take the news so much in his stride that you almost wonder if perhaps in some intuitive way he did not know that it had been Jacob all along and blessed him anyway, believing in his heart that he would make the worthier successor. Rebecca, the mother, had favored the younger son from the start, so of course there were no hard words from her. In fact, only Esau behaved as you might have expected. He was furious at having been cheated, and he vowed to kill Jacob the first chance he got. But for all his raging, nobody apparently felt very sorry for him, because the truth of the matter is that Esau seems to have been pretty much of a fool.

One remembers the story of how, before being cheated out of the blessing, he sold his birthright for some bread and some lentil soup simply because Jacob had come to him at a time when he was ravenously hungry after a long day in the fields — his birthright looking pale and intangible beside the fragrant reality of a good meal. So, although everybody saw that Esau had been given a raw deal, there seems to have been the feeling that maybe it was no more than what he deserved, and that he probably would not have known what to do with a square deal anyway.

In other words, far from suffering for his dishonesty, Jacob clearly profited from it. Not only was the blessing his, not to mention the birthright, but nobody seems to have thought much the worse of him for it, and there are no signs in the narrative that his conscience troubled him in the least. The only price he had to pay was to go away for a while until Esau's anger cooled down; and although one can imagine that this was not easy for him, he was more than compensated for his pains by the extraordinary thing that happened to him on his way.

For anyone who is still trying to find an easy moral here, this is the place to despair: because in the very process of trying to escape the wrath of the brother he had cheated, this betrayer of his father camped for the night in the hill country to the north, lay down with a stone for his pillow, and then dreamed, not the nightmare of the guilty, but a dream that nearly brings tears to the eyes with its beauty. The wonderful unexpectedness of it — of life itself, of God himself. He dreamed of a great ladder set up on the earth with the top of it reaching into heaven and the angels ascending and descending upon it; and there above it in the blazing starlight stood the Lord God himself, speaking to Jacob words of great benediction and great comfort: "The land on which you lie I will give to your descendants, and your descendants will be like the dust of the earth, and behold, I am with you and will keep you wherever you go."

Do not misunderstand me about moralists. The ecclesiastical body to which I am answerable as a minister would, I am sure, take a rather dim view of it if I were to say, "Down with moralists!" But as a matter of fact that is neither what I want to say nor what I feel. Moralists have their point; and in the long run, and very profoundly too, honesty *is* the best policy. But the thing to remember is that one cannot say that until one has said something else first. And that something else is that, practically speaking, dishonesty is not a bad policy either.

I do not mean extreme dishonesty — larceny, blackmail, perjury, and so on — because practically speaking that is a bad policy, if only on the grounds that either it lands the individual in jail or keeps him so busy trying to stay out of jail that he hardly has time to enjoy his ill-gotten gains once he has gotten them. I mean Jacob's kind of dishonesty, which is also apt to be your kind and mine. This is a policy that can take a man a long way in this world, and we are fools either to forget it or to pretend that it is not so.

This is not a very noble truth about life, but I think that it is a truth nonetheless, and as such it has to be faced, just as in their relentless wisdom the recorders of this ancient cycle of stories faced it. It can be stated quite simply: the shrewd and ambitious man who is strong on guts and weak on conscience, who knows very well what he wants and directs all his energies toward getting it, the Jacobs of this world, all in all do pretty well. Again, I do not mean the criminal who is willing to break the law to get what he wants or even to take somebody's life if that becomes necessary. I mean the man who stays within the law and would never seriously consider taking other people's lives, but who from time to time might simply manipulate them a little for his own purposes or maybe just remain indifferent to them. There is no law against taking advantage of somebody else's stupidity, for instance. The world is full of Esaus, of suckers, and there is no need to worry about giving a sucker an even break because the chances are that he will never know what hit him anyway. In fact, a sucker is by definition the man who never knows what hit him and thus keeps on getting hit — if not us, by somebody else, so why not by us?

And the world is full of Isaacs, of people who cannot help loving us no matter what we do, and whose love we are free to use pretty much as we please, knowing perfectly well that they will go on loving us anyway — and without really hurting them either, or at least not in a way that they mind, feeling the way they do. One is not doing anything wrong by all this, not in a way the world objects to, and if he plays it with any kind of sensitivity, a man is not going to be ostracized by anybody or even much criticized. On the contrary, he can remain by and large what the world calls a "good guy," and I do not use that term altogether ironically either. I mean "gooder" than many, good enough so that God in his infinite mercy can still touch that man's heart with blessed dreams.

Only what does it all get him? I know what you expect the preacher to say: that it gets him nothing. But even preachers must be honest. I think it can get him a good deal, this policy of dishonesty where necessary. It can get him the invitation or the promotion. It can get him the job. It can get him the pat on the back and the admiring wink that mean so much. And these, in large measure, are what we mean by happiness. Do not underestimate them.

Then it comes time for Jacob to go home again. He has lived long enough in the hill country to the north, long enough to marry and to get rich. He is a successful man and, as the world goes, a happy man. Old Isaac has long since died, and there is every reason to think that Esau is willing to let bygones be bygones. Good old Esau. Jacob wants to go home again, back to the land that God promised to Abraham, to Isaac, and now to him, as a gift. A gift.

God's gift. And now Jacob, who knows what he wants and what he can get and how to get it, goes back to get that gift. And I mean *get,* and you can be sure that Jacob means it too.

When he reaches the river Jabbok, which is all that stands between him and the promised land, he sends his family and his servants across ahead of him, but he remains behind to spend the night on the near shore alone. One wonders why. Maybe in order to savor to its fullest this moment of greatest achievement, this moment for which all his earlier moments have been preparing and from which only a river separates him now.

And then it happens. Out of the deep of the night a stranger leaps. He hurls himself at Jacob, and they fall to the ground, their bodies lashing through the darkness. It is terrible enough not to see the attacker's face, and his strength is more terrible still, the strength of more than a man. All the night through they struggle in silence, until just before morning, when it looks as though a miracle might happen. Jacob is winning. The stranger cries out to be set free before the sun rises. Then, suddenly, all is reversed.

He merely touches the hollow of Jacob's thigh, and in a moment Jacob is lying there crippled and helpless. The sense we have, which Jacob must have had, that the whole battle was from the beginning fated to end this way, that the stranger had simply held back until now, letting Jacob exert all his strength and almost win, so that when he was defeated he would know that he was truly defeated, so that he would know that not all the shrewdness, will, and brute force that he could muster were enough to get this. Jacob will not release his grip, only now it is a grip not of violence but of need, like the grip of a drowning man.

The darkness has faded just enough so that for the first time he can dimly see his opponent's face. And what he sees is something more terrible than the face of death — the face of love. It is vast and strong, half ruined with suffering and fierce with joy, the face a man flees down all the darkness of his days until at last he cries out, "I will not let you go, unless you bless me!" Not a blessing that he can have now by the strength of his cunning or the force of his will, but a blessing that he can have only as a gift.

Power, success, happiness, as the world knows them, are his

who will fight for them hard enough; but peace, love, joy are only from God. And God is the enemy whom Jacob fought there by the river, of course, and whom in one way or another we all of us fight — God, the beloved enemy. Our enemy because, before giving us everything, he demands of us everything; before giving us life, he demands our lives — our selves, our wills, our treasure.

Will we give them, you and I? I do not know. Only remember the last glimpse that we have of Jacob, limping home against the great conflagration of the dawn. Remember Jesus of Nazareth, staggering on broken feet out of the tomb toward the Resurrection, bearing on his body the proud insignia of the defeat that is victory, the magnificent defeat of the human soul at the hands of God.

BARBARA BROWN TAYLOR

Beginning at the End

Few enemies intimidate a preacher more than the familiarity that breeds numbness. People have heard the old, old story before. The good news is not news to them — and frankly, it no longer sounds as good as it used to, either. The interest that such folk bring to sermons is therefore mild.

Some preachers spy low expectations of this kind and endeavor to meet them. Others strive desperately for novelty. The wisest show a discipline born of confidence in the gospel itself: it will show its beauty and grace if only we have the intelligence to dress it in simple clothes of excellent quality.

"Beginning at the End" is an almost pure example of the disciplined and deceptively simple parable sermon. By apt use of image and analogy (notice the way breezes keep cooling people in this sermon), by sturdy and revealing diction, by a discerning portrait of the ways of God and of human beings, Barbara Brown Taylor quietly sharpens the point of the parable until she finally sticks us with it. Then she gives it the twist of grace so that it stays. Then she stops.

Beginning at the End

[Jesus said,] "For the kingdom of heaven is like a house-holder who went out early in the morning to hire laborers for his vineyard. After agreeing with the laborers for a denarius a day, he sent them into his vineyard. And going out about the third hour he saw others standing idle in the market place; and to them he said, 'You go into the vineyard too, and whatever is right I will give you.' So they went. Going out again about the sixth hour and the ninth hour, he did the same. And about the eleventh hour he went out and found others standing; and he said to them, 'Why do you stand here idle all day?' They said to him, 'Because no one has hired us.' He said to them, 'You go into the vineyard too.' And when evening came, the owner of the vineyard said to his steward, 'Call the laborers and pay them their wages, beginning with the last, up to the first.' And when those hired about the eleventh hour came, each of them received a denarius. Now when the first came, they thought they would receive more; but each of them also received a denarius. And on receiving it they grumbled at the householder, saying, 'These last worked only one hour, and you have made them equal to us who have borne the burden of the day and the scorching heat.' But he replied to one of them, 'Friend, I am doing you no wrong; did you not agree with me for a denarius? Take what belongs to you, and go; I choose to give to this last as I give to you. Am I not allowed to do what I choose with what belongs to me? Or do you begrudge my generosity?' So the last will be first, and the first last."

Matthew 20:1-16

The parable of the laborers in the vineyard is a little like cod liver oil: you know Jesus is right; you know it must be good for you; but that does not make it any easier to swallow. Along with the parable of the prodigal son, today's parable is one of those stories of forgiveness so radical that it offends, because it seems to reward those who have done the least while it sends those who have worked the hardest to the end of the line.

"So the last will be first, and the first last," Jesus says, scrambling the usual order of things, challenging the sacred assumption by which most of us live our lives — namely, that the front of the line is the place to be, that the way to win God's attention is to be the best person, the hardest worker, the first one into the vineyard in the morning and the last one to leave at night. Only according to today's reading, where that will get you is exactly nowhere. According to the parable of the laborers in the vineyard, those at the end of the line will not only be paid as much as those at the front; they will also be paid *first*. It is just not fair.

One thing that often helps me understand hard stories like this one is to see where they fit. At what point in his life does Jesus tell the story? Where is he and what is he doing? To whom is he talking? What has just happened and what happens next?

If you turn to the nineteenth chapter of Matthew, for instance, to the paragraph just before this parable, you find out that Peter has just asked Jesus what he and the other disciples can expect in the way of reward for their loyalty to Jesus. They have given up everything to follow him, Peter points out. What will he give them in return? Jesus promises them twelve thrones in the world to come. "But many that are first will be last," he says, "and the last first." Then he tells the parable of the laborers in the vineyard.

That is what happens *before* the story. What happens *after* it is that James's and John's mother comes up to Jesus and makes a special case for her two sons, asking Jesus to *give* them the best thrones in the kingdom, one on his left and one on his right. Politely but firmly, Jesus lets her know that she doesn't know what she is talking about, because his throne will not be made out of gold and jewels but out of wood and nails, in the shape of a cross.

It helps to know where the parable fits, that both before and after Jesus tells it his own disciples are jockeying for position, wanting good seats in the kingdom, competing for the best seats, each of them trying to be first in line when the doors are propped open and the show begins.

Have you ever done that? I remember waiting in line for the Saturday afternoon matinee at the local movie theatre when I was a little girl. It was summertime, and there were always lots of us there. Our parents would drop us off in the heat of the afternoon, giddy at the prospect of a couple hours' peace and quiet. We stood in the shade of the awning outside and waited for the box office to open, our dollar bills burning holes in our pockets as we debated the economics of popcorn versus junior mints or milk duds.

We were loud and boisterous, standing so close together that we could smell each other — that damp, healthy smell that children give off in the summertime. Our friends would arrive, and we would shout their names, motioning them over to claim the places we had saved for them. The children behind us would complain bitterly, and so would we when the same thing happened in front of us, but it was all part of the game.

Where every one of us wanted to be was right up there at the front of the line. That was the best place to be, not only because you were the first inside, but because you were there when the moment came, when the doors were unlocked and the timid-looking manager pushed them open, so that a great wave of cold air rolled out of the dark theatre and hit you like a blast from the arctic, an icy promise of everything that waited for you inside. That was the moment everyone waited for, and those who had won places at the front of the line got the very best of it.

I cannot imagine anything more disheartening than if the manager had come outside and reversed the order, telling those of us at the front of the line to stay put, while he invited those at the end of the line — those who had just arrived, those who were not even hot yet from standing in the sun — to enter the theatre first. I think I would have cried; I certainly would have booed, because it would not have been fair. Those of us at the front of the line had *earned* our reward; we knew it, and so did everyone else. On what grounds would anyone *dare* reverse the order?

According to today's story, the manager just feels like being generous. Those are his grounds. He can do whatever he wants to do in his own vineyard, and what he wants is to let the last be first and the first be last. Everyone will be paid; no one will go home empty-handed. He simply wants to reverse the order and pay everyone the same thing, regardless of how long they have stood in the sun.

Some of them have been there since dawn, mind you. Early that morning the householder went to the marketplace, to the corner where those without steady jobs hang out, and he hired a handful of them to work in his vineyard for the day. He offered them a denarius — a fair day's wage — and they agreed, but by nine in the morning it was clear that there was more work than they could do. So the householder went back to the corner again, and again at noon, and again at three in the afternoon, bringing more workers back with him each time, after promising to pay them whatever was right.

Finally, at five in the afternoon, with only one hour left before dark, he goes back to the corner and finds a few men still standing idle. Rounding them up, he takes them back to the vineyard, where they help the others finish up the day's work. Then comes the moment they have all been waiting for. The blazing sun goes down, a cool breeze stirs the dusk, and the householder calls his steward to give them all their pay.

Beginning with the last to be hired, he presses a denarius into each of their hands. When they gasp out loud, the others strain to see, and a murmur goes through the crowd. The householder has turned out to be a very generous man! If he pays the latecomers a whole denarius for just one hour's work, then those who arrived at dawn are about to be rich!

But before they can do the arithmetic in their heads, the steward has paid them all — one denarius, one denarius, one denarius — whether they came at dawn and slaved all day or showed up at five to work the last hour, their pay is the same, and the murmurs at the front of the line quickly turn to grumbling. "These last worked only one hour, and you have made them equal to us," say the first to be hired, their faces all sunburned and their clothes sweated through. "You have made them equal to us who have borne the burden of the day and the scorching heat."

That is when the householder reminds them that he has kept his part of the bargain, that he has paid them exactly what they agreed to be paid, and what business is it of theirs what he pays the others? The vineyard is his, the money is his. Isn't he allowed to do what he wants to with what belongs to him? "Or do you," he says, "begrudge my generosity?"

You bet they do. Like most human beings, they have an innate sense of what is fair and what is not. Equal pay for equal work is fair; equal pay for unequal work is not fair. Rewarding those who do the most work is fair; rewarding those who do the least is not fair. Treating everyone the same is fair; treating everyone the same when they are *not* the same is not fair.

Life is so often not fair. You have heard the stories: a state employee arrives at her desk early every morning, answering the telephone until her tardy co-workers appear. She skips lunch in order to catch up on the filing and stays late to fill out reports for her supervisor, who has learned that she is the only one in the department who knows what is going on. When annual raises are due, he calls her into his office and explains that, while she has done a superlative job, there will be no merit increases this year. Salaries will be increased across the board, with everyone receiving the same amount, because he thinks that will do more for group morale. It is not fair.

Or a man cares for his elderly mother, taking her into his own home when she becomes too frail to live by herself, and although he has three brothers and sisters, he rarely hears from them. They call from time to time to tell him how grateful they are, but none of them offers to help. "They have problems of their own," his mother tells him, patting his hand. "I just thank God for you." Then she dies, and suddenly the whole family appears, grieving as if they had been there all along. At the lawyer's office they are all ears. The man who has spent most of his savings caring for his mother sits and listens with his head in his hands as the will is read. "I leave my estate to be divided equally among my four dear children," it reads, "because I love them all the same." It is just not fair.

Life is not fair, which is why it seems all that much more important that God should be. God should be the *one* authority whom you can count on to reward people according to their efforts, who keeps track of how long you have worked and how hard you have worked and who does not let people break into line ahead of you. God should be the *one* manager who polices the line, walking up and down to make sure everyone stays where he or she belongs, so that the first remain first and the last wait their turns at the end of the line. Life may not be fair, but God should be.

But it is not so, according to today's story. According to today's story, God is the householder who puts the same amount of money into a stack of little white envelopes and instructs his steward to pass them out beginning at the *end* of the line, with those who arrived last and worked least. Moving from that end of the line toward the front, where those who arrived first and worked most are standing, the steward does what he is told, but depending on where he is in the line the response he gets is quite different.

At the end of the line, with the last and the least, there is a lot of cheering, a lot of laughter and backslapping, while nearer the front, with the first and the most, there is loud grumbling and great hostility, so that the steward hands over the envelopes faster and faster, ready to run for his life. In every case, the pay is the same — a fair day's wage — but how it is received depends entirely on what each man believes he *deserves*. Those who have gotten more than they think they deserve are jubilant, while those who have gotten less are furious. "Take what belongs to you, and go," the householder tells them. "Am I not allowed to do what I choose with what belongs to me?"

The most curious thing about this parable for me is where we locate ourselves in line. The story sounds quite different from the end of the line, after all, than it does from the front of the line; but isn't it interesting that ninety-nine percent of us hear it from front row seats? *We* are the ones who have gotten the short end of the stick; *we* are the ones who have been cheated. We are the ones who have gotten up early and worked hard and stayed late and all for what? So that some backward householder can come along and start at the wrong end of the line, treating us just like the ne'er-do-wells who don't even get dressed until noon!

That is how most of us hear the parable, but it is entirely possible that we are mistaken about where we are in line. Did you ever think about that? It is entirely possible that, as far as God is concerned, we are halfway around the block, that there are all sorts of people ahead of us in line, people who are far more deserving of God's love than we are, people who have more stars in their crowns than we will ever have.

They are at the front of the line, and we are near the end of it for all sorts of reasons. No one told us about it, for one thing. We did not know there *was* a line until late in the day. But even if we had, we might not have done much about it. We know all kinds of things we do not do much about. There are so many things we mean to do that we never get around to doing, and there are so many things we mean not to do that we end up doing anyway. Even when we manage to do our best, things get in the way: people get sick, businesses fail, relationships go down the drain. There are a lot of reasons why people wind up at the end of the line, and only God can sort them all out.

But suppose for a moment that it is *you* back there, craning your neck for even a glimpse of the theatre, knowing you will never make it, that all the tickets will be gone long before you get there, and that you are about to have one more long hot afternoon on your hands while everyone else is laughing and eating popcorn inside the cool, dark theatre. It makes you want to cry; it makes you want to give up, when all of a sudden a stir goes through the crowd. The manager appears out of nowhere and walks right up to you, a stack of blue tickets in his hand. "We're starting at this end today," he says, handing you your ticket, and everyone at the end of the line begins to cheer.

God is not fair. For reasons we may never know, God seems to love us indiscriminately, and seems also to enjoy reversing the systems we set up to explain why God should love some of us more than others of us. By starting at the end of our lines, with the last and the least, God lets us know that his ways are not our ways, and that if we want to see things his way we might question our own notions of what is fair, and why we get so upset when our lines do not work.

God is not fair, but depending on where you are in line that can sound like powerful good news, because if God is not fair then there is a chance that we will get paid more than we are worth, that we will get more than we deserve, that we will make it through the doors even though we are last in line — not because of who *we* are but because of who *God* is.

God is not fair; God is *generous,* and when we begrudge that generosity it is only because we have forgotten where we stand. On any given day of our lives, when the sun goes down and a cool breeze stirs the dusk, when the work is done and the steward heads toward the end of the line to hand out the pay, there is a very good chance that the cheers and backslapping, the laughter and gratitude with which he is greeted will turn out to be our own. Amen.

JÜRGEN MOLTMANN

The Pharisee and the Tax Collector

Theologian Karl Barth once remarked that he wanted the biblical text to govern, as much as possible, both the content and the form of his sermons. Jürgen Moltmann learned a good deal of theology from Barth, and, as this sermon shows, he appears to have heeded his teacher Barth on matters homiletic as well. Indeed, "The Pharisee and the Tax Collector" tracks the form and content of the Lukan parable like a stylus in a groove. Almost every sentence of the sermon has been drawn from some feature of the text. Even the structure of the sermon grows out of the narrative shape of the text, as is shown by the division of the sermon into "scenes" based upon the dramatic texture of the parable.

The Pharisee and the Tax Collector

Vindicate me, O LORD,
for I have walked in my integrity,
and I have trusted in the LORD without wavering.
Prove me, O LORD, and try me;
test my heart and my mind.
For thy steadfast love is before my eyes,
and I walk in faithfulness to thee.

I do not sit with false men,
nor do I consort with dissemblers;
I hate the company of evildoers,
and I will not sit with the wicked.

I wash my hands in innocence,
and go about thy altar, O LORD,
singing aloud a song of thanksgiving,
and telling all thy wondrous deeds.

O LORD, I love the habitation of thy house,
and the place where thy glory dwells.
Sweep me not away with sinners,
nor my life with bloodthirsty men,
men in whose hands are evil devices,
and whose right hands are full of bribes.

But as for me, I walk in my integrity;
redeem me, and be gracious to me.
My foot stands on level ground;
in the great congregation I will bless the LORD.

Psalm 26, "The Pharisee's Psalm"

"Two men went up into the temple to pray, one a
Pharisee and the other a tax collector. The Pharisee stood
and prayed thus with himself, 'God, I thank thee that I
am not like other men, extortioners, unjust, adulterers,
or even like this tax collector. I fast twice a week, I give
tithes of all that I get.' But the tax collector, standing far
off, would not even lift up his eyes to heaven, but beat
his breast, saying, 'God, be merciful to me a sinner!' I
tell you, this man went down to his house justified rather
than the other."

Luke 18:10-14

Luke reports that Jesus told this parable "to certain people who
trusted in themselves that they were righteous and despised others."
If we want to understand the parable and experience its healing
effect on ourselves, we must stop looking round elsewhere for these
"certain people who trusted in themselves." We — you and I —
are these people ourselves. The story tells that two people once
went to the temple, quite by chance at the same time. They did
not know each other personally, but they were well enough known
in Jerusalem as typical of certain groups. The one was a Pharisee,
the other a tax collector. The one was a good man, the other a real
crook. The one led a decent moral and religious life. The other
was mixed up in dirty business. The Pharisee belonged to the group
of people who were active in religious and social affairs. He knew
what the essential thing in life is: to do the will of God according
to the law. He knew what is important in human society: the
distinction between good and evil. The middle classes, honest
working people, and people who were trying to rise in the social
scale all followed this honorable and respectable discipline. Tax
collectors were more or less at the other end of Jerusalem society.
These men were collaborationists with the Roman occupying
power. To put it bluntly, they were traitors to their country. By
demanding higher taxes than were actually due, they made sure of
their own cut. To put it bluntly again, their business was corruption.

We have all come to church, to our temple, this morning. Most of us do not know one another personally, but the types we represent are of course well enough known in the town. In the parable the local coloring is taken from Jerusalem society. In this congregation the coloring belongs to the local newspaper. I imagine that few of us are as good, as noble, or as honorable as the Pharisee in the story. But I do not suppose that many of us are as repellent as the corrupt tax collector. Each of us is a mixture somewhere between the two, part Pharisee, part tax collector; sometimes a Pharisee, sometimes a tax collector. This is what we are known to be — known to other people and known to ourselves. But who are we really? Who knows our Pharisee's soul and who knows our tax collector's soul? Who is going to heal the conflict within us and among us?

Those two men, then, typical examples of Jerusalem society, went to the temple to pray. It is there, in the way they present themselves to God, that Jesus pins them down and pronounces judgment on them. *In prayer* the two men reveal themselves before God Almighty. Under the heaven of his law they present what they think is the truth about themselves — the one with the aim of being confirmed in his righteousness, the other so that he may at least find mercy for his sins. Both subject themselves to the same standard.

We, too, came to church this morning "to pray," if presenting oneself to God and uttering what weighs on one's mind is praying. We, too, are seeking assurance about ourselves and about other people before the God who is supposed to be our mainstay and provide us with a firm orientation. We, too, are hungering for recognition, for without recognition no one can live. We, too, are seeking mercy in the things about ourselves that neither we nor anyone else can describe as good. If we are willing, let us in the Spirit this morning put ourselves alongside those two kinds of people in the parable and see what we can discover from them about ourselves.

The Drama Begins: Scene One

The Pharisee appears on the stage. We will stop calling him "the Pharisee," because through long Christian tradition the Pharisee has become the villain, the bogeyman. He has also unfortunately become the figure of odium in which Christian anti-Judaism is crystallized: Jew Süss, Shylock, the Pharisees, the Jews — and God has rejected them. So we shall simply call the Pharisee "the good man."

Well, the good man takes the stage and strikes a pose. With face uncovered, head held high, and hands outspread, he utters his prayer of thanksgiving, the prayer of innocence itself. It sounds like the annual reports we are given to read at the end of the year. Or like an election speech. He presents himself, righteous and good as he is, and waits for the applause. The God whom he thanks is merely the heavenly echo of the human ego that displays itself here in all its glory. But what has the good man actually to offer?

What he offers is merely *a negative identity,* like so many political and ecclesiastical election candidates, with their vapid alternatives. "I thank thee that I am not" like the others — the wicked, the unjust, the adulterers, or that repulsive tax collector over there in the corner. But what he is, actually and positively, he is unable to say. Neither God nor man could draw any positive conclusions from these negative premises. It is surely a scanty identity that is acquired by being able to say who one is not. Who am I? Well, I am certainly not an exploiter, but I am not a "radical" either. Of course I am not a Marxist or Leninist — but needless to say I am not a police spy. Anyone who can only talk about himself like this has a totally aggressive identity. He has found no certainty in himself and is evidently suffering from lack of personality; so his anxiety builds up negative figures of this kind, with the aim of tracing a demarcation line between himself and other people. Anyone who can only thank God for all the things he is not can talk a long time without ever arriving at his real self. He beats about the bush. He slinks round himself, trying to mark off his own limits. What he has to thank God for is really nothing, nothing at all. Instead of being sorry for the unpleasant tax collector in the corner, he uses him, too, merely as a doormat, so that he can stand a little higher himself. He condemns "the others" in himself. He condemns "the others" in general, and the tax collector in particular, in order to set himself in the proper light.

How many people do this? How often do we do it? Why? Out of anxiety and inner insecurity. Really, the good man is lying. Who is most ready to judge and least prepared to save, like this man here? It is precisely the person who does not take the good seriously and who deceives God and himself. He condemns the wicked most severely and is incessantly prepared to condemn the godless. And the person he is really judging without realizing it is himself.

So with a negative personal identity one has not much to show for oneself — before God, oneself, or other people.

The good man only arrives at something positive when he diverts attention from his person and points to his "good works": he fasts twice a week and gives ten percent of his income for the poor. Is that not something? That is worth talking about! We could all take a leaf out of his book. Fasting twice a week and giving ten percent — that would level up conditions between the rich and poor nations in the world. Fasting twice a week and giving ten percent — that could be the new life-style for authentic Christian living. Fasting twice a week and giving ten percent — with that, deserts could be irrigated, slums cleared, and poor nations developed. Fasting twice a week and giving ten percent was the great theme of the Assembly of the World Council of Churches in Uppsala in 1968. Even though in the end the money was less than planned, there was still enough to build up Interchurch Aid, Overseas Aid, and Bread for the World. So what more is needed? Another few percent? Or is what is lacking something quite different? In 1975 a well-known European church leader came to the Assembly of the World Council of Churches in Nairobi armed with large donations of money. He invited the heads of the African churches to come and discuss how these gifts could best be distributed. They never appeared. Why not? They gave this as their reason: "We don't want your money. We want you yourselves. We certainly need help, unfortunately. But we need brothers even more. Who are you?" they asked us.

So what is lacking in the twice-weekly fast and the ten percent? It is the human person who opens himself and gives himself. What is lacking is humanity, brotherliness, solidarity, and friendship. It is only these things that can prevent the receiver from feeling humiliated by the help he is given. So with positive attainments — fasting twice a week and giving ten percent — we still have nothing to show for ourselves, nothing to show before God, other people, or ourselves. The person who does a great deal, has a great deal, and gives a great deal, but is nothing in himself, is — yes, who is he really? A good person or a poor person? It seems to me that he is a dangerous person. People like that are not good to live among.

Scene Two

The tax collector enters. Again, we shall stop calling him "the tax collector." The long tradition of Christian sympathy has made this tax collector the prototype of the repentant sinner — the petty criminal who can be reformed, so to speak. Here we shall simply call him "the bad man." All his repentance cannot ultimately blind us to the fact that the man is corrupt through and through. Sympathy is completely out of place.

So the bad man comes on stage. But we can hardly see him. He stands to one side and "far off," as our Bible translates it. He does not venture out into the floodlights, where the good man stands, but stays in the twilight, the shadows. And that is the proper place for him.

He does not venture to look up to the Holy of Holies. Nor has he any reason to do so. He does not thank God with open hands. And they are certainly too dirty. He beats his breast. A pity he did not beat it harder still. He cries: "God, be merciful to me a sinner!" And in saying that he is at last uttering the complete truth about himself. For he is "a sinner," a bad man — before God, before the law, before the standards of his own people, and before himself. If anyone can still be merciful to him, it can only be God.

What has the bad man to offer? No fasts and no ten percent — or if ten percent, then probably ten percent in tax evasion. So he does not even begin to render an account of himself. This bad man accepts everything he has done, fully and completely, without beating about the bush. He takes everything on himself and acknowledges what he is to his own self: "I, sinner." In saying this he strips himself naked. There is nothing else he can do. And yet, just by doing this, he *himself* is left. For in this very way the tax collector arrives at the truth about himself, as the sinner he is. It is a bitter truth. It is a truth destructive of all respect — a truth that might well be called suicidal. For a sinner has forfeited his rights. He no longer has any supporters. No one can save him. But it is *his* truth, it is he himself, his dignity in all his shame. And so God arrives at his rights. By giving judgment for God and not himself, he throws himself entirely on God's mercy. With this he reminds God and himself that the outskirts of the law are kindly: the Lord "gives grace to the humble," we read in Proverbs 3:34 (NIV).

What has the bad man to offer? *Himself*. Nothing else? No, nothing else. He has nothing. He can do nothing. But he is here. He is this sinner. He finds room *in his own person* for everything he has done wrong: "I, sinner." And with this, corrupt though he is, he acquires a positive, personal identity. He does not blacken other people in order to set off his own virtues. He immediately begins to talk about himself. "God, be merciful to me a sinner." A person who talks like this is an honest person. We know where we are with him. The bad man is not a dangerous person. One can live among "sinners" like this.

Scene Three

We have now been to the temple, first with the good man and then with the bad man. We have talked first to the one and then to the other. That was not quite right, because the men are in the temple *at the same time*. They are dependent on one another. If we simply look at them individually, we spoil the parable. For really the Pharisee and the tax collector are the two opposite extremes of one and the same society. The Pharisee, as his name tells us, is someone apart only because of his aloofness from everything that makes him impure — which means from impure sinners and tax collectors as well. He becomes someone special only through his condemnation of other people who are not as he is. So he needs these "others," and ultimately the tax collector too. Without them he would not be what he purports to be. The tax collector is in a similar position, but in reverse. For he would not feel like a sinner if it were not for these "special people" who in comparable situations simply do not prove to be corruptible. If it were not for the Pharisee, the tax collector would only be doing "what everyone else does," people who "after all are no better than us," as we say. Leonhard Ragaz perceived a truth when he said about this parable: "The Pharisee is to blame for the tax collector: he pushed him into the religious and social bondage in which the law ceased to matter to him any more." Of course the Pharisee is not to blame for the tax collector's tax evasions, but it is true that he turns him into the sinner, the outcast, the man with a stigma. Through his public condemnation he pins the tax collector down and takes away his every hope.

In almost every group, whether in the church or in society as a whole, there are the "high fliers" who dominate everything — the top of the class, the leaders, the people who decide what is good and what is bad. And then there are the people at the bottom of the ladder, "the dregs," whom the group or society uses as a way of acquiring a profile for itself, because they embody everything that is "wicked." Pharisees and tax collectors are the exponents of a social gulf, the gulf between "the good" and "the bad," "the just" and "the unjust," "God's children" and "people who hate God," "believers" and "unbelievers." Whenever this gulf is fixed, a merciless struggle begins — the struggle between the supposedly "good" people and the allegedly "bad" ones. Because in this struggle everyone is either a friend or an enemy, it is bound to end with the apocalyptic extermination of the allegedly "bad" people. How does this conflict arise? It has its genesis in the social gulf that the parable stylizes through the Pharisee and the tax collector. And how does the gulf arise? It has its genesis in "the good man." He claims the good as his own property and presents it as just that. All possession is dangerous because it brings anxiety with it. But the possession of the good is the most appalling danger of all, because it rips open the gap between the good and the bad. Because there are no steps leading from one side of the gap to the other, the conflict ends in the single alternative: life or death. Whenever industrial struggles, or struggles for property and social power, or differences of belief in the church are bound up with this gulf between good and bad — and when are they not? — hell is let loose, unfortunately in the quite literal sense. Every socialist molehill then turns into an apocalyptic mountain. Every deviating opinion seems then to be accompanied by the smell of brimstone.

Do not let us deceive ourselves, here in this church either. We may be sitting quite amiably next to one another; but this frightful struggle between "the good people" and "the bad ones" is latent in us, too, and can break out at any moment.

Scene Four: Finale

The person telling the parable enters the stage and pronounces sentence. Jesus introduces his judgment with weighty solemnity: "I tell you. . . ." Here Jesus is speaking in the name of God himself. This is a shock that shatters even the language of the parable. In the first place, no one can know what two people prayed in the temple except the God to whom they prayed. Secondly, Jesus' "I tell you" follows directly on the tax collector's cry, "God, be merciful to me a sinner." It is the divine "I" that Jesus uses and that utters itself through his words. And what does this divine judgment say?

It declares the tax collector and sinner to be righteous "rather than" the just Pharisee. "This man went down to his house justified rather than the other." Some manuscripts leave out "rather than the other" altogether. Then the pronouncement sounds harsher still. The tax collector went down to his house justified. The Pharisee is not even worth talking about anymore. What does this mean?

Jesus declares that, in God's eyes, right is on the side of the tax collector, not the Pharisee. Jesus declares that the tax collector is not merely granted the grace he prayed for. "God, be *merciful* to me a sinner" was what he asked for. "He went down to his house *justified*" — that is the response. The answer is far greater than the request. If Jesus had only wanted to say how inconceivably good God can be, then he would merely have had to say: the Pharisee went to his house justified, and God had mercy on the tax collector. Then each of them would have received his due, and Jesus would have been as "well-balanced" as we are always being told to be today. And everyone would have been quite content — including ourselves.

But the radical from Nazareth turns everything upside down: the sinner goes home justified, while to the righteous man God is not even gracious. This is hard for all the "good" people — and extremely surprising for the "bad" ones. If we appeal to the importance of good and bad in the social order, we might even say that it menaces society.

If we look at the Pharisee and the tax collector, each for himself, as individuals, then Jesus' judgment really is incomprehensible — and indeed unjust. But when we perceive the devilish gulf that the Pharisee opens up between himself and the tax collector, when he seizes the good for himself and pushes the other man into evil, then Jesus' judgment about justification becomes a liberating judgment — for the tax collector first of all, and then really for the Pharisee too. Ultimately it is not these individual people who are in question, but the vicious circle in which the one person becomes guilty because of the way he judges the other, and in which social and psychological death is disseminated through self-righteousness and the condemnation of others.

We will only be liberated from this vicious circle when we face ourselves and God with the judgment of Jesus and the tax collector's confession. And we all — I too — belong to the "certain people" who, when it comes to the point, exalt themselves by disparaging others. And with this we lose sight of ourselves and God and other people.

Jesus' justifying judgment brings about a splendid inward and outward deliverance. God condemns the good person who I want to be, but am not, and accepts the bad person who I do not want to be, but am.

In community with Jesus, people have continually discovered that God accepts our tax collector's soul and rejects our Pharisee's soul. In community with Jesus, "the friend of sinners and tax collectors," we see that we are loved — and how much we are loved — in the place where we do not want to be at all: in community with the people we despise. In community with Jesus, we discover that doors open — the door to the repressed self in our inmost heart, and the door to the repressed "other" who is at our side.

"God, be merciful to me a sinner." That is the truth, the whole truth, and nothing but the truth in us. No one can go beyond this. Happy is the person who enters into it, rests in it, and continually returns to it. "We are beggars, that's the truth," as Luther put it.

"This man went down to his house justified." That is the still greater truth of God about us. This is Jesus for us, Jesus beside us, and Jesus with us. Happy is the person who lives in this assurance. For "if God be for us, who can be against us?"

Before the sermon we listened to what is sometimes called "the Pharisee's psalm," Psalm 26. In the spirit of what we have heard, let us now pray "the tax collector's psalm," Psalm 51, so that we may learn who we in truth are, "beloved sinners," and may go to our homes justified.

> Have mercy on me, O God,
> according to thy abundant mercy
> blot out my transgressions.
> Wash me thoroughly from my iniquity,
> and cleanse me from my sin!
>
> For I know my transgressions,
> and my sin is ever before me.
> Against thee, thee only, have I sinned,
> and done that which is evil in thy sight,

so that thou art justified in thy sentence
and blameless in thy judgment. . . .

Behold, thou desirest truth in the inward being;
therefore teach me wisdom in my secret heart. . . .

Create in me a clean heart, O God,
and put a new and right spirit within me.
Cast me not away from thy presence,
and take not thy holy Spirit from me.
Restore to me the joy of thy salvation,
and uphold me with a willing spirit. . . .

FRED B. CRADDOCK

Have You Ever Heard
John Preach?

In this biographical sermon, Fred Craddock presents John the Baptist in two ways at once. John is both a figure in biblical history and an eccentric revival preacher, thundering from a tent pitched somewhere on an asphalt parking lot. Thus Craddock faithfully reproduces the biblical portrait of John, the first-century precursor of Jesus, but also hints that John is our contemporary, a country evangelist whose message challenges, and even threatens, because John puts people "in the presence of God." And that, of course, is what nobody wants and what everybody wants.

Craddock updates John by blurring the lines between the times (teenagers in this sermon are "sitting around on the hoods of the camels") and by haunting us with the sermon title, at once a refrain and a distressingly serious question. All along, Craddock's artful images stitch together two worlds — in fact, two kinds of worlds: we wake "from a dream of palaces and patios to find the roof leaks and the rent's due," but we also find that a fresh snowfall can transform yesterday's "ugly garbage dumpster [into] a mound to the glory of God."

Fred B. Craddock, "Have You Ever Heard John Preach?" from *Best Sermons 4*, edited by James W. Cox, pp. 10-17. Copyright © 1991 by HarperCollins, Publishers. Reprinted by permission of HarperCollins, Publishers, Inc.

Have You Ever Heard John Preach?

The beginning of the gospel of Jesus Christ, the Son of God. As it is written in Isaiah the prophet,

"Behold, I send my messenger before thy face,
who shall prepare thy way;
the voice of one crying in the wilderness:
Prepare the way of the Lord,
make his paths straight — "

John the baptizer appeared in the wilderness, preaching a baptism of repentance for the forgiveness of sins. And there went out to him all the country of Judea, and all the people of Jerusalem; and they were baptized by him in the river Jordan, confessing their sins. Now John was clothed with camel's hair, and had a leather girdle around his waist, and ate locusts and wild honey. And he preached, saying, "After me comes he who is mightier than I, the thong of whose sandals I am not worthy to stoop down and untie. I have baptized you with water; but he will baptize you with the Holy Spirit."

Mark 1:1-8

If Jesus were here tonight, and I had asked for names of preachers most influential for whom we're grateful, his voice would have listed the name John the Baptist. There is no question about that. There is no human being more influential upon the life and career of Jesus than John. We don't know how their association began. We know that a day came, an hour came when Jesus untied the apron strings, lifted the carpenter's apron over his head, put it on the bench, and left the shop. We don't know why that day, that hour, just then. We do know the eighteen solid years, we understand that. They had to be. They had to be silent years — you don't hear roots growing. They had to be silent years. Jesus had a wise mother — she didn't push him out into the show windows of the world like a child star. She let him grow.

But why this day, why this hour? I don't know. He may have heard the groaning and crying from south of town. When Jesus was a teenager, the Romans rounded up in Nazareth and environs a lot of people they considered to be troublemakers or suspected to be such and hanged them on poles, like power poles running along the road south of town, and the screaming of the women and sisters and daughters and wives and the moaning of the victims could not have gone unnoticed by young Jesus. Maybe he still remembers, and he can't stay a carpenter anymore. I don't know.

It might have been the lessons droned away in the synagogue that nobody heard but everybody heard. It might have been a mother's prayer over the kitchen stove. It might have been the stirrings of God in his heart in ways mysterious still to us and probably to him. It might have been that the word came into town about John in the desert. Have you heard John? Have you heard John? Maybe that was it, because Jesus left. He went through the dark gap of the Valley of Jezreel into the heated Jordan valley to the desert country in the south of Palestine where this man, this extraordinary man, was preaching.

They became close. They were already close, Luke said. Luke says they were about the same age — within six months of each other, Jesus being at that time thirty years old. Luke says they were cousins, their mothers being kin — Elizabeth the old woman and Mary the young girl. Maybe they already were close. We don't understand. We don't know. We don't have the information. But Jesus came to John. Heard John. Was with John. Was influenced by John.

The whole New Testament announces that this is one of the most extraordinary figures in the history of God's work in the world. Mark calls John the beginning of the gospel of Jesus Christ. John, in his Gospel, starts with that marvelous poem, this hymn to Christ, and twice he interrupts it by saying, "Now there was a man sent from God whose name was John; he was not the light." Why does he interrupt his own song with a little prose footnote

that says, "I'm not singing about John"? Because that man was so
great, some would think, "Ah, that's John." Like Herod Antipas
after John was dead, when he heard about Jesus, he said, "That's
John again."

Luke says in the Book of Acts that there was a very eloquent
preacher who came from North Africa to Corinth, Greece, and
wanted to preach in the church, and his first sermon was "John, the
Christ of God." He had to be straightened out on one minor detail,
and then he was all right. Luke says that when Paul went to Asia and
stopped in the great city of Ephesus he found a little gathering of
disciples, and he met with them, and he talked with them, and they
said, "We're followers of John." Did you know that by the year 50
on three continents there were groups following John?

And the power of that man over Jesus. He baptized Jesus.
The first sermon that Jesus ever preached was the sermon of his
model, his leader, John. Repent, the kingdom of heaven is at hand.
Same sermon. But what did you expect? It was his first sermon.
All of the synoptics say that he did not even begin his preaching
until John's ministry was shut up in prison. And the silencing of
that great man said to Jesus, You continue. And so he came into
Galilee, preaching like John.

They were so much alike. Herod said of Jesus, "That's John
again." According to Acts, the resurrected Christ, the postglorious
Christ, just before ascending quoted John the Baptist. When Jesus
got word that John had been killed, he said to his disciples, "Let's
go somewhere else." And they got in a boat and crossed the sea.
But he owed the man a funeral, and so he said to the crowd, "What
did you go out to see? A man dressed up in fine clothes? They
belong in king's houses. What did you go out to see? A reed shaken
by the wind? Oh, no, no. A prophet? Greater than a prophet. In
fact," said Jesus, "there has never been anybody born of woman
greater than John the Baptist." You cannot study the life of Jesus
unless you study John.

What an extraordinary man. Did you ever hear him preach?
A lot of people did. If you take all the Gospels together, all the
Gospels together, they came from what today we would call Leb-
anon, Syrophoenicia, Syria, Jordan, Israel, Arabia. Think about it.

In the desert. Standing under the burning sun, sand swirling in your rice, people standing together who had sworn on their mother's grave, "I wouldn't be caught dead with those people!" Jews and Arabs standing together because, when the Word of God is preached, you tend to forget why it is you hate this person next to you.

Oh, a lot of people came. I'm sure some of them came out of curiosity. I can imagine the teenagers in that country, sitting around on the hoods of the camels, nothing to do. "Have you heard of John?" "No." "Well, let's go out there." "What are you doing?" And they go out; I'm sure there was a lot of that. And you can't blame them. He was an oddity. He had long hair, and when I say he had long hair, I don't mean he just had long hair. It wasn't like the young businessmen in Atlanta with a little ponytail. He never cut his hair. I mean, he *never* cut his hair. He had a long beard, not a neat beard like some of you have. I mean, he had never trimmed his beard. He was a Nazarite. And he was strange. He dressed in an unusual way — camel's hair and a leather band around the waist. And his food — he never went home with anybody for lunch, and I'm sure nobody accepted his invitation. "I'll take a rain check on that, John." He lived in the desert.

But they came. All the Gospels say the crowds came. Left the plow in the furrow, left the bread in the oven, turned school out early. Have you ever heard John preach? Absolutely riveting, I'm sure. Fred Robertson used to say that here was no chef offering up fancy dishes. He broke the bread of God with his bare hands and said, "Eat it and live." He was no politician trying to make *yes* sound like *no* and *no* sound like *yes*. He said, "The judge is coming, and I'm here to serve subpoenas." He was no candle in the sanctuary; he was a prairie fire with a stump or a rock as his pulpit. The sun and moon and stars as chandeliers. And the Jordan River, his baptistry. And they came. And I imagine listening to his sermons was like the kind of meal you have after holidays. After all that sweet stuff and fruitcake and turkey and again turkey — and how many ways can you fix turkey? And you finally give up and just have some cornbread and milk and vegetables. That's what it was like. It must have been. And the persuasive form of his character.

We used to talk a lot about the character of the preacher being important for preaching. But I'm listening to it now from the rhetoricians. The old Greek rhetoric professors used to say, "For all of your oratory, the most persuasive part of your argument is your character." And there's John, the rough grain of his character shining through. What he said and what he was cut out of the same cloth. And it must have been persuasive, because all the multitudes came out there. And when the sermon was over, they came over and said, "John, what are we to do?" And he said, "If you have any food, share it. If you have any clothes, share them." The tax collectors came and said, "What are we to do?" He said, "Don't take any more than is your due." And the soldiers were standing on the rim of the crowd, and when everybody else was gone, they shuffled awkwardly up to the pulpit and said, "Any word for us?" And he said, "No violence and don't intimidate the people and don't forage around here trying to supplement your income. Be content with your wages."

Persuasive. Did you ever hear him preach? It's kind of frightening. Oh, not just the images he used. He did use some strong images. Ax at the root of the tree. God can raise up children of Abraham from these stones. The winnowing fork is in his hand. Wheat and chaff. Chaff is burned, save the wheat. Are you ready? Repent! (Pause.) It's kind of, you know . . . But that's not what was frightening about it. What's frightening about listening to John preach is that he puts you in the presence of God. And that's what everybody wants, and that's what everybody doesn't want. Because the light at the altar is different from every other light in the world.

In the dim lamps of this world, we can compare ourselves with each other, and all of us come off looking good. We convince ourselves that God grades on the curve, and what's the difference? We're all okay. And then you come into the presence of God, and you're at the altar, and it's all different. For if our hearts condemn us, think of this — God is greater than our hearts and knows everything. It's called, in literature, a moment of truth. The whining is over. There's no way to modulate the human voice to make a whine acceptable. The whining is over. The excusing is over. It's the school, it's the church, it's the board, it's the government. It isn't! All that's over. It just stops. Like a skipping rock across the water, when it slows down — boom. Like waking from a dream of palaces and patios to find the roof leaks and the rent's due. Like shutting off the stereo, and you still hear the rat gnawing in the wall. That's just the fact of it.

In my mind, I serve God. But there's another force in my life, and I say, "I'm going to do that." I don't do it. I say, "I'll never do that." I do it. Crucified between the sky of what I intend and the earth of what I perform. That's the truth. You know what the moment of truth is. We all want it; we don't want it. We don't talk about it a lot. I don't like to talk religion carelessly and carefreely, like some people do. They're just full of Jesus talk and Spirit talk everywhere and all. I just can't do that. But that doesn't mean it isn't there. You can bury it as deep as a bone — it's there. If you live in the fast lane or the slow, it doesn't matter — it's there. You don't have to be down-and-out — that's a mistake many of the churches make. They think you can minister to people only when they're down-and-out, got a crisis, family falling apart, got fired, on drugs, this and that, and in swoops the church. "Can I help you?"

Look, the people who are up walking around and doing great, they have the same need. That's not the difference. We don't wait until somebody's down-and-out, circling overhead like a vulture. "One of these days you'll go down, and then we can help you." And finally there you are up over a little general store, in one room, 15-watt bulb swinging overhead, and you're on a bare mattress, cigarette butts floating in urine and stale beer, and then we come and say, "You need the Lord." That's what the person needed before.

You see, it doesn't matter whether you're on the central podium at the Olympics crying through the national anthem with that gold medal around your neck or you're wheeled into the service in a chair because you have muscular dystrophy. Your need is the same. It doesn't matter if you're at the peak of your income power or lean your face into the post office window and say, "Are the checks late again?" It's all the same. It doesn't matter if you have bowed your neck at the university to receive the doctoral hood or you're a fifty-three-year-old enrolled in a literacy class — it's all the same.

Now those moments come to us, sometimes in an afternoon that you spend in the monastery of your mind, sometimes in some violent exchange. But they come. Glen Adsett, a schoolmate of years ago, ministered mostly in China. He was under house arrest in China when the soldiers came one day and said, "You can return to America." They were celebrating, and the soldiers said, "You can take two hundred pounds with you." Well, they'd been there for years. Two hundred pounds. They got the scales and started the family argument — two children, wife, husband. Must have this vase. Well, this is a new typewriter. What about my books? What about this? And they weighed everything and took it off and weighed this and took it off and weighed this and, finally, right on the dot — two hundred pounds. The soldiers asked, "Ready to go?" "Yes." "Did you weigh everything?" "Yes." "You weighed the kids?" "No, we didn't." "Weigh the kids." And in a moment, typewriter and vase and all became trash. Trash. It happens.

When I was pastoring in Tennessee, there was a girl about seven years old who came to our church regularly, to Sunday school, and sometimes her parents let her stay for the worship service. They didn't come. We had a circular drive at that church. It was built for people who let their children off and drove on. We didn't want to inconvenience them, so we had a circular drive. But they were very faithful — Mom and Dad. They had moved in there from New Jersey with the new chemical plant. He was upwardly mobile, they were both very ambitious, and they didn't come to church. There wasn't really any need for that, I guess. But on Saturday nights, the whole town knew of their parties. They gave parties, not for entertainment, but as part of the upwardly mobile thing. That determined who was invited — the right people, the one just above, finally on up to the boss. And those parties were full of drinking and wild and vulgar things. Everybody knew. But there was a beautiful girl every Sunday.

One Sunday morning I looked out, and she was there, and I thought, "Well, she's with her friends." But there were Mom and Dad. And after the sermon, at the close of the service, as is the custom at my church, came an invitation to discipleship. And Mr. and Mrs. Mom and Dad came to the front. They confessed faith in Christ. Afterward, I said, "What prompted this?" They said, "Well, do you know about our parties?" And I said, "Yeah, I heard about your parties." They said, "Well, we had one last night again, and it got a little loud, and it got a little rough. And there was too much drinking. And we waked our daughter, and she came downstairs, she was on about the third step. And she saw that we were eating and drinking, and she said, 'Oh, can I give the blessing? God is great, God is good, let us thank him for our food. Goodnight, everybody.' She went back upstairs. 'Oh, my land, it's time to go, we gotta be going. We've stayed. . . .' Within two minutes the room was empty." Mr. and Mrs. Mom and Dad are picking up crumpled napkins and wasted and spilled peanuts and half-sandwiches and taking empty glasses on trays to the kitchen. And with two trays, he and she meet beside the sink on either side, and they look at each other, and he expresses what both are thinking: "Where do we think we're going?" The moment of truth.

Did you ever hear John preach? Most refreshing thing in the world. Most refreshing thing in the world. He said, "God's Messiah is coming. The kingdom is at the door. God's Messiah is right next door." What a thrilling thing! Oh, of course, everybody jumped at that, like it was going to be the cure for everything. They were going to be turned around, of course, because their old motto, "Where the Messiah is, there is no misery," was going to be reversed: "Where there is misery, there is the Messiah." But they didn't know it then. How exciting it was, and hope-filling it was. Oh, not everything was going to be fixed. That's not the point of the kingdom of God, to fix everything. Some things cannot be fixed. Some things happen in our lives, in our relationships, that all the king's horses and all the king's men can't put together again. That's just the way it is.

Do you remember that couple in Thomas Hardy's novel? They had a daughter named Elizabeth, and Elizabeth died. And they agreed that if they had another child and it was a girl, they would name her Elizabeth, and maybe it would help. And they had another child, and it was a girl, and they named her Elizabeth. And it didn't help. And they realized they could have had fifty daughters and named them all Elizabeth — they would still miss Elizabeth. Some things you don't fix. But this is what John said: "The Messiah is coming; get ready by repenting and confessing your sins." And they confessed their sins and were washed in the Jordan, and they were forgiven. They were forgiven. They were forgiven. What's that like? The Bible has so many images for that — new creation (don't let that slip past you). New creation? Morning has broken like the first morning? Yeah. Blackbird like the first bird? Yeah. New creation, that's what the Bible calls it. The Bible calls it a new beginning. Picture a child, third grade, trying to do arithmetic, in a hurry, bell's about to ring, teacher's fussing, "Hurry up, children," try to erase a mistake, tear the paper, make a black smear, start to cry, teacher comes by, "Oh, my goodness," and teacher slides a new sheet of paper there and says, "Why don't you just start over?"

The Bible calls it a new birth. You've been to that window, haven't you? The maternity ward, the nursery, and all that stuff up there in that big window? And all the men outside trying to figure out which one it is? You know, Julie is in there somewhere, and I know she's the prettiest one, and you can't read those little old bands where the arm comes down and the hand joins and there's a deep wrinkle and there's that band, and it's so small, and you say, "Well, I think that's . . ." And the Bible says, That's what it is, that is it. And John offered that.

The Bible says it's like a snowfall. You get up in the morning early, and you look out: about four inches and there's not a print in it yet. And you look across the alley, and what yesterday afternoon was the ugly garbage dumpster is now a mound to the glory of God. That's what the Bible calls it. And John is offering it. Did you ever hear John preach? If you haven't, you will. Because the only way to Nazareth is through the desert. Well, that's not really true. You can get to Nazareth without going through the desert. But you won't find Jesus.

DOUGLAS E. NELSON

Raging Faith

Douglas E. Nelson brought to his preaching a spiky sense of humor, special angles of vision on human defection and divine grace, and a poet's feel for language. He also brought a wide knowledge, not only of Scripture and of Christian tradition, but also of the world's great fiction, poetry, and drama — particularly Shakespeare and Greek tragedy, much of which he had by memory.

In the following sermon, we can spot wonderful seepage from Nelson's reading into his preaching. A biblical figure comes to life here with dramatic, almost unnerving plausibility. The source of this sermon is a single narrative of a singular Gentile. More immediately, the source is the preacher's discernment that Naaman the Syrian faces a brutal dilemma: he can do something ridiculously faithful, or he can rot in his litter.

Douglas E. Nelson, "Raging Faith," from *Is There Any Word from the Lord?* by Douglas E. Nelson. Used by permission of the Session of the First Presbyterian Church of New Haven, Connecticut.

Raging Faith

"Are not Abana and Pharpar, the rivers of Damascus, better than all the waters of Israel? Could I not wash in them and be clean?" So he turned and went away in a rage.

2 Kings 5:12

Could you blame the man? If the Jordan waters had sizzled when he stepped into the shallows it wouldn't have been surprising. And yet this man has been always on the list of classic examples of faith. Our Lord threw the name at the little stuffy dignitaries of Nazareth. Many lepers in Israel — but only Naaman the Syrian was cleansed. You may recall that the reference was not appreciated.

We are involved with a continuing discussion of the shapes of belief. What pattern does human experience find in the search for God? You heard the narrative read to you — and I am sure you remembered having heard it often. After all, preachers cannot resist preaching about it. Just where, would you say, does this man's belief take form? I ask because it seems to me we all need to ponder that question.

Is it belief, for instance, that leaps so quickly to life back there in Damascus? For long months the splendid palace of this great man has been a gloomy place. Servants tiptoe instead of clattering. The ornate tables in the banquet hall gather dust, for in this household there will be no more social occasions. Every day messengers come from the king to ask for the latest bulletins on Naaman's condition. Officers from the general staff drop by — not for orders but for news. Less important people too, a steady stream of them — privates and noncommissioned officers, clumsily stammering at the back gate for word of the chief. They have followed him into dozens of battles and across deserts and mountain ranges, and every man of them would die for him. But nobody can, of course. Naaman must do his own dying, slowly and repulsively. No glory here, and no dignity, just the slow crumbling of his body into pallid rot. The man is a leper. Everyone loves him. No one dares come near him.

Then a little slave girl makes a hesitant remark about a great healer in her native Israel, and inside of hours the general's palace is in an uproar. Orders from the sickroom go down the chain of command. Across the city bugles call a veteran infantry division from barracks, and the elite cavalry squadrons of the army set feverishly to work on their equipment.

Is this belief? A man nearly dead, setting himself for long, agonized days of travel — all because some superstitious child babbled some bit of homesick gossip? Just imagine what the journey would be like, in a suffocating closed litter, jolting across the hills, dust and flies and torment at every slight jar. Was this why his faith ranks so high in the records? William James, I think it is, describes faith as a mountain climber making a desperate leap across a crevasse to save his life. As a full illustration of faith it leaves much to be desired, but it has its truth. I think, for many of us, belief has never been a logical progression from premise to conclusion. We believe, or we seek to believe, because the alternatives have not one shred of promise — slammed doors, with never a glimmer of light showing at the cracks. For Naaman it is not that the prattle of a slave girl is particularly plausible. It is just that, unless this turns out to be true, he will go on to putrid helplessness and then die.

Well, they arrive, this splendid array of troops, banners, glittering chariots, and shiny officers. Oh yes, and out there at a safe distance the general and his litter, just far enough from the lead squadron that the sickening stench will not carry. A word or two, muffled by the curtains, and an officer dismounts to knock on the door of a shanty. All that magnificence, after all that distance, at the door of a shed. A few words at the door, and the officer comes back white with fury. The shabby, insolent unmentionable in there won't even come out. Just go wash in the Jordan seven times. The troops curse savagely and glare at Elisha's hovel, fingering their swords. And Naaman is so infuriated that he almost snarls an order to teach that scum a lesson. The least the lout could do would be to come out and try — a few prayers and incantations, a bit of waving of the hands and muttering of mysterious words!

Wash in the Jordan? That muddy, miserable little creek? Are not Abana and Pharpar, the rivers of Damascus, better than all the waters of Israel? Could I not wash in them and be clean?

Yes, it takes belief to come this far, and human belief expects drama. Naaman has no faith in any humdrum, trivial little prescription. Pay a million dollars? Gladly — after all, the crisis calls for something imposing. Move a mountain or storm a fortress? Willingly! Leprosy calls for something rather impressive.

It was a very wise man, and a very brave one, who reasoned with the sick, savage general. Yes, you could have done something with grandeur to it. Why not try this little thing? And now the stillness lasts for a long, tense moment. Then the muffled voice gives an order, and the litter moves down to the gravelly edge of the Jordan. And Naaman drags his tortured body to the ground, lurches and stumbles into the water, and slowly dips. And again, and again, and again.

What shape of belief do you glimpse here? The leap of credulity back there at the start? The grim holding of courage and purpose over the endless miles? Naaman couldn't have told anyone the answer. As a matter of fact, he didn't understand the whole matter. He was wrong, you know, in what little theology he had. He was comparing water — Abana and Pharpar, rivers of Damascus, and this insignificant little puddle, Jordan. What mattered, of course, was not which water the man got into but the man who got into the water.

Surely this is part of the structure of belief — the humility to take a little step instead of waiting for a great one. The readiness of a man or woman to accept an unexpected answer. And so very often the growth does come like that. We touch God where we had not dreamed he would be. We meet him in some utterly unplanned event — perhaps not on our knees but at a lunch counter, possibly not in some thrill of reverence but in a crisis of emptiness.

We may, if we choose, go back in sullen disappointment to our starting place. Or we may take that slow, unsteady step, out beyond our comprehension and into the Jordan.

SUSAN PLOCHER THOMAS

Parables and Children's Sermons

Anyone who thinks of Jesus' parables as lullabies about lost lambs or about seed and soil has missed their point. To be sure, Jesus' parables lifted those who heard in them the mystery of grace. But the parables also turned up the palms and wrinkled the brows of the merely mystified, and menaced the self-satisfied. Indeed, the parables sometimes stirred up more snakes than they killed — so much so that, in the end, Jesus was crucified not in spite of his parables but, in part, because of them.

In this sermon, Susan Plocher Thomas preaches less about a parable than about parables, and especially about the risks of hearing them. She knows that alert listening to — and preaching on — a Jesus parable is like plugging in an electric hair dryer while standing in a puddle of draining bathwater. You may find the experience more thrilling than you had hoped.

Susan Plocher Thomas, "Parables and Children's Sermons." Used by permission of the author.

Parables and Children's Sermons

The scribes and the chief priests tried to lay hands on
him [Jesus] at that very hour, but they feared the people;
for they perceived that he had told this parable against
them.

Luke 20:19

In my former parish, we used to feature "children's sermons"
regularly — that is, a brief story or object lesson directed at the
children in the congregation, who would gather around the pastor
while the sermon was being presented. I had been introduced to
this practice when I was an intern — and after my first few sermons
in my rural internship parish had learned the most important lesson
one can learn about children's sermons. No, it's *not* "Don't ever
ask the children a question like 'And what do *your* mommy and
daddy do right before they go to sleep?' if you're trying to make
a point about regularized prayer" — although taking care how you
phrase a question *is* a valuable lesson to learn as an intern!

No, the most important lesson I learned was that, if I *really*
wanted to get something across to the congregation, I didn't worry
about getting it so clearly into my "regular" sermon. I just made
sure I got it into the children's sermon. Because that was the one
that was heard, even though it was, as it were, *over*heard. Practi-
tioners of children's sermons warn against just such a use — preaching to the adults under the guise of preaching to the children —
but I found this to be extremely effective on occasion. And what
parent or person who works with children hasn't used a similar
technique with children — discussing loudly with an adult partner
what might happen if little Joey does (or doesn't) do such a thing,
knowing that little Joey is around the corner overhearing every
word?

Well, Luke tells us Jesus did the same thing with this parable
of the wicked tenant farmers who abused three servants and finally

killed the owner's son, all of whom simply came to collect the
proportion of the produce that had been contracted for in the
landlord/tenant agreement. When Jesus tells this parable, he has
just finished a confrontation with the chief priests, scribes, and
elders who asked him (while he was teaching in the temple), "By
what authority do you do these things?" Jesus, as was typical for
him, countered with a question. This one was about John the
Baptist's authority to baptize — and the leaders know they are
caught. They can't answer that the authority was from heaven,
because then Jesus would ask why, if that were so, they didn't
believe John. They can't answer that it was by his own or human
authority, because they know John was popular with the people
who are now listening to Jesus, and they fear the anger of the
people. So they equivocate and say they don't know. Jesus, seeing
through them, therefore refuses to give them the satisfaction of an
answer to *their* question about where *his* authority to teach and
heal comes from.

Having finished this parry with the religious leaders, who now
presumably are gathered in a disgruntled little knot at the edge of
the crowd, Jesus proceeds to tell the people (not the religious
leaders, but the people) the parable of the wicked tenants. Jesus,
however, speaks loudly enough to be overheard.

And — to their credit, I suppose, at least in this regard — the
clergy are neither deaf nor stupid, for they perceive, Luke tells us,
that Jesus really was directing this parable at (or against) them.
They overhear the story they were intended to overhear, and they
properly apply it to themselves.

However, what they did with that realization is something
else, and it is part of the unfolding story of Jesus on his way to his
death by crucifixion. The clergy properly understood the parable
— that is, that *they* were the wicked tenants who had become
arrogant and wished to keep for themselves that which they only
held in trust. But the realization of who they were in the story
didn't bring them to repentance; rather, it strengthened their re-
solve to get rid of this person who was calling them to account —
in short, it incited them even more to play their roles in character.
Luke tells us they would have taken things into their own hands

right then and there — taken the beloved son outside and killed
him right then — except that they feared what the people would
do, the people who were hanging on Jesus' every word.

Now, that the religious leaders caught on to the point of
Jesus' parable so quickly, and saw themselves in it, is a bit unusual.
Normally, the parables of Jesus, coming as they do out of common
life and familiar scenes, look safe at first glance. But Clarence
Jordan, author of the *Cottonpatch Version of the Bible,* calls the
parables Trojan Horses. They look harmless — and then *Bam!*
they've gotcha. It's as if Jesus lit a stick of dynamite, Jordan says,
covered it over with an interesting story, and presented it to his
hearers (or overhearers). By the time these good people got these
parables unwrapped, he and his disciples were a few miles down
the road. Chances are, they could hear the explosion.

So we can see that the folks who overheard this parable, being
clergy, were especially quick on the unwrapping of the interpretation. They'd been taught that, you know, in seminary. Unfortunately, right understanding is not a sure path to change of heart
— as is clear from their response. We might remember that, we
who have tended to see education as the key to social change. Right
understanding is no sure path to a change of heart.

But hearing — or *over*hearing — the word that is meant for
us is still most certainly our task. What sounds harmless may, when
we have taken it home, be devastating. What we must pray for each
other is that the explosion and the shattering will cause changes of
heart, realignments of priorities, reformation — personal and social.

I have begun to approach the word — and particularly Jesus'
parables — with care. In my bathroom is one of those handheld
hair dryers a lot of people have, and recently I've been noticing a
tag near the electric plug that starts out with the words, "To reduce
the risk of electrocution . . ." In big gold letters — "To *reduce* the
risk of electrocution . . ." — as if electrocution is the norm and
here are a few helpful hints that might bring the chances down a
little — you know, delay the inevitable a while.

Hearing Clarence Jordan's description of how the parables
work makes me wonder if *they* ought not to carry a similar warning.
"To reduce the risk of explosion . . ."; "to reduce the risk of being

called to account . . . "; "to reduce the risk of self-recognition . . . "; "to reduce the risk of being addressed by God . . . " — do what?

Well, first, try not to hear what might be intended for you in God's word.

Then, if you do hear, try not to understand.

If you do understand, try not to respond.

If you do respond, try to put your shattered illusions back together with a glue that makes an even tighter bond than the one you had before (there are many such glues now on the market).

And finally, don't come along the rest of the way to Gethsemane, Calvary, and the dawn of the third day. Because the risks are great, there are no warning tags, and you will *surely* overhear much more that is intended for you.

Amen.

CHARLES L. RICE

From the Sixteenth Floor

All sermons try, one way or another, to move listeners to new heights from which they may gain fresh perspective, but few name the floor. Charles Rice imaginatively hauls the pews to an elevator and lifts us and the rest of the congregation to the sixteenth floor of an office building from which we can see "both the city and the sky" from a different angle. What do we see from this angle? We see pain. All around the city we see the kind of pain that leads to despair and then to anguished prayer.

The first, and longest, part of the sermon arises from a contemporary poem by Richard Selig. The biblical text appears only at the end of the sermon, and then somewhat abruptly. But when it comes, we see something else from the sixteenth floor, something besides pain: we see that our prayers have been answered in a startling way.

From the Sixteenth Floor

And when he drew near and saw the city he wept over it,
saying, "Would that even today you knew the things that
make for peace! But now they are hid from your eyes."

Luke 19:41-42;
see also Psalm 127; Luke 19:29-40

Pardoning this borough for its evil,
I look past the tops of buildings, to where
The sky is. Remembering that man's malice,
This man's fate; the former's cunning,
The latter's jeopardy — seeing the sky,
Placid in spite of soot and heartache,
I am reminded to pray. Redemption,
Like our janitor, comes as we go home:
A stooped man turning out the lights.

Richard Selig[1]

It is hard to see a city from its streets.
  Perhaps you have to get up above it, say to the sixteenth floor.
  There is the city at your feet, the throb of its business a steady
roar,

  its mingled joy and pain appearing as one organism,
    streets alive with the intertwined lives of persons
    who are no more than dots in motion.

1. Selig, in *A Pocket Book of Modern Verse*, ed. Oscar Williams (New York: Washington Square Press, 1965), p. 610. First published in Richard Selig, *Poems* (Dublin: The Dolmen Press, 1962), distributed in the United States by Dufour Editions.

From that height it is hard to sort out the hospital from the office building.

But imagination, the more conscious of persons for being at a distance, dwells on one man's malice, another man's fate,

> the man in a hospital gown,
>> and another, briskly striding, in a starched white shirt,
>> one anesthetized against his jeopardy,
>> the other vigorous in his cunning.

But that is the city, the place of "business is business" and business as usual, and the place where people die as surely as they go home from work at the end of the day.

You can see a city whole from the sixteenth floor, and seeing it you may fall to despair,
> or to not caring.

But from an eyrie you can also see the sky:
> I look past the tops of buildings, to where
> The sky is. . . .
> . . . .
> Placid in spite of soot and heartache.

You can live in a place like New York and see that bluest of skies as seldom as you see the faces around you,

> lost in endlessly fascinating canyons,
>> heartache obscured by well-furnished windows and
>> well-planned faces,
>> the sky unnecessary and soot-shrouded.

But from the sixteenth floor, you can see the sky.

Up there, in view of the placid blue, you may be able, even while looking down on malice and fate,

> cunning and jeopardy,

to pardon this borough for its evil, to forgive and accept, and that is something very different from not caring.

You don't pardon out of hand what you see from the sixteenth floor.

The city at your feet is not at all like the office at your back,

this efficient place with unseen people ready every night for your daily manipulation.

Out in the city, unlike the office, you can't even clear the air of soot, to say nothing of heartache, by pushing buttons and sending memoranda.

Standing above the city you come to see that the life which threads its streets and moves behind blank windows is out of your control.

And so you are reminded to pray, and in praying to live with the city's malice and pain without resignation.

From the sixteenth floor, a man sees both the city and the sky, and he is likely to feel humble and hopeful, to come to compassion for the dying as well as the cunning.

We are on the sixteenth floor.

We can only imagine how the earth appears to the astronaut—

his sense of the world in its wholeness,
   a small blue ball floating in space with three billion
   people aboard.

Seeing earth from 50,000 miles out has given us a new feeling for the human community.

From out there the geographical boundaries and ancient
   rivalries of man seem petty indeed.

From space, the earth returns to the appearance of creation: one earth for all of God's children.

In such a world, the law of survival is not nature red in tooth and claw — any more than it is the city's competition and individualism — but compassion and cooperation.

But how shall that become clear to us, as clear as the sky?

The times are upon us, clearing our vision, getting us up to heights where we can see.

The theologian would say that the time is eschatological.

Crisis presses us to think about the *meaning* of our life together.

> People in the city are hurting —
> 　hurting each other,
> 　　hurting themselves by hurting one another,
> 　　　just hurting.

Increased visibility and enforced proximity will not let us escape the questions: Who is my neighbor? Why do I feel so uncomfortable in the elevator with these people who live in the same building with me? What *is* a community?

T. S. Eliot's Stranger puts the question:

> 　　　"What is the meaning of this city?
> Do you huddle close together because you love
> 　each other?"
> What will you answer? "We all dwell together
> To make money from each other"? or "This is a
> 　community"?
> And the Stranger will depart and return to the desert.
> O my soul, be prepared for the coming of the Stranger,
> Be prepared for him who knows how to ask questions.[2]

We know the answer to the question.

Knowing it, how shall we pardon "this borough for its evil"?

---

2. T. S. Eliot, *The Collected Poems, 1909-1962* (New York: Harcourt Brace Jovanovich, Inc., 1963), p. 103.

Only if we know what Richard Selig knows: the redemption of the city is not finally in our hands.

The lesson is late, but we are learning that human community is a creation of the spirit.

Our technology has reared skyscrapers,
   our science has produced enough food for all the people,
      our genius has made man mobile, as free as the jet
      and the automobile.
But we live in jeopardy,
   next door to hunger,
      in cities where we cannot walk in the parks,
         choking on our own wastes.

Technology, research, efficiency — the hallmarks of our society — will certainly play their part in rebuilding the city that they have built.

But they cannot redeem the city.

As the air becomes more choked, the fact becomes more clear that our salvation lies in the recovery of faith and humanity.

However much we dislike the overused word, the city's problem is "spiritual."

Or as the poet puts it, there is hope of salvation in the man who leaves his business, the engineering of the town, to look out over the city,

   to *feel* for it,
      and then to be reminded to pray.
                     . . . Redemption,
   Like our janitor, comes as we go home.

Let us, so to speak, come down to earth.

What does it mean to say that the redemption of the city comes after we have closed up shop, that salvation arrives after we have done all that we can do?

Take a specific problem, the pollution and ravaging of man's environment — air, water, countryside.

The very face of the land — like a man's countenance, which with passing years reveals his affections — reflects the soul of a people.

The soot which blankets our cities,
    the ugliness which litters our avenues and highways,
        our thickening rivers,
        the glut of murderous automobiles belching the poison
        of irresponsible individualism at its worst:
our soul is laid bare by what we are doing to the land.

Having gained the world and lost our soul, we are losing the world.

The ecological crisis reveals our spiritual poverty, the price of materialism.

To our madness for wealth, novelty, and power, even the air we breathe and the water that is life itself can be sacrificed.

As St. Augustine knew, when men cease to love best the City of God, the city of man becomes a slum.

Looking out upon the city that we have built, we see our souls.

We need not, however, dwell on soot and sewage.

We could speak of the ignored elderly, unwanted by their busy families and written off as a loss by a glamorous, high-living society;

    the scorned poor, an affront to our self-image;
        the neglected sick, who can't pay their own way and
        embarrass a society built around the myth of the
        self-made man.

They are all part of the landscape of a city where economic success and personal fulfillment are equated, where power is supremely valued and ultimately trusted.

That landscape is a jungle, where people prey upon each other.

All right, so we are up on the sixteenth floor.
We've seen the city, and ourselves.
So what do we *do*?

That is the first question an American would ask.

The point of this sermon is, however, that the first movement of the faithful man is not action but prayer.

Praying is getting up on the sixteenth floor where we can see the city and feel for it.

Before we do anything, or after we have done all we can — as you like — we are called to pray, remembering that redemption comes after we go home.

For it is God who put us here together, who can put it in our hearts to love each other.

What life have you if you have not life together?
There is no life that is not in community,
And no community not lived in praise of God.
. . . .
We build in vain unless the Lord build with us.
Can you keep the city that the Lord keeps not with you?
. . . .
Where there is no temple there shall be no homes.[3]

The words sound quaint, but they are no less true.

Our redemption draws near when we trust only in the God of love.

The compounding crises of our time, even as they spur us to action, remind us to pray.

When you get up on the sixteenth floor, and see our city clearly, you are moved, not to send memos or push buttons, but to pray.

Though we are God's servants in saving the city — called to bend our energies to build houses,

harness energy,
control population,
to push buttons, send memos, and man laboratories —

from the sixteenth floor it is clear that

3. Eliot, pp. 101-3.

> . . . Redemption,
> Like our janitor, comes as we go home:
> A stooped man turning out the lights.

The gospel tells the story of Jesus' coming to Jerusalem riding upon a lowly donkey.

> And when he drew near and saw the city he wept over it, saying, "Would that even today you knew the things that make for peace!" (Luke 19:41-42)

Not long after that, he carried a cross to the hilltop outside Jerusalem.

Nailed up there, he had a good view of the city.

ELIZABETH ACHTEMEIER

Of Children and Streets and the Kingdom

Elizabeth Achtemeier's sermon gives prophetic voice to children who have been bullied, neglected, or even sold. Achtemeier wants the kingdom of God to come for them. But is the kingdom "some never-never land in the sweet by-and-by"? Or is the kingdom wonderfully mundane? Could it be "life on this earth — life transformed to accord with the will and purpose of God"?

Expertly handling and weaving together the Old and New Testament lessons, Achtemeier proposes a fragrant and earthy version of a central biblical reality. Remarkably, in Zechariah and in Achtemeier, the kingdom of God is a public park that is fit for children.

Of Children and Streets and the Kingdom

And the word of the LORD of hosts came to me, saying, "Thus says the LORD of hosts: I am jealous for Zion with great jealousy, and I am jealous for her with great wrath. Thus says the LORD: I will return to Zion, and will dwell in the midst of Jerusalem, and Jerusalem shall be called the faithful city, and the mountain of the LORD of hosts, the holy mountain. Thus says the LORD of hosts: Old men and old women shall again sit in the streets of Jerusalem, each with staff in hand for very age. And the streets of the city shall be full of boys and girls playing in its streets. Thus says the LORD of hosts: If it is marvelous in the sight of the remnant of this people in these days, should it also be marvelous in my sight, says the LORD of hosts? Thus says the LORD of hosts: Behold, I will save my people from the east country and from the west country; and I will bring them to dwell in the midst of Jerusalem; and they shall be my people and I will be their God, in faithfulness and in righteousness."

Zechariah 8:1-8

At that time the disciples came to Jesus, saying, "Who is the greatest in the kingdom of heaven?" And calling to him a child, he put him in the midst of them, and said, "Truly, I say to you, unless you turn and become like children, you will never enter the kingdom of heaven. Whoever humbles himself like this child, he is the greatest in the kingdom of heaven."

Matthew 18:1-4

"Thy kingdom come, thy will be done, on earth as it is in heaven." We pray every Sunday for God to bring in the kingdom of heaven, but I wonder if we really want it. Do we really want the kingdom of God to come? That is the question. Certainly every time we celebrate the Lord's Supper, we look forward to the coming of that kingdom. In the words of Paul, as often as we eat the bread and drink the cup, we proclaim the Lord's death *until he comes.* Indeed, the Lord's Supper is understood in the Christian church as a foretaste of that final, messianic banquet in the new age, when God's kingdom will have come in its fullness and God's work with his world will have been brought to completion. But it probably is a real question whether any of us wants to attend that final banquet. At least it is a question whether we want to attend it soon. Jesus taught, in his parables, that the kingdom of God was like a pearl of great price, or like a treasure uncovered in a field, that was so valuable and so desirable that men were willing to sell everything they had in order to obtain it, but few of us would be willing to make that sacrifice. We are not all that sure that we want the kingdom of God to come. And the reasons for that are very clear.

In the first place, we are a very comfortable people. We like our life as it is. Despite all the problems that we Americans have with our marriages or money or jobs or families, we really are fairly contented. Polls have occasionally been taken of the American public in which it has been repeatedly shown that some sixty to seventy-five percent of us are satisfied with our lives. Preachers, and indeed our writers and artists, are accustomed to painting very gloomy pictures of us. For example, Nathan Scott has said that "At the center of our literature is a narrative of estrangement and alienation: the story told is a tale of our abandonment in some blind lobby, or corridor of time. And in that dark, no thread." But I am not sure such literature is an accurate portrayal of our everyday lives. After all, most of us have families and friends whom we enjoy and jobs that keep us busy and happy and a religious faith that sustains us in the rougher moments. And while we may pray every Sunday for the kingdom of God to come, we probably would add, "but not yet." "Thy kingdom come, O Lord, but maybe not just now."

Besides, we might well ask, in the second place, have we not achieved here in the United States a way of living that is just about as close to heaven on earth as we are likely to get? For the first time in history, those of us in the Western world have built societies in which most human beings no longer have to worry about the basic necessities of life. Ever since the human race began, its societies have been concerned about one thing — how to stay alive: about where the next meal is coming from, about providing shelter to live in, about having clothes enough to protect themselves against the elements.

Certainly that was true of the inhabitants of Jerusalem, who listened to Zechariah's preaching about the kingdom. They were a ragtag bunch of refugees who had managed to survive the Babylonian destruction of their country in 587 B.C. Some of them had spent years of exile in Babylonia and then had been allowed to return to Palestine. Others, who were among the poorer classes, had been allowed to remain in Palestine all along, and they had simply scraped out a living in that devastated land as best they could. But now, in the year 518 B.C., when this passage in Zechariah was written, all of the inhabitants of Jerusalem were in desperate straits. Their temple was still a burned-out ruin. Their city walls were nothing but rubble. Drought and blight withered their crops, and hunger was rampant. Inflation, caused by a shortage of goods, ate up their meager earnings. They no longer even had a king or a national government. They were just a tiny, impoverished subprovince in the vast Persian empire. Their life was a matter of grubbing for the basic necessities of life, so it is no wonder that they heard Zechariah gladly when he preached this passage to them about the coming of the kingdom of God. They needed something better — and that is still true for most of the peoples on this earth. Most peoples need something better, because they still have to worry about simply managing to exist.

But that is no longer true for most of us in the U.S. We no longer worry about getting enough to eat. On the contrary, we worry about getting too fat. We even worry about our dogs and cats getting too fat, so we put them on diets, too. We are so free of anxiety about the basic necessities of life that we can just worry about which computer system to buy, or about how many we should plan on for the party Friday night, or about which fast-food chain puts the most beef in its hamburgers. We have pretty well got it made, we think, so who wants to leave all that for some unknown realm called the kingdom of God? Who wants to give up the good life in America for some ethereal realm in the sky?

And perhaps that is the third reason we do not really want the kingdom of God to come — because we think of it as some vague realm way off in heaven somewhere, separated from all the good things that we so enjoy in this life.

We have very strange conceptions of the kingdom of God. Usually we think of it as a place in heaven where we will go after we die. And our pictures of the kingdom have been very much influenced by all those fanciful stories of pearly gates and angels flying about. We have inherited those pictures from a hundred different sources: from such literature as *Pilgrim's Progress,* from the art of Rubens and Michelangelo, from Negro spirituals that sing of golden slippers walking the golden streets, and from the imagery and symbolism of the Bible itself. We have even put all those pictures into our hymns: "Holy, holy, holy," runs the second verse of the well-known hymn, "all the saints adore thee/Casting down their golden crowns around the glassy sea/Cherubim and seraphim falling down before thee/ Who were, and art, and evermore shalt be." None of that makes very much sense to us, nor does it appear too appealing. And so we may pray in the Lord's Prayer for God's kingdom to come, but we are not sure we want it. Seek ye first the kingdom of earth, is our motto, and let heaven take care of itself.

Now certainly, in the Bible, there is a reality to heaven. It is the dwelling place of God the Father, Son, and Holy Spirit. And the Bible simply strains at the limits of human language to describe that dwelling place. But alongside that, our Old Testament lesson from the prophet Zechariah gives us another, different, supplementary picture of the kingdom of God. And it is a picture that participates very much in the realities of this earth. Let me read it to you again:

> Thus says the LORD: I will return to Zion, and will dwell in the midst of Jerusalem, and Jerusalem shall be called the faithful city. . . . Old men and old women shall again sit in the streets of Jerusalem, each with staff in hand for very age. And the streets of the city shall be full of boys and girls playing in the streets. (Zech. 8:3-5)

What is the kingdom of God, according to the prophet Zechariah? It is a public park! It is a park where old people are no longer cold and lonely and ill and senile, but participants in a community. It is a public park where the elderly can sit together and bask in the sun, and talk and laugh over the good old days in full vigor and clear mind and satisfaction of life.

The kingdom of God is a public park where little children can run and play in its squares, in safety and fun and delight. It is a place where no pervert is waiting to lure one of them away with offers of candy; where no drug pusher is lurking to tempt the older children to try a brightly colored pill. It is a place where no child is abused or unwanted or malnourished, and where there is not even a bully among the group, shoving and taunting the littler ones until they break into tears. The kingdom of God, says Zechariah, is a public park where the streets are safe for children.

You see, the kingdom of God, according to the Bible, is not some never-never land in the sweet by-and-by. Most of the Bible really is not very interested in heaven. No, the kingdom of God is life on this earth — life transformed to accord with the will and purpose of a loving God. The Lord's Prayer does not say, "Thy kingdom come in heaven." It says, "Thy kingdom come on earth, even as it is in heaven." God works to accomplish his will for the earth. He works to fulfill his purpose and intention for human life in the world here and now. He presses on toward the time when this solid, everyday, common land of ours will become the good place that he intended in the beginning for it to be.

And in the light of all that, it is very clear that we do not yet have it made, that we are not yet living in the kingdom of God — not even here in the U.S.A. For in the kingdom of God, our streets will be safe for our children. And right now, they are certainly far from being fit places for our little ones. Few parents would send their child into any one of our parks now to play unaccompanied, because our parks are not fit for children. On the streets of Los Angeles, children as young as ten or eleven sell themselves as prostitutes. And as for the streets of the world — well, children scrounge for garbage in the streets of Calcutta and Saigon. Children in northern Ethiopia are dying by the hundreds every day. Children in El Salvador fall victim, with their parents, to the murderous sweeps of death squads.

And since that be true, can we not and must we not daily, earnestly pray, "Thy kingdom come, thy will be done, on earth as it is in heaven"? O Lord, bring in the time when our streets will be fit for our children! For if that time is not coming, then there really is not much point to all that you and I are doing, is there? If Zechariah's vision is not the goal of human history, then there is no purpose to our sojourn on this globe.

The kingdom of God — a place where little children can play — yes, that is very much a goal for which we pray and yearn and struggle.

Zechariah further tells us in our Old Testament lesson that the kingdom will not have come until our children are also fit for our streets. And that means that you and I have work to do. Now do not misunderstand me. Certainly we human beings, by our own efforts, cannot create the kingdom. Only God can work such a radical transformation of society. But having been given Zechariah's vision of what God's final purpose is for this planet of ours, we can at least say yes to that purpose of good and try to live our lives in accordance with it. And that means we have work to do as parents and grandparents, as teachers and examples and leaders. It is not enough that we accept God's purpose by working in society to make our streets fit for children; we also have to work in our homes and schools and churches to raise children who are fit for our streets.

I shall never forget the story of the group of civic-minded club members who met one day with the juvenile court judge to ask him what the most important thing was that they could do to improve their community. The judge replied in six simple words: "Be at home for your children." Now that is not to disparage all the efforts such groups make to improve conditions in our communities — those efforts must be made, and we are deeply indebted to our volunteers. It also is not to ignore the fact that we all have jobs we have to attend to. But it is to emphasize that question that we constantly should be asking ourselves: are we raising children who are fit for our streets?

A child who has not been taught right from wrong is not fit to be loosed on society. A child who has had no discipline is a child without limits on her selfishness. A child who has not been loved and encouraged and praised and hugged is a child who can never love others. And yes, a child who has not been taught that there is a sovereign God to whom he is responsible is a child who will never use his God-given talents wisely and who therefore will have no purpose and meaning for his life. Are we raising children who can contribute to their fellow human beings, who know how to love God and neighbor? Or are we perpetuating the evils of life in the offspring entrusted to us? Those are the questions we always must ask. Are we raising children who are fit to receive the kingdom of God?

Maybe we can raise such children, good Christians, only if we ourselves are fit. Maybe our children will be ready for the kingdom only if we ourselves, as parents and grandparents and leaders and citizens, are also ready for it.

Our Lord came preaching the kingdom of God, the New Testament tells us, and in parable after parable he instructed us how to become citizens of it. We cannot earn our way into the kingdom of God, he said, by our own good deeds and our own fine works. For the kingdom is simply a gift given to all workers, equally, in the vineyard. Nor can we buy our way into God's peaceable realm, no matter how much our liquid capital. We may be able to buy the best clothes and sirloin steak and even a summer place. We may be able to purchase the latest technology and support the strongest military. But we cannot buy that kingdom of God that Zechariah pictures, with its peace and contentment, its secure joy, and its happy elders and children. Indeed, taught Jesus, it is very hard for a rich person to enter the kingdom of God at all; for you see, rich people tend to depend on themselves and their wealth, when what we have to do to be citizens of the kingdom — whether we be rich or poor or middle-class — is to depend solely on God and his working in our lives. We have to trust him.

And so it finally comes down, it seems, to that story we heard for our New Testament lesson, that story in which Jesus took that little child and set him in the midst as an example. It finally comes down to humbly depending on our God as a child depends on his father. For in the kingdom of God, God is truly king. He rules. He orders life. His will is done. And until we stop trying to be our own gods and goddesses, until we cease making decisions apart from his will given us in the Scriptures, until we stop thinking that anything goes and start asking what God wants, until we quit relying on our own petty strength to live righteous and meaningful and decent lives in this world, we will never be ready to live in the kingdom of God, and neither will our children. It is no wonder that Zechariah can picture that happy public park in his prophecy, because the happiness in that park depends on something else — it depends on the fact that God dwells in the midst of the city and orders and rules its life.

And so you see, if our children are to be fit for the streets of any city, they have to be raised by parents and adults who depend on the will and power of God. They have to be raised by adults who themselves have become humble, as a little child is humble. They have to be guided by parents who can truly pray, "Our Father . . . *thy* kingdom come, *thy* will be done, on earth as it is in heaven."

But if we can truly pray that prayer, good Christians, if we can want God's will for our lives and for the lives of our children, with all our hearts and minds and strength, then maybe we and our children will be ready to receive our King and his kingdom that is coming. For the kingdom comes, friends, it surely comes. Make no mistake about it.

It began to come that night when that one Child, who is fit for all streets, in all places and all times, was born in the city of Bethlehem. It began when God himself, incarnate in that Child, drew near to us and took up his dwelling in our midst, in fulfillment of Zechariah's promise. It began when that one Child, grown up, died on a cross and was raised by his Father and became the victor over all the evil and violence, all the ugliness and death that haunt our communities. And so we know in Jesus Christ that Zechariah's promise will finally be fully fulfilled, and that our city, and the cities of the world, will become faithful cities. God will dwell in the midst of us, as our Ruler and Father. And old men and old women shall again sit in the park, each with staff in hand for very age. And the streets of our city shall be full of boys and girls, playing in the squares.

O Lord, thy kingdom come — yea, quickly come — on earth as it is in heaven. Amen.

THE AIMS
OF THE SERMON

Most congregations have had the experience of sitting through a sermon that was tolerably clear, orderly, and biblical but that nonetheless failed to move anybody. Why? If asked about it, members of the congregation might express dissatisfaction provoked by the aimlessness of the sermon they heard. What was the point? listeners want to ask. Where was the sermon going? What was the preacher trying to *do* with this sermon?

Good preachers have aims and outcomes in mind as they prepare to enter a pulpit. But, of course, not just any aim will do. No conscientious preacher deliberately uses a sermon to expand a personal power base, for instance, or to dazzle listeners with rhetorical pyrotechnics, or to bully or entertain a congregation. Neither do alert preachers assume and try to feed a lay appetite for specialized biblical and theological data. As Harry Emerson Fosdick once remarked, preachers who shape a sermon to answer such questions as, "Whatever did become of the Jebusites?" may arouse no more than polite dismay. Moreover, sermons that work at cross-purposes with their texts (the text warns; the sermon comforts) will likely generate a real, even if unexpressed, buzz of confusion in listeners. So sermons must do more than pursue some aim, even if they must not do less.

Depending on their text and occasion, good sermons warn, comfort, or evangelize. They prophesy, counsel, teach, or rebuke. They deconstruct popular opinion or reinforce it. Always, one way or another, they proclaim gospel truth.

KARL BARTH

Jesus Is Victor

Before they counsel, instruct, warn, or comfort, preachers proclaim. They seek first the kerygma, and find that all these other things naturally follow.

Nobody in the twentieth century believed in the priority of proclamation more fiercely than Karl Barth. Even Barth's massive theology is "fascinatingly exasperating, or exasperatingly fascinating," as theologian Rowan Williams once put it, in part because it, too, proclaims great and mysterious things with a kind of "that's the way it is" air of certainty and finality.

"Jesus Is Victor" proclaims resurrection and does so repeatedly. Barth's fingerprints are all over this sermon, not least in his scorn for pretty "rejuvenation of nature" approaches to Easter, and in his insistence that the Easter word is clear, potent, and therefore intolerable to a world obscured by its own shadows and follies. Beyond all else, such a world needs to hear the word of Easter victory that is the centerpiece of Christian proclamation.

Karl Barth, "Jesus Is Victor," from Karl Barth and Eduard Thurneysen, *Come Holy Spirit: Sermons,* published by T. & T. Clark Ltd. Used by permission.

Jesus Is Victor

And you did he make alive, when ye were dead through
your trespasses and sins, wherein ye once walked according to the course of this world. . . . But God, being rich
in mercy, for his great love wherewith he loved us, even
when we were dead through our trespasses, made us alive
together with Christ . . . and raised us up with him and
made us to sit in the heavenly places in Christ Jesus.

Ephesians 2:1-2, 4-6, ASV

What is Easter? The Bible answers: resurrection, resurrection of
Jesus from the dead; and that means: the living God, forgiveness
of sins, the empty tomb, conquered death — in a word, Jesus is
victor. But really, are these answers? Answers which we understand,
with which we may do something? Are these clear, plain, understandable words, from which light streams forth? Are they not rather
hard to understand, hazy words, which follow one another, which
only involve us in deeper enigmas? May we not say to ourselves,
"We have had enough of these old questions, these enigmas of life
which daily puzzle us? We do not care to deal with these old, nor
with these newer, greater questions. Life is hard and dismal. We
have little enough light; and we come to church that we may receive
more light in order that the little light we have may not be made
dimmer, or be stolen from us."

Perhaps we are deep in doubt. We do not understand life, and
we do not understand ourselves. We are afraid of life. There are so
many dark shadows around us that we can scarcely find the way.
After all, is there really a way out? Does life have a meaning? And
along comes Easter and says, "God, the living God, exists. God
lives. God triumphs." "Yes, that is *the* question," you reply. "It is
with this question that I struggle. *That* is what I do not understand, and no assumption of the Bible or of a preacher helps me
over my difficulties. The darkness becomes extremely black just

when you speak about that. Just then the question starts to burn as a freshly inflicted wound. The living God — if only I could grasp and understand that! If that would only speak to me!"

Or it may be you are not a brooding person. Your situation is quite different. You are an active, or, at least, an ambitious, striving, progressive person. But you chafe beneath your failures and weaknesses, and with all your progress they still cleave to you. Perhaps you have lived for years under the curse of a moral trespass. And no one knows why you secretly slip back into your old faults and feel so ashamed of yourself. Perhaps others know it, they can see it on you. Anyway, it is a curse, an imprisonment in which you are held. You know: "There is a worm eating away at the roots of my life, and it disturbs whatever might grow out of these roots." And you do not know how to be done with it. You — your better self — are bound with chains to another, a baser I, which you must detest, and yet you cannot slough it off, because it belongs to you. You miserable person, who shall deliver you from the body of this death! And here comes Easter and says: "Forgiveness of sins! Broken chains! If God is for us, who can be against us?" "Yes," you sigh, "how wonderful it would be, but it is just my burden, my misery, that I do not experience *anything* like that. This shout of joy cannot well up out of my own experience any more after all these countless failures that I have endured. Let shout who will, but rejoicing is not for me. On the contrary, forgiveness means freedom, and I first discover what chains and fences really are when we speak of freedom."

Or, finally: We must die. The untold dark moment will come for us all, when the end comes, at the place where this world sinks away and where we have to bid farewell to the realities of this life with all of its lights and shades. Where do we go then? What will be left of us? From our position we can answer nothing. As far as our human thinking and living is concerned, that is the last word. A grave-mound, a few frail flowers, that is all that is left. O enigma of dying, O enigma of life, which faces us at the exit of life. And yet, again Easter comes and speaks the unheard of word about the conquest of death, the empty grave; and this word is for us the most unheard of, and the hardest to believe. Who can understand it? Where all ends, there all really begins. Are we not tempted to say: "O, cease this talk, we have done once-for-all with this terrible enigma of dying. You are ripping open the old wounds anew when you speak of it!"

The final summing up of all this which is told us at Easter is: Jesus is victor! Jesus — is it not He who was born in humblest lowliness, who died on the cross crying the cry of a derelict of God, He who forgave sins but who collapsed under the burden of sin, He, the humble, smitten by His fate; and of all those laden with grief, is He not the most burdened man of Nazareth? And He is to be *victor*?

Yes, it is always a difficult, a dark truth, a word that scarcely can be tolerated by our ears — that word "resurrection." That is to say, it is not necessarily hazy. What it really means is clear — too clear; plain — only too plain. It means what it says: something mighty, crystal-clear, complete. It signifies: That is the world, that is life with its imprisonments and tragedies of sorrow and of sin, life with its doubts and unanswered questions, life with its grave-mounds and crosses for the dead, a unique enigma, so immense that all answers are silent before it. Nothing, absolutely nothing, can one do who is in this fate, sin and death, with its thousandfold festering need; nothing can one do to stop it; everything is too insignificant to fill up this vacuum. Admit it; it negates everything; there is no way out! There might be the possibility of a miracle happening — no, not *a* miracle, but *the* miracle, the miracle of *God* — God's incomprehensible, saving intervention and mercy, the all-inclusive renewal that leads from death to life that comes from Him, God's creation-word, God's life-word, and that means resurrection from the dead! Resurrection, not progress, not evolution, not enlightenment, but what the word means, namely, a call from heaven to us: "Rise up! You are dead, but I will give you life." That is what is proclaimed here, and it is the only way that the world can be saved. Take away this summons, and make something else of it, something smaller, less than the absolute whole, less than the absolute ultimate, or less than the absolutely powerful, and you have taken away all, the unique, the last hope there is for us on earth.

Perhaps, we still allow the word "resurrection" to *please* us very well. Yes, we reach out our eager hands toward it. Who is there that does not eagerly desire the promise of freedom, life, and hope for the future! But that which disturbs us and which we will not endure, which we scarcely or absolutely will not and cannot admit, is the divine encroachment which all this presupposes, and that is our distress, the awfulness of our chains, the imprisonment which we suffer, from which there is no escape. We will gladly let anyone tell us about the love of God; we rejoice when it is ardently proclaimed to us. But do we not see that all this is meaningless patter if we are not at the same time shocked as by a crash of lightning with a sense of the depth of our lost condition to which the love of God had to stoop? We do not like to see that we are deeply imprisoned, and that it is true, so irrefutably true, that we cannot, absolutely cannot, in any way help ourselves; that it is true, we are a people who live in the shadow and darkness of death; that this is true, and is proclaimed to us in, with, and under the word "resurrection" — oh, that is for us the bitter, unacceptable, and unendurable truth which stirs us to rebellion. That is the darkness in the clear word "resurrection." Oh, yes, we gladly allow it to be proclaimed to us, *but* that the victory in *no* sense grows or issues *from us,* that it is *God's* victory, and that this victory is contrary to our wishes, and comes as a result of our impotent helplessness — this is what we do not care to hear at all. "Ye were dead in your sins and trespasses, in which ye walked according to the course of this world. But God, who is rich in mercy, has made us alive with Christ." If only we could take the words "God has made us alive" by themselves, without that word "but" which precedes it, and which so emphatically refers to our "being dead in our sins"! Nevertheless, it is true that wherever that crystal-clear word "resurrection" shall resound and be heard and understood, the prior word must be resounded and heard and perceived, which is — "Death." It must be seen and understood that in the midst of life, even in blooming and healthy life, there is a yawning chasm, a deep pit that cannot be filled by any art or power of man. Only one word is sufficient to cover this chasm, to fill this pit, and that is the word: "Jesus is victor!" — the word "resurrection." First of all, one must see and realize that all the paths of life upon which we walk are the same, now or at any later time, in that they all lead to the same edge of the precipice, over which there is no bridge man can build in any case, but which in incomprehensible fashion has been made manifest in the resurrection of Jesus Christ from the dead. Who would partake in this resurrection must first have seen this chasm, have discovered this pit.

And life is not easy; on the contrary, it becomes dead in earnest and difficult wherever this word "resurrection" resounds, because this word is serious. It throws clear light upon our existence, and in the clarity of it we see how dark our existence is. It proclaims true freedom to us and lets us painfully discover our prison chains. It tells us that the one and only and last refuge is God. But it tells us that only because it tells us that all our positions on life's battlefield are lost and that we must vacate them. Against this fact we defend ourselves. We do not tolerate this assessment and pronouncement upon our lives, which inheres in the resurrection proclamation. For that reason we deny the resurrection, or we at least minimize it. We alter it. We seek to minimize this maximum word. We seek to bedim that illuminating light that falls upon our existence. We denature that truth of its unconditional, wonderful, divine essence. We alter it into something human.

And then, in our preaching on Easter day, we say something about the rejuvenation of nature, or the romantic reappearing of the blossoms, or the revival of the frozen torpid meadows. We interpret the message that Jesus is victor, not in its literal sense, but we interpret it as a symbol or a human idea. In that case the message tells us that the world is not so bad off. After each and all evils there naturally follows something good. One must not lose his courage! Only hope! And should it be that we stand beside graves and we talk about the resurrection, we should not think of it as a literal resurrection, but rather as a continuation of life in a spiritual sense, in a limbo-like, mystic beyond, or, perhaps, in the memory of those loved ones who survive, or in those acts and deeds which the deceased one left behind. We may seek to be satisfied with this sort of resurrection. We may get along very well for some time with the comfort that death is not so terrible. One must just not lose his courage! We may succeed for a long time with the romantic reappearing of the blossoms and the rejuvenation of spring, and thus forget the bitterness of present reality. It may be that, even as

we stand beside the graves of loved ones, we might find contentment in the thought of a spiritual continuation of this life. But the
remarkable thing about it is that the real truth of the resurrection
seems to be too strong for us, because it will not suffer itself to be
hidden or concealed in these harmless clothes. It always breaks
forth, through all these romantic dreams about reappearing blossoms and the comforts which men offer each other, whereby we
have concealed it; it rises up and shouts at us, asking us: "Do you
really think that is all I have to say to you? Do you really believe
that is why Jesus came to earth, why He agonized and suffered,
why He was crucified and rose again on the third day, to become
merely a symbol for the truth — which really is no truth — that
eventually everything will be all right?"

And it is remarkable that this resurrection truth has a com-
panion, namely life itself. Life itself stands up and, grasping us, asks:
"Do you really think that by this easy and convenient way you can
solve me? Do you not yet understand what I am all about? Do not
the riddles of your existence, your sin and your futile battles against
it, your death, which you are daily approaching, do not these things
give you enough to think about that you imagine you can come
through all these dark things without an absolutely mighty, absolutely true, an absolutely ultimate word of victory that is the vital
core of life? This mighty, true word of victory is resurrection! Is all
this still obscure to you? Ah, this *word* is certainly not dark, it is
your *life* that is dark. The world is dark because mankind is imprisoned." But we will not admit it. And as long as we will not admit
it, the word "resurrection" will be a difficult word, a rock of offense,
hard and offensive, because it is so sincere and because we cannot
honestly face it without having to admit that life is difficult, that
the world is dark, that death is not child's play, and that we are not
done with our sins. No cultural education, no art, no evolutionary
development helps me beyond my sins. I must receive assistance
from the ground up. Then the steep walls of our security are broken
to bits, and we are forced to become humble, poor, pleading. Thus
we are driven more and more to surrender and give up all that we
have, surrender and give up those things which we formerly used
to protect and defend and hold to ourselves against the voice of

the resurrection's truth, which spoke to us so mightily out of the facts of life. Thus we edge over very close to the place where we can hear the great "but" which immediately follows, "But God who is rich in mercy, because of his great love wherewith he loved us even when we were dead through our trespasses, made us alive together with Christ."

"*But God*" — Yes, *there* resurrection is proclaimed. *There* eventuates a new emancipating beginning in the very midst of human transiency. There a new door opens, when all other exits are barricaded. There a new page is turned, the old is past, turned over and laid back. "But God, who is rich in mercy" — a tremendous, new, and unexpected possibility opens to us after all possibilities are exhausted; a great, radiant freedom bursts forth after you harbored no more hope that you could escape the imprisonment of your character and your circumstances, your troubles and your burdens. "But God!" Perhaps you have not yet reckoned in earnest with that phrase. But you must now reckon with it and with nothing else. Perhaps you will now remark: "I cannot understand it, I do not sense it, I have not yet experienced it. It does not harmonize with my experience. I am not pious, not religiously inclined. In short, I do not have any rational ground to trust myself to it." But I might reply: "Do you not understand that the resurrection is a goal for which there is no rational ground, which requires no reason, to which no human support, human knowledge, or human experience can be brought to prove or make it true? It is not a question as to whether *you* can *grasp* it or not, whether there is some supporting proof of it; but the main question is whether you have that freedom which is without ground or support, without knowledge, proof, or experience in the midst of your impasse, darkness, and the afflictions of your life and death."

Do you have that freedom to breathe and be happy about this "but God"? That is the primary question. Are you free enough to let your life come to such a point, where without your assistance "even though you are dead in your sins" this is true: "But God, who is rich in mercy. . . ." Yes, truer than your sin, truer than all your experiences and your thoughts, truer than all your doubts and afflictions, truer than death, graves, and hell. This freedom God will gladly give you, this freedom to breathe in His atmosphere, even though you have a thousand griefs; this freedom to rise from the dead in the victorious power of Christ, even though you are a sinner and a mortal. This is the Easter message.

This is the Easter gospel. Why do we not believe it? Why do we always strive against this mighty "but God, who is rich in mercy . . ."? Why do we not crash through the imprisoning wall of our thought-life, which keeps us from the great resuscitation that can become our possession? Why is not this gospel preached from every pulpit? Why is it not heard in all our human constraints, upon all deathbeds, and at the side of all graves? Why do we not really know that all have been made alive through the mercy of God? And even when we do know it, why is it not *the one* and *only* truth against which there is not anything of importance to invalidate it, because it pierces everything, suspends everything, and renews everything? These questions are synonymous with the question: Why do we still think that we can live our life without God, even for one hour? Have we not yet sunk deep enough to see how little progress we can make alone? Yes, that is the enigma of all enigmas about which a great, single, tragic wonderment reigns in heaven — the fact that man thinks he can live and die in his own strength. On the one hand we find life with all its need and its enigmas, and on the other is God with all the lights and powers of the heavenly world, and in the midst is man in whom both seek to unite, whose existence shall become the stage upon which God desires to meet the needs of man, a stage of the resurrection, for that is resurrection. But man will not surrender his life to it; he rebels, he does not understand and will not believe, he hides himself even in the resurrection!

Yet all we can say is to repeat, "But God, who is rich in mercy . . ."; God will have done with this enigma, the enigma of our unbelief. He has already done with it. For the resurrection is not simply *one* word, *one* idea, *a* program. Resurrection is *fact*. Resurrection has happened. The contradiction is broken. The life of man has already become the stage of the divine triumphant mercy. Jesus Christ has risen from the dead. Let us ask God that He may conquer us through his word.

C. S. LEWIS

The Weight of Glory

C. S. Lewis, perhaps the most celebrated Christian writer of the twentieth century, combined straight thinking with deep passion for the things of faith. Alarmingly learned in both philosophy and literature, Lewis wrote as a kind of rationalist romantic, or romantic rationalist, a kindler of fires in quite various people. For decades, some of these people have been children, drawn to the deep magic of Lewis's keen imagination, laser-like prose, and avuncular readiness to tell cracking good stories — stories that can arouse old hungers even in the young.

"The Weight of Glory," one of Lewis's few sermons, aims to analyze a big, but mysterious, biblical theme. (The sermon title and part of its theme come from 2 Corinthians 4:17.) Christians sing and speak of glory, but what is it? More particularly, what shall we make of our longing for it, the "inconsolable secret" of which we may be privately ashamed?

The last paragraph of this sermon is classic in twentieth-century Christian literature.

The Weight of Glory

. . . The New Testament has lots to say about self-denial, but not about self-denial as an end in itself. We are told to deny ourselves and take up our crosses in order that we may follow Christ; and . . . nearly every description of what we shall ultimately find if we do so contains an appeal to desire. . . . Indeed, if we consider the unblushing promise of reward and the staggering nature of the rewards promised in the Gospels, it would seem that our Lord finds our desires not too strong, but too weak. We are halfhearted creatures, fooling about with drink and sex and ambition when infinite joy is offered us, like an ignorant child who wants to go on making mud pies in a slum because he cannot imagine what is meant by the offer of a holiday at the sea. We are far too easily pleased.

. . . Now, if we are made for heaven, the desire for our proper place will be already in us, but not yet attached to the true object. . . . In speaking of this desire for our own far-off country, which we find in ourselves even now, I feel a certain shyness. I am almost committing an indecency. I am trying to rip open the inconsolable secret in each one of you — the secret which hurts so much that you take your revenge on it by calling it names like Nostalgia and Romanticism and Adolescence; the secret also which pierces with such sweetness that when, in very intimate conversation, the mention of it becomes imminent, we grow awkward and affect to laugh at ourselves; the secret we cannot hide and cannot tell, though we desire to do both. We cannot tell it because it is a desire for something that has never actually appeared in our experience. We cannot hide it because our experience is constantly suggesting it, and we betray ourselves like lovers at the mention of a name. Our commonest expedient is to call it beauty and behave as if that had settled the matter. Wordsworth's expedient was to identify it with certain moments in his own past. But all this is a cheat. If Wordsworth had gone back to those moments in the past, he would not have found the thing itself, but only the reminder of it; what he remembered would turn out to be itself a remembering.

The books or the music in which we thought the beauty was located will betray us if we trust to them; it was not *in* them, it only came *through* them, and what came through them was longing. These things — the beauty, the memory of our own past — are good images of what we really desire; but if they are mistaken for the thing itself, they turn into dumb idols, breaking the hearts of their worshippers. For they are not the thing itself; they are only the scent of a flower we have not found, the echo of a tune we have not heard, news from a country we have never yet visited. Do you think I am trying to weave a spell? Perhaps I am; but remember your fairy tales. Spells are used for breaking enchantments as well as for inducing them. And you and I have need of the strongest spell that can be found to wake us from the evil enchantment of worldliness which has been laid upon us for nearly a hundred years. Almost our whole education has been directed to silencing this shy, persistent, inner voice; almost all our modern philosophies have been devised to convince us that the good of man is to be found on this earth. And yet it is a remarkable thing that such philosophies of Progress or Creative Evolution themselves bear reluctant witness to the truth that our real goal is elsewhere. When they want to convince you that earth is your home, notice how they set about it. They begin by trying to persuade you that earth can be made into heaven, thus giving a sop to your sense of exile in earth as it is. Next, they tell you that this fortunate event is still a good way off in the future, thus giving a sop to your knowledge that the fatherland is not here and now. Finally, lest your longing for the transtemporal should awake and spoil the whole affair, they use any rhetoric that comes to hand to keep out of your mind the recollection that even if all the happiness they promised could come to man on earth, yet still each generation would lose it by death, including the last generation of all, and the whole story would be nothing, not even a story, for ever and ever. . . .

Do what they will, then, we remain conscious of a desire which no natural happiness will satisfy. But is there any reason to suppose that reality offers any satisfaction to it? "Nor does the being hungry prove that we have bread." But I think it may be urged that this misses the point. A man's physical hunger does not prove that man will get any bread; he may die of starvation on a raft in the Atlantic. But surely a man's hunger does prove that he comes of a race which repairs its body by eating and inhabits a world where eatable substances exist. In the same way, though I do not believe (I wish I did) that my desire for Paradise proves that I shall enjoy it, I think it a pretty good indication that such a thing exists and that some men will. A man may love a woman and not win her; but it would be very odd if the phenomenon called "falling in love" occurred in a sexless world.

Here, then, is the desire, still wandering and uncertain of its object and still largely unable to see that object in the direction where it really lies. Our sacred books give us some account of the object. . . .

The promises of Scripture may very roughly be reduced to five heads. It is promised (1) that we shall be with Christ; (2) that we shall be like him; (3) with an enormous wealth of imagery, that we shall have "glory"; (4) that we shall, in some sense, be fed or feasted or entertained; and (5) that we shall have some sort of official position in the universe — ruling cities, judging angels, being pillars of God's temple. . . .

I turn . . . to the idea of glory. There is no getting away from the fact that this idea is very prominent in the New Testament and in early Christian writings. Salvation is constantly associated with palms, crowns, white robes, thrones, and splendor like the sun and stars. All this makes no immediate appeal to me at all, and in that respect I fancy I am a typical modern. Glory suggests two ideas to me, of which one seems wicked and the other ridiculous. Either glory means to me fame, or it means luminosity. As for the first, since to be famous means to be better known than other people, the desire for fame appears to me as a competitive passion and therefore of hell rather than heaven. As for the second, who wishes to become a kind of living electric lightbulb?

When I began to look into this matter, I was shocked to find such different Christians as Milton, Johnson, and Thomas Aquinas taking heavenly glory quite frankly in the sense of fame or good report. But not fame conferred by our fellow creatures — fame with God, approval or (I might say) "appreciation" by God. And then, when I had thought it over, I saw that this view was scriptural; nothing can eliminate from the parable the divine *accolade*, "Well done, thou good and faithful servant." With that, a good deal of what I had been thinking all my life fell down like a house of cards. I suddenly remembered that no one can enter heaven except as a child; and nothing is so obvious in a child — not in a conceited child, but in a good child — as its great and undisguised pleasure in being praised. Not only in a child, either, but even in a dog or a horse. Apparently what I had mistaken for humility had, all these years, prevented me from understanding what is in fact the humblest, the most childlike, the most creaturely of pleasures — nay, the specific pleasure of the inferior: the pleasure of a beast before men, a child before its father, a pupil before his teacher, a creature before its Creator. I am not forgetting how horribly this most innocent desire is parodied in our human ambitions, or how very quickly, in my own experience, the lawful pleasure of praise from those whom it was my duty to please turns into the deadly poison of self-admiration. But I thought I could detect a moment — a very, very short moment — before this happened, during which the satisfaction of having pleased those whom I rightly loved and rightly feared was pure. And that is enough to raise our thoughts to what may happen when the redeemed soul, beyond all hope and nearly beyond belief, learns at last that she has pleased Him whom she was created to please. There will be no room for vanity then. She will be free from the miserable illusion that it is her doing. With no taint of what we should now call self-approval she will most innocently rejoice in the thing that God has made her to be, and the moment which heals her old inferiority complex forever will also drown her pride deeper than Prospero's book. Perfect humility dispenses with modesty. If God is satisfied with the work, the work may be satisfied with itself; "it is not for her to bandy compliments with her Sovereign." I can imagine someone saying that he dislikes my idea of heaven as a place where we are patted on the back. But proud misunderstanding is behind that dislike. In the end that Face which is the delight or the terror of the universe must be turned upon each of us either with one expression or with the other, either conferring glory inexpressible or inflicting shame that can never be cured or disguised. I read in a periodical the other day that the fundamental thing is how we think of God. By God himself, it is not! How God thinks of us is not only more important, but infinitely more important. Indeed, how we think of him is of no importance except insofar as it is related to how he thinks of us. It is written that we shall "stand before" him, shall appear, shall be inspected. The promise of glory is the promise, almost incredible and only possible by the work of Christ, that some of us, that any of us who really chooses, shall actually survive that examination, shall find approval, shall please God. To please God . . . to be a real ingredient in the divine happiness . . . to be loved by God, not merely pitied, but delighted in as an artist delights in his work or a father in a son — it seems impossible, a weight or burden of glory which our thoughts can hardly sustain. But so it is.

And now notice what is happening. If I had rejected the authoritative and scriptural image of glory and stuck obstinately to the vague desire which was, at the outset, my only pointer to heaven, I could have seen no connection at all between that desire and the Christian promise. But now, having followed up what seemed puzzling and repellent in the sacred books, I find, to my great surprise, looking back, that the connection is perfectly clear. Glory, as Christianity teaches me to hope for it, turns out to satisfy my original desire and indeed to reveal an element in that desire which I had not noticed. By ceasing for a moment to consider my own wants I have begun to learn better what I really wanted. When I attempted, a few minutes ago, to describe our spiritual longings, I was omitting one of their most curious characteristics. We usually notice it just as the moment of vision dies away, as the music ends, or as the landscape loses the celestial light. What we feel then has been well described by Keats as "the journey homeward to habitual self." You know what I mean. For a few minutes we have had the illusion of belonging to that world. Now we wake to find that it is no such thing. We have been mere spectators. Beauty has smiled, but not to welcome us; her face was turned in our direction, but not to see us. We have not been accepted, welcomed, or taken into the dance. We may go when we please, we may stay if we can: "Nobody marks us." A scientist may reply that since most of the things we call beautiful are inanimate, it is not very surprising that they take no notice of us. That, of course, is true. It is not the physical objects that I am speaking of, but that indescribable something of which they become for a moment the messengers. And part of the bitterness which mixes with the sweetness of that message is due to the fact that it so seldom seems to be a message intended for us, but rather something we have overheard. By bitterness I mean pain, not resentment. We should hardly dare to ask that any notice be taken of ourselves. But we pine. The sense that in this universe we are treated as strangers, the longing to be acknowledged, to meet with some response, to bridge some chasm that yawns between us and reality, is part of our inconsolable secret. And surely, from this point of view, the promise of glory, in the sense described, becomes highly relevant to our deep desire. For glory means good report with God, acceptance by God, response, acknowledgment, and welcome into the heart of things. The door on which we have been knocking all our lives will open at last.

Perhaps it seems rather crude to describe glory as the fact of being "noticed" by God. But this is almost the language of the New Testament. St. Paul promises to those who love God not, as we should expect, that they will know him, but that they will be known by him (1 Cor. 8:3). It is a strange promise. Does not God know all things at all times? But it is dreadfully re-echoed in another passage of the New Testament. There we are warned that it may happen to anyone of us to appear at last before the face of God and hear only the appalling words, "I never knew you. Depart from me." In some sense, as dark to the intellect as it is unendurable to the feelings, we can be both banished from the presence of Him who is present everywhere and erased from the knowledge of Him who knows all. We can be left utterly and absolutely *outside* — repelled, exiled, estranged, finally and unspeakably ignored. On the other hand, we can be called in, welcomed, received, acknowledged. We walk every day on the razor edge between these two incredible possibilities. Apparently, then, our lifelong nostalgia, our longing to be reunited with something in the universe from which we now feel cut off, to be on the inside of some door which we have always seen from the outside, is no mere neurotic fancy, but the truest index of our real situation. And to be at last summoned inside would be both glory and honor beyond all our merits and also the healing of that old ache.

And this brings me to the other sense of glory — glory as brightness, splendor, luminosity. We are to shine as the sun, we are to be given the Morning Star. I think I begin to see what it means. In one way, of course, God has given us the Morning Star already: you can go and enjoy the gift on many fine mornings if you get up early enough. What more, you may ask, do we want? Ah, but we want so much more — something the books on aesthetics take little notice of. But the poets and the mythologies know all about it. We do not want merely to *see* beauty, though, God knows, even that is bounty enough. We want something else which can hardly be put into words — to be united with the beauty we see, to pass into it, to receive it into ourselves, to bathe in it, to become part of it. That is why we have peopled air and earth and water with gods and goddesses and nymphs and elves — that, though we cannot, yet these projections can enjoy in themselves that beauty, grace, and power of which Nature is the image. That is why the poets tell us such lovely falsehoods. They talk as if the west wind could really sweep into a human soul; but it can't. They tell us that "beauty born of murmuring sound" will pass into a human face; but it won't. Or not yet. For if we take the imagery of Scripture seriously, if we believe that God will one day *give* us the Morning Star and cause us to *put on* the splendor of the sun, then we may surmise that both the ancient myths and the modern poetry, so false as history, may be very near the truth as prophecy. At present we are on the outside of the world, the wrong side of the door. We discern the freshness and purity of morning, but they do not make us fresh and pure. We cannot mingle with the splendors we see. But all the leaves of the New Testament are rustling with the rumor that it will not always be so. Some day, God willing, we shall get *in*. When human souls have become as perfect in voluntary obedience as the creation is in its lifeless obedience, then they will put on its glory, or rather that greater glory of which Nature is only the first sketch. For you must not think that I am putting forward any heathen fancy of being absorbed into Nature. Nature is mortal; we shall outlive her. When all the suns and nebulae have passed away, each one of you will still be alive. Nature is only the image, the symbol; but it is the symbol Scripture invites me to use. We are summoned to pass in through Nature, beyond her, into that splendor which she fitfully reflects. . . .

Meanwhile the cross comes before the crown and tomorrow is a Monday morning. A cleft has opened in the pitiless walls of the world, and we are invited to follow our great Captain inside. The following him is, of course, the essential point. That being so, it may be asked what practical use there is in the speculations which I have been indulging. I can think of at least one such use. It may be possible for each to think too much of his own potential glory hereafter; it is hardly possible for him to think too often or too deeply about that of his neighbor. The load, or weight, or burden of my neighbor's glory should be laid on my back, a load so heavy that only humility can carry it, and the backs of the proud will be broken. It is a serious thing to live in a society of possible gods and goddesses, to remember that the dullest and most uninteresting person you can talk to may one day be a creature which, if you saw it now, you would be strongly tempted to worship, or else a horror and a corruption such as you now meet, if at all, only in a nightmare. All day long we are, in some degree, helping each other to one or other of these destinations. It is in the light of these overwhelming possibilities, it is with the awe and the circumspection proper to them, that we should conduct all our dealings with one another, all friendships, all loves, all play, all politics. There are no *ordinary* people. You have never talked to a mere mortal. Nations, cultures, arts, civilizations — these are mortal, and their life is to ours as the life of a gnat. But it is immortals whom we joke with, work with, marry, snub, and exploit — immortal horrors or everlasting splendors. This does not mean that we are to be perpetually solemn. We must play. But our merriment must be of that kind (and it is, in fact, the merriest kind) which exists between people who have, from the outset, taken each other seriously — no flippancy, no superiority, no presumption. And our charity must be a real and costly love, with deep feeling for the sins in spite of which we love the sinner — no mere tolerance, or indulgence which parodies love as flippancy parodies merriment. Next to the Blessed Sacrament itself, your neighbor is the holiest object presented to your senses. If he is your Christian neighbor, he is holy in almost the same way, for in him also Christ *vere latitat* — the glorifier and the glorified, Glory Himself, is truly hidden.

PAUL TILLICH

You Are Accepted

In perhaps the best known and most admired of his sermons, Paul Tillich eloquently explores the meaning and power of sin and grace. In his characteristic way, Tillich correlates theological and existential ideas, inviting listeners to join him in pondering the common human sense of alienation. To do so is to begin a descent into ourselves, a penetration of "the deeper levels of our life," the levels where we struggle "between separation and reunion, between sin and grace."

As always, Tillich wants to accomplish more than merely educating his listeners and more than fleshing out experientially a couple of old theological bones. He has a kerygmatic aim as well, maybe even an evangelistic one: Tillich wants his listeners to experience the accepting grace of God. Hence the power of the sentences that precede Tillich's refrain, "You are accepted. *You are accepted.* . . ." Hence the beauty and power of the refrain itself. This part of the sermon has become one of the most-quoted sections in all of Tillich's works.

You Are Accepted

Moreover the law entered, that the offence might
abound. But where sin abounded, grace did much more
abound.

Romans 5:20, KJV

These words of Paul summarize his apostolic experience, his religious message as a whole, and the Christian understanding of life.
To discuss these words, or to make them the text of even several
sermons, has always seemed impossible to me. I have never dared
to use them before. But something has driven me to consider them
during the past few months, a desire to give witness to the two
facts that appeared to me, in hours of retrospection, as the all-
determining facts of our life: the abounding of sin and the greater
abounding of grace.

There are few words more strange to most of us than "sin"
and "grace." They are strange, just because they are so well known.
During the centuries they have received distorting connotations
and have lost so much of their genuine power that we must seriously
ask ourselves whether we should use them at all, or whether we
should discard them as useless tools. But there is a mysterious fact
about the great words of our religious tradition: they cannot be
replaced. All attempts to make substitutions, including those I have
tried myself, have failed to convey the reality that was to be expressed; they have led to shallow and impotent talk. There are no
substitutes for words like "sin" and "grace." But there *is* a way of
rediscovering their meaning, the same way that leads us down into
the depth of our human existence. In that depth these words were
conceived; and *there* they gained power for all ages; *there* they must
be found again by each generation, and by each of us for himself.
Let us therefore try to penetrate the deeper levels of our life, in
order to see whether we can discover in them the realities of which
our text speaks.

Have the men of our time still a feeling of the meaning of sin? Do they, and do we, still realize that sin does *not* mean an immoral act, that "sin" should never be used in the plural, and that not our sins, but rather our *sin* is the great, all-pervading problem of our life? Do we still know that it is arrogant and erroneous to divide men by calling some "sinners" and others "righteous"? For by way of such a division, we can usually discover that we ourselves do not *quite* belong to the "sinners," since we have avoided heavy sins, have made some progress in the control of this or that sin, and have been even humble enough not to call ourselves "righteous." Are we still able to realize that this kind of thinking and feeling about sin is far removed from what the great religious tradition, both within and outside the Bible, has meant when it speaks of sin?

I should like to suggest another word to you, not as a substitute for the word "sin," but as a useful clue in the interpretation of the word "sin": "separation." Separation is an aspect of the experience of everyone. Perhaps the word "sin" has the same root as the word "asunder." In any case, *sin is separation.* To be in the state of sin is to be in the state of separation. And separation is threefold: there is separation among individual lives, separation of a man from himself, and separation of all men from the Ground of Being. This threefold separation constitutes the state of everything that exists; it is a universal fact; it is the fate of every life. And it is our human fate in a very special sense. For *we* as men know that we are separated. We not only suffer with all other creatures because of the self-destructive consequences of our separation but also know *why* we suffer. We know that we are estranged from something to which we really belong, and with which we *should* be united. We know that the fate of separation is not merely a natural event like a flash of sudden lightning, but that it is an experience in which we actively participate, in which our whole personality is involved, and that, as fate, it is also *guilt.* Separation that is fate *and* guilt constitutes the meaning of the word "sin." It is *this* which is the state of our entire existence, from its very beginning to its very end. Such separation is prepared in the mother's womb, and before that time, in every preceding generation. It is manifest in the special actions of our conscious life. It reaches beyond our graves into all the succeeding generations. It is our existence itself. *Existence is separation!* Before sin is an act, it is a state.

We can say the same things about grace. For sin and grace are bound to each other. We do not even have a knowledge of sin unless we have already experienced the unity of life, which is grace. And conversely, we could not grasp the meaning of grace without having experienced the separation of life, which is sin. Grace is just as difficult to describe as sin. For some people, grace is the willingness of a divine king and father to forgive over and again the foolishness and weakness of his subjects and children. We must reject such a concept of grace; for it is a merely childish destruction of a human dignity. For others grace is a magic power in the dark places of the soul, but a power without any significance for practical life, a quickly vanishing and useless idea. For others grace is the benevolence that we may find beside the cruelty and destructiveness in life. But then, it does not matter whether we say "life goes on," or whether we say "there is grace in life"; if grace means no more than this, the word should, and will, disappear. For other people, grace indicates the gifts that one has received from nature or society, and the power to do good things with the help of those gifts. But grace is more than gifts. In grace something is overcome; grace occurs "in spite of" something; grace occurs in spite of separation and estrangement. Grace is the reunion of life with life, the reconciliation of the self with itself. Grace transforms fate into a meaningful destiny; it changes guilt into confidence and courage. There is something triumphant in the word "grace": in spite of the abounding of sin grace abounds much more.

And now let us look down into ourselves to discover there the struggle between separation and reunion, between sin and grace, in our relation to others, in our relation to ourselves, and in our relation to the Ground and aim of our being. If our souls respond to the description that I intend to give, words like "sin" and "separation," "grace" and "reunion" may have a new meaning for us. But the words themselves are not important. It is the response of the deepest levels of our being that is important. If such a response were to occur among us this moment, we could say that we have known grace.

Who has not, at some time, been lonely in the midst of a social event? The feeling of our separation from the rest of life is most acute when we are surrounded by it in noise and talk. We realize then much more than in moments of solitude how strange we are to one another, how estranged life is from life. Each one of us draws back into himself. We cannot penetrate the hidden center of another individual; nor can that individual pass beyond the shroud that covers our own being. Even the greatest love cannot break through the walls of the self. Who has not experienced that disillusionment of all great love? If one were to hurl away his self in complete self-surrender, he would become a nothing, without form or strength, a self without self, merely an object of contempt and abuse. Our generation knows more than the generation of our fathers about the hidden hostility in the ground of our souls. Today we know much about the profusive aggressiveness in every being. Today we can confirm what Immanuel Kant, the prophet of human reason and dignity, was honest enough to say: there is something in the misfortune of our best friends that does not displease us. Who among us is dishonest enough to deny that this is true also of him? Are we not almost always ready to abuse everybody and everything, although often in a very refined way, for the pleasure of self-elevation, for an occasion for boasting, for a moment of lust? To know that we are ready is to know the meaning of the separation of life from life, and of "sin abounding."

The most irrevocable expression of the separation of life from life today is the attitude of social groups within nations toward each other, and the attitude of nations themselves toward other nations. The walls of distance, in time and space, have been removed by technical progress; but the walls of estrangement between heart and heart have been incredibly strengthened. The madness of the German Nazis and the cruelty of the lynching mobs in the South provide too easy an excuse for us to turn our thoughts from our own selves. But let us just consider ourselves and what we feel, when we read, this morning and tonight, that in some sections of Europe all children under the age of three are sick and dying, or that in some sections of Asia millions without homes are freezing and starving to death. The strangeness of life to life is evident in the strange fact that we can know all this, and yet can live today, this morning, tonight, as though we were completely ignorant. And I refer to the most sensitive people among us. In both mankind and nature, life is separated from life. Estrangement prevails among all things that live. Sin abounds.

It is important to remember that we are not merely separated from one another. For we are also separated from ourselves. *Man Against Himself* is not merely the title of a book, but rather also indicates the rediscovery of an age-old insight. Man is split within himself. Life moves against itself through aggression, hate, and despair. We are wont to condemn self-love; but what we really mean to condemn is contrary to self-love. It is that mixture of selfishness and self-hate that permanently pursues us, that prevents us from loving others, and that prohibits us from losing ourselves in the love with which we are loved eternally. He who is able to love himself is able to love others also; he who has learned to overcome self-contempt has overcome his contempt for others. But the depth of our separation lies in just the fact that we are not capable of a great and merciful divine love toward ourselves. On the contrary, in each of us there is an instinct of self-destruction, which is as strong as our instinct of self-preservation. In our tendency to abuse and destroy others, there is an open or hidden tendency to abuse and to destroy ourselves. Cruelty toward others is always also cruelty toward ourselves. Nothing is more obvious than the split in both our unconscious life and conscious personality. Without the help of modern psychology, Paul expressed the fact in his famous words, "For I do not do the good I desire, but rather the evil that I do not desire." And then he continued in words that might well be the motto of all depth psychology: "Now if I should do what I do not wish to do, it is not I that do it, but rather sin which dwells within me." The apostle sensed a split between his conscious will and his real will, between himself and something strange within and alien to him. He was estranged from himself, and that estrangement he called "sin." He also called it a strange "law in his limbs," an irresistible compulsion. How often we commit certain acts in perfect consciousness, yet with the shocking sense that we are being controlled by an alien power! That is the experience of the separation of ourselves from ourselves, which is to say "sin," whether or not we like to use that word.

Thus, the state of our whole life is estrangement from others and ourselves, because we are estranged from the Ground of our being, because we are estranged from the origin and aim of our life. And we do not know where we have come from, or where we are going. We are separated from the mystery, the depth, and the greatness of our existence. We hear the voice of that depth; but our ears are closed. We feel that something radical, total, and unconditioned is demanded of us; but we rebel against it, try to escape its urgency, and will not accept its promise.

We cannot escape, however. If that something is the Ground of our being, we are bound to it for all eternity, just as we are bound to ourselves and to all other life. We always remain in the power of that from which we are estranged. That fact brings us to the ultimate depth of sin: separated and yet bound, estranged and yet belonging, destroyed and yet preserved, the state that is called despair. Despair means that there is no escape. Despair is "the sickness unto death." But the terrible thing about the sickness of despair is that we cannot be released, not even through open or hidden suicide. For we all know that we are bound eternally and inescapably to the Ground of our being. The abyss of separation is not always visible. But it has become more visible to our generation than to the preceding generations, because of our feeling of meaninglessness, emptiness, doubt, and cynicism — all expressions of despair, of our separation from the roots and the meaning of our life. Sin in its most profound sense, sin, as despair, abounds among us.

"Where sin abounded, grace did much more abound," says Paul in the same letter in which he describes the unimaginable power of separation and self-destruction within society and the individual soul. He does not say these words because sentimental interests demand a happy ending for everything tragic. He says them because they describe the most overwhelming and determining experience of his life. In the picture of Jesus as the Christ, which

appeared to him at the moment of his greatest separation from
other men, from himself, and from God, he found himself accepted
in spite of his being rejected. And when he found that he was
accepted, he was able to accept himself and to be reconciled to
others. The moment in which grace struck him and overwhelmed
him, he was reunited with that to which he belonged, and from
which he was estranged in utter strangeness. Do we know what it
means to be struck by grace? It does *not* mean that we suddenly
believe that God exists, or that Jesus is the Savior, or that the Bible
contains the truth. To believe that something *is,* is almost contrary
to the meaning of grace. Furthermore, grace does not mean simply
that we are making progress in our moral self-control, in our fight
against special faults, and in our relationships to men and to society.
Moral progress may be a fruit of grace; but it is not grace itself,
and it can even prevent us from receiving grace. For there is too
often a graceless acceptance of Christian doctrines and a graceless
battle against the structures of evil in our personalities. Such a
graceless relation to God may lead us by necessity either to arrogance or to despair. It would be better to refuse God and the Christ
and the Bible than to accept them without grace. For if we accept
without grace, we do so in the state of separation, and can only
succeed in deepening the separation. We cannot transform our lives,
unless we allow them to be transformed by that stroke of grace. It
happens; or it does not happen. And certainly it does *not* happen
if we try to force it upon ourselves, just as it shall not happen so
long as we think, in our self-complacency, that we have no need of
it. Grace strikes us when we are in great pain and restlessness. It
strikes us when we walk through the dark valley of a meaningless
and empty life. It strikes us when we feel that our separation is
deeper than usual, because we have violated another life, a life which
we loved, or from which we were estranged. It strikes us when our
disgust for our own being, our indifference, our weakness, our
hostility, and our lack of direction and composure have become
intolerable to us. It strikes us when, year after year, the longed-for
perfection of life does not appear, when the old compulsions reign
within us as they have for decades, when despair destroys all joy
and courage. Sometimes at that moment a wave of light breaks into

our darkness, and it is as though a voice were saying: "You are accepted. *You are accepted*, accepted by that which is greater than you, and the name of which you do not know. Do not ask for the name now; perhaps you will find it later. Do not try to do anything now; perhaps later you will do much. Do not seek for anything; do not perform anything; do not intend anything. *Simply accept the fact that you are accepted!*" If that happens to us, we experience grace. After such an experience we may not be better than before, and we may not believe more than before. But everything is transformed. In that moment, grace conquers sin, and reconciliation bridges the gulf of estrangement. And nothing is demanded of this experience, no religious or moral or intellectual presupposition, nothing but *acceptance*.

In the light of this grace we perceive the power of grace in our relation to others and to ourselves. We experience the grace of being able to look frankly into the eyes of another, the miraculous grace of reunion of life with life. We experience the grace of understanding one another's words. We understand not merely the literal meaning of the words, but also that which lies behind them, even when they are harsh or angry. For even then there is a longing to break through the walls of separation. We experience the grace of being able to accept the life of another, even if it be hostile and harmful to us, for, through grace, we know that it belongs to the same Ground to which we belong, and by which we have been accepted. We experience the grace that is able to overcome the tragic separation of the sexes, of the generations, of the nations, of the races, and even the utter strangeness between man and nature. Sometimes grace appears in all these separations to reunite us with those to whom we belong. For life belongs to life.

And in the light of this grace we perceive the power of grace in our relation to ourselves. We experience moments in which we accept ourselves, because we feel that we have been accepted by that which is greater than we. If only more such moments were given to us! For it is such moments that make us love our life, that make us accept ourselves, not in our goodness and self-complacency, but in our certainty of the eternal meaning of our life. We cannot force ourselves to accept ourselves. We cannot compel anyone to accept himself. But sometimes it happens that we receive the power to say yes to ourselves, that peace enters into us and makes us whole, that self-hate and self-contempt disappear, and that our self is reunited with itself. Then we can say that grace has come upon us.

"Sin" and "grace" are strange words, but they are not strange things. We find them whenever we look into ourselves with searching eyes and longing hearts. They determine our life. They abound within us and in all of life. May grace more abound within us!

WILLIAM H. WILLIMON

What Time Is It?

Conversational, quiet, reflective, sometimes ironic, "What Time Is It?" asks its central question with the same leisure as those who think there is plenty of time for grace. The preacher of this evangelistic sermon is in no hurry: he has time to explore two views of history, two kinds of parables, two views of life's pace and God's grace.

But then someone dies; and the mood of the sermon darkens, and its pace quickens. We get addressed with more urgency. Shadows lengthen, and signs appear: it is later than we think. And then the ending — as sudden and lethal as a shot to the heart.

In pace, tone, and emotional dynamics, Willimon's sermon keeps up, movement by movement, with the progress of its own discussion.

William H. Willimon, "What Time Is It?" originally appeared in the July–August 1985 issue of *Preaching*. Reprinted by permission of *Preaching* and of the author.

What Time Is It?

"From the fig tree learn its lesson: as soon as its branch becomes tender and puts forth its leaves, you know that summer is near. So also, when you see all these things, you know that he is near, at the very gates. Truly, I say to you, this generation will not pass away till all these things take place. Heaven and earth will pass away, but my words will not pass away.

"But of that day and hour no one knows, not even the angels of heaven, nor the Son, but the Father only. As were the days of Noah, so will be the coming of the Son of man. For as in those days before the flood they were eating and drinking, marrying and giving in marriage, until the day when Noah entered the ark, and they did not know until the flood came and swept them all away, so will be the coming of the Son of man. Then two men will be in the field; one is taken and one is left. Two women will be grinding at the mill; one is taken and one is left. Watch therefore, for you do not know on what day your Lord is coming. But know this, that if the householder had known in what part of the night the thief was coming, he would have watched and would not have let his house be broken into. Therefore you also must be ready; for the Son of man is coming at an hour you do not expect."

Matthew 24:32-44

A woman of my acquaintance has thrown away her watch and decided to have nothing more to do with clocks. "I have freed myself from the tyranny of time," she says. She has had it with bourgeois, middle-class punctuality. She will now live as if every day were a vacation at the beach.

Something in me would like to be her, free from time's

tyranny, measuring time as did my ancestors — through the gentle passage of seasons, sunrise and sunset, not seconds, minutes, hours, punching in and punching out.

I have been conditioned into the chronology of the academy. I used to wonder why faculty meetings lasted so long. Days, weeks spent discussing, evaluating, pondering. The Dean announces that coffee hour has been changed from ten to ten thirty.

"Well, I believe we ought to reflect upon that," says one. "What are the larger issues, the basic philosophical questions surrounding coffee hour?" says another. Three days later, we are still pondering.

Before you laugh at us academics, I remind you that, as scholars, we are in the business of cautious observation and careful deliberation. Many a good thesis has been ruined because its author rushed to judgment, failed to weigh carefully all the facts, prematurely eliminated a possible solution. The key to good research is patience, restraint, caution.

"Scholars don't make good managers," says one management theorist. "They are trained not to decide."

The story is told that the physicist, Max Planck, died and went to heaven. St. Peter met him at the gate saying, "Professor Planck, this door goes to the Kingdom of Heaven, while this door leads to a discussion about the Kingdom of Heaven." As a scholar, you know which one he chose.

The word "decision" comes from the Latin meaning "to cut off," "to sever." Better to discuss, defer, refer to a committee for further consideration. Why go on record believing that the earth is round when someone may discover next year that it's really flat? Wait. Observe. Be patient. There's still time.

No wonder that many prudent people simply decide not to decide. They drift, or sit quietly in a corner, watching the vast, multicolored parade go by. One day they may decide, but not now, not with so many options. Not today. We mustn't prematurely close out the possibilities. Each time we take account of our lives, look back on where we have come, the roads taken and not taken, we know: Life is the sum of all the choices we make, or refuse to make.

"Men at forty close doors more softly," says the poet. Only a fool would rush to close one door prematurely by opening another. Best to wait until all of the evidence is in, until the data has been collected. Wait. Decisions are for tomorrow.

And there will always be a tomorrow. It's in the Bible. "There is nothing new under the sun," says the writer of the Book of Ecclesiastes. Something comes, something goes; thus it has ever been, thus it will ever be. Life is one thing after another in endless procession. Ecclesiastes has a Greek view of history. For the Greeks, time is a circle. There is no beginning to the world; no end either. Everything is a circle. There is a time to be born, a time to die, a time to plant, a time to reap, a time to build up, a time to tear down.

Over and over again it goes, eternally rising and falling and rising again. This is time, said the Greeks. There will always be tomorrow. Wisdom belongs to those who wait, who carefully weigh all possibilities, collect as much information as possible, consider all sides of an issue, and be moderately cautious. Why hurry? There will always be tomorrow.

Besides, as Christians we know that, even if we make the wrong decision (or, more to the point, no decision at all), there is always grace. A young boy asked for his inheritance from his father. He then took the money out to the "far country" to live the "good life." But his plan turned sour. He lost all of his money in loose living and was soon reduced to the level of a pig. Yet all was not lost for this prodigal. He returned home, penitent and broken, and his waiting father received him with joy, threw a party for him, and all was forgiven.

Matthew tells a story. A man goes out at dawn and hires some workers for his vineyard. Later in the day, he goes out and hires some more men to work. Late in the afternoon, an hour or so before quitting time, he hires yet more workers. When the day ends, he calls all the workers together and pays them all — the same wage. The ones who have been out sweating since dawn get paid as much as those who only got in an hour before dusk. There is grumbling. "Do you begrudge my generosity?" the master asks the grumbling workers.

And we love that little parable. Because it means that what we hoped is right: There is still time. So what if you haven't got your life together today? Don't worry. The father waits. You may be the eleventh-hour worker who will get as much grace from God as those who have been at it since infancy. God's kingdom is like that, says Jesus. God is gracious. There will always be a tomorrow for decisions and homecomings. Why trouble ourselves about the now when there is always grace for the future?

All would be well if Matthew told only one parable, the one about the laborers in the vineyard. We could let grace be grace, a gift a gift, and drift on through today to an ever-open tomorrow. But Matthew tells other stories: A group of girls are invited to a wedding party. They mean to go get oil for their lamps, but it was first one thing and then another. When the call finally goes out, "Come to the party!" the oil is gone. By the time they go out and buy oil, alas, the door is shut. The party has begun without them. They bang at the door, they cry out, they claw at the door! But no, the door is shut. They had their chance. It's over now. There will be no tomorrow.

Or today's lesson from Matthew: When you see the fig tree blossom, you know what time it is. Noah knew the time. When Noah built the ark his neighbors ate and drank at backyard patio parties. They looked over the fence and saw the old man feverishly hammering away at the ark. If they had only known: The clouds gathering on the horizon were to spoil more than their picnic!

Thieves don't send engraved announcements to alert you of a nocturnal visit, says Jesus. And that's the way God is, life is — sometimes it comes upon you like a thief in the night.

Jesus, Jew that he was, had no Greek view of history. Unlike the Greeks, Israel viewed history, not as a never-ending circle, but as a straight line, a line with a beginning and an end. The world begins in Genesis with God's creation of the world and ends in Revelation. There is a beginning and an end to all things. Someday, there will be no tomorrow.

The invitation is given. When it is rejected, it goes elsewhere. The door is opened. Then it is shut. The gavel goes down, the ticking clock is silent, the little up-and-down line on the monitor becomes straight, and it is over. There is no tomorrow.

That's a word which isn't popular these days, is it? We would rather Matthew tell us about eleventh-hour workers who get grace rather than about procrastinators who end up out in the cold. Ninety-nine percent of Americans like the story of the prodigal son better than the story of the foolish virgins or the thief in the night.

And that was possibly the way it was for the church of Matthew's day. The time of crisis was over. It's hard to live every day, day in, day out, as if there were no tomorrow. Jesus had said that he was returning soon to reclaim the faithful. But where was he? The church had waited, and waited. By the time this Gospel was written the church had been waiting for maybe seventy-five or eighty years for the return of Christ, and that's a long time to stand on tiptoes. It's hard to maintain a sense of crisis for eighty years!

Therein is the problem. "There will always be a tomorrow," some must have said. "After all, there have been about 29,000 tomorrows since Jesus told us he would return for us." The once taut church relaxed, loosened its grip, settled down in the everydayness of things.

And that, our story today indicates, is dangerous. To live as if there will always be a tomorrow is to live like a fool. The best-selling religious book of all time is called *The Late Great Planet Earth*. Fifty million people paid good money to read Hal Lindsey's view of the end. Yet it isn't only Jerry Falwell, Hal Lindsey, and James Watt talking this way. The gathering ecological crisis, the threat of nuclear war, international monetary problems — suddenly everyone is talking apocalyptic but the church, the liberal, contented church, which long ago made peace with the present and dared not think about tomorrow.

Next year, next administration, maybe we'll sit down with the Russians and talk disarmament. There's still time.

It is so easy to be fooled. Here we sit with all this substantial stone enclosing us. This church has been here for fifty years, so it's not too foolish to assume that we'll be here fifty more. You'll come home to your fiftieth reunion and everyone will look exactly as they do now, right?

A few Sundays ago, after the service was ended in this vast, eternal-looking, neo-Gothic place, tourists were milling around in the nave, looking at windows and admiring the carving. A man slumped to the floor. His wife cried out. The Duke emergency team was called. Later she told me that they had moved to North Carolina a month ago. Early retirement it was to be in this climate more hospitable than Iowa. They were in Durham to walk in the

Duke gardens and to see the Chapel. He had no history of heart trouble. She went in to see the Chapel. She left a widow.

Who are we kidding? We who smile and go about our business, raise our children, build our houses, go to football games, take afternoon naps — all under the shadow of the great, dark mushroom cloud. The flash, the roar, the rush of wind and rubble, and, for the whole race, there is no tomorrow.

Is that why not everyone thinks it's such a grand idea to return for Homecoming? These occasions make time seem so linear, life so finite, the bitter-sweet realization that the ever-rolling stream of time bears all our dreams away?

It was at the funeral of her beloved husband when she asked if she could say a word to the gathered congregation: If you are going to love somebody, she said with tears in her eyes, do it today. If you are going to tell someone they are special, that their life has touched yours, do it today. She had become wise the hard way.

Jesus says you and I can live any way we want. We can put off life as if there were always a tomorrow. We can make it all look so secure and solid and eternal. Yet, for me, for you, for us all, there will be one day when there is no tomorrow. The invitation comes, the door opens, and light shines through, the word is spoken, the waters rise, the bell tolls, and it is time; for good or ill, it is time.

"Of that day and hour no one knows. . . . Watch."

When I was serving a little church in rural Georgia, one of my members had a relative who died, and Patsy and I went to the funeral as a show of support for the family. The funeral was in a little, hot, crowded, off-brand Baptist country church. Well, I had never seen anything like it. They wheeled the coffin in; the preacher began to preach. He shouted, fumed, flayed his arms.

"It's too late for Joe," he screamed. "He might have wanted to do this or that in life, but it's too late for him now. He's dead. It's all over for him. He might have wanted to straighten his life out, but he can't now. It's over."

What a comfort this must be to the family, I thought.

"But it ain't too late for you! People drop dead every day. So why wait? Now is the day for decision. Now is the time to make your life count for something. Give your life to Jesus!"

Well, it was the worst thing I ever heard. "Can you imagine a preacher doing that kind of thing to a grieving family?" I asked Patsy on the way home. "I've never heard anything so manipulative, cheap, and inappropriate. I would never preach a sermon like that," I said. She agreed. She agreed it was tacky, manipulative, calloused. "Of course," she added, "the worst part of all is that what he said was true."

HARRY EMERSON FOSDICK

The Importance of
Doubting Our Doubts

Harry Emerson Fosdick was known for his "project" or "life-situation" method of pastoral preaching. He would begin a sermon by describing and analyzing a concrete human problem. Only after he had taken time to make firm contact with his listeners in this way would he turn to the resources of the Christian faith for a response.

One virtue of this approach was its economy: Fosdick was able to counsel hundreds simultaneously. Moreover, though he regularly preached to large crowds in the vast sanctuary of New York's Riverside Church, Fosdick's empathy created the intimate atmosphere of a one-on-one pastoral care conversation. In fact, hearers would often report that, as they heard Fosdick preach, they had the sense of being personally addressed.

Notice in the sermon before us how Fosdick peers behind the pious faces of his hearers and spots questions and uncertainties there. Notice also that hearers — or readers — who have had their minds read may then be ready to have their hearts pierced and healed.

Harry Emerson Fosdick, "The Importance of Doubting Our Doubts," from *What Is Vital in Religion* by Harry Emerson Fosdick, pp. 89-99. Copyright 1955 by Harper & Brothers. Copyright renewed 1983 by Elinor F. Downs and Dorothy Fosdick. Reprinted by permission of HarperCollins, Publishers, Inc.

The Importance of Doubting Our Doubts

In the vocabulary of religion the word "doubt" has a bad significance. Have you ever heard a preacher use it in a favorable sense? Faith is the great word. Faith is the victory that overcomes the world, and is not doubt its chief enemy? So the word "doubt" has been exiled to religion's semantic doghouse.

But that does not solve the problem. Once more today I feel what I commonly feel when I face worshiping congregations. You look so pious. You are so reverent. You listen so respectfully to Scripture and anthem. You sing so earnestly the resounding hymns. Yet I know and you know that in every life there is something else which our worship does not express — doubts, questions, uncertainties, skepticisms. Every one of us, facing the Christian faith, must honestly say what the man in the Gospel story said to Jesus: "Lord, I believe; help thou mine unbelief." Especially in these days, so disturbing to placid, docile faith about God and man, how applicable are the Bishop's words in Browning's poem:

> With me, faith means perpetual unbelief,
> Kept quiet like the snake 'neath Michael's foot,
> Who stands calm just because he feels it writhe.

Concerning this problem, which in one way or another we all face, I offer two preliminary observations. First, doubt is not a "snake"; the capacity to doubt is one of man's noblest powers. Look at our world today and see the innumerable beliefs and practices, from communism up and down, which ought to be doubted! The great servants of our race have been distinguished by the fact that in the face of universally accepted falsehoods they dared stand up and cry: I doubt that! Without the capacity to doubt there could be no progress — only docile, unquestioning acceptance of the status quo and its established dogmatisms.

Think of the scientific realm! The earth is flat, the sun circles round it — when such ideas were everywhere accepted, a few bravely dared to disbelieve them. Every scientific advance has started with skepticism. When we think of the scientific pioneers we emphasize their faith, their affirmative belief in new ideas and possibilities. Right! But in the experience of the pioneers themselves their first poignant struggle, their initial critical venture, centered in perilous and daring disbelief. Galileo was right when he called doubt the father of discovery.

But, someone says, when we turn from science to religion, we want faith — faith in God, in Christ, in the human soul. Of course we want faith! But anyone who thinks he can achieve great faith without exercising his God-given capacity to doubt is oversimplifying the problem. Jesus himself was a magnificent doubter. Wild ideas of a war-making Messiah who would overthrow Rome were prevalent in his time. He doubted them. "An eye for an eye and a tooth for a tooth" was the true law, they said. He doubted it. He saw men trusting in long prayers, broad phylacteries, rigid Sabbath rules, dietary laws as essential to true religion, and he doubted them all. He saw men believing in ancient traditions just because they were ancient, and he poured his skepticism on such reactionaries: "It was said unto them of old time, but I say unto you." Samaritans are an inferior race was the popular idea, but he scorned it; a good Samaritan, he said, is better than a bad priest. We are saved by Jesus' faith, we say. Yes, but just as truly as any scientific pioneer did, he reached his faith through his daring doubts. My friends, we sing the praises of the great believers. So do I! But who can worthily express our unpayable indebtedness to the brave doubters, who in perilous times, when false ideas dominated men's minds and spoiled their lives, saved the day with their courageous disbelief? Let us sing their praises too!

To someone here, struggling with this problem, I am saying first: Don't despise your capacity to doubt! Honor it! It is one of your noblest attributes.

My second preliminary observation is that the sturdiest faith has always come out of the struggle with doubt. There are only two ways in which we can possess Christian faith. One is to inherit it, borrow it, swallow it without question, take it over as we do the cut of our clothes without thinking about it. Some here may be able to do that, but your faith then is not really *yours*. You never fought for it. As one student said: "Being a Methodist, just because your parents were, is like wearing a secondhand hat that does not fit." No! Great faith, if it is really to be one's very own, always has to be fought for.

One who does not understand this, does not understand the Bible. It is a book of faith, we say. To be sure it is! But it is also a book filled with the struggles of men wrestling with their doubts and unbelief. Listen to Gideon crying, "If the Lord is with us, why then has all this befallen us?" Listen to the Psalmist:

My tears have been my food day and night,
While they continually say unto me,
    Where is thy God?

Listen to Job complaining to God: "I cry unto thee, and thou dost not answer me," or to Jeremiah calling God "a deceitful brook" and "waters that fail," and crying, "Cursed be the day on which I was born!"

The Bible only a book of faith? But listen to Ecclesiastes: "Vanity of vanities, all is vanity. . . . That which befalleth the sons of men befalleth beasts . . . as the one dieth, so dieth the other; yea, they have all one breath; and man hath no preeminence above the beasts." Indeed, listen to our Lord himself on Calvary! He is quoting the twenty-second psalm. He knows it by heart: "My God, my God, why hast thou forsaken me? Why art thou so far from helping me?" I am talking to someone here who is struggling with his doubts. The Bible is your book, my friend. All its faith was hammered out on the hard anvil of doubt.

The trouble is that most Christians know about the faith of the great believers but not about their inner struggles. All Yale men here, and many more of us too, remember William Lyon Phelps. What a radiant Christian faith he had! But listen to him in his autobiography: "My religious faith remains in possession of the field only after prolonged civil war with my naturally sceptical mind." That experience belongs in the best tradition of the great believers. John Knox, the Scottish Reformer — what a man of conviction! Yes, but remember that time when his soul knew "anger, wrath and indignation, which it conceived against God, calling all his promises in doubt." Increase Mather — that doughty Puritan — what a man of faith! Yes, but read his diary and run on entries like this: "Greatly molested with temptations to atheism." Sing Luther's hymn, "A Mighty Fortress Is Our God," and one would suppose he never questioned his faith, but see him in other hours. "For more than a week," he wrote, "Christ was wholly lost. I was shaken by desperation and blasphemy against God."

I speak for the encouragement of someone here struggling with his unbelief. The noblest faith of the church has come out of that struggle. No man really possesses the Christian faith until he has fought for it. So Browning put it:

> The more of doubt, the stronger faith, I say,
> If faith o'ercomes doubt.

That brings us to the vital issue. How does faith overcome doubt?

Today I emphasize one central matter in the experience of the great believers: they went honestly through with their disbeliefs until at last they began to doubt their doubts. How important that process is! When it was first suggested that steamships could be built which would cross the ocean, multitudes were skeptical. One man proved it could not be done. He wrote a book proving that no steamship could carry enough fuel to keep its engines going across the ocean. Well, the first steamship that crossed the Atlantic and landed in New York Harbor carried a copy of that book. Ah, my skeptical disbeliever, you would have been a wiser man had you carried your doubt a little further until you doubted your doubts! I am preaching this sermon because I want someone here not to stop doubting, but to go through with his skepticism until he disbelieves his disbelief.

Let us apply this first to our faith in God! Someone here is struggling with doubts about God. Well, there are many ideas of God that ought to be doubted. The Bible itself progresses from one discarded idea of God to a nobler concept of him because men dared to doubt. But when it comes to surrendering belief in God and becoming an atheist, have you ever carried your doubts through to *that* conclusion? See where that lands you! No God! Nothing ultimately creative here except protons and electrons going it blind! All creation, as one atheist says, only "a curious accident in a backwater"! Everything explained by the chance collocation of physical elements! All the law-abiding order and beauty of the world, all the nobility of human character at its best, explained as though the physical letters of the alphabet had been blown together by a chance wind into the thirteenth chapter of First Corinthians! Christ himself and all he stands for — nothing, as it were, nothing but the physical notes of the musical scale tossed by purposeless winds until accidentally they fell together into the Ninth Symphony! Can you really believe that? Is not that utterly incredible?

In the United States today we face a strong trend back toward religious faith, and one reason, I think, lies in what we are saying now. Many in this last generation surrendered to skepticism, went through with it to its conclusion, until they began finding their disbelief unbelievable.

So Robert Louis Stevenson became a man of radiant faith, but he did not start that way. He started by calling the religion he was brought up in "the deadliest gag and wet-blanket that can be laid on man." He started by calling himself "a youthful atheist." Then, as he grew up, began what Gilbert Chesterton called his "first wild doubts of doubt." "The church was not right," wrote Stevenson, "but certainly not the antichurch either." "'Tis a strange world," he said, "but there is a manifest God for those who care to look for him." Then at last he began talking about his "cast-iron faith." "Whether on the first of January or the thirty-first of December," he wrote, "faith is a good word to end on." So he went through with his skepticism until he found his disbelief unbelievable.

I thank God now that that experience of Stevenson's was mine too. When I started for college my junior year, I told my mother that I was going to clear God out of the universe and begin all over to see what I could find. I could not swallow the Christian faith unquestioningly. I had to fight for it. And so it's mine! Every doubt raised against it, every question asked about it, I have faced often with agony of mind. I am not afraid of atheism; of all my disbeliefs I most certainly disbelieve that! And now in my elder years what a Christian of the last generation said I understand: "Who never doubted never half believed."

Let us apply this truth now not only to faith in God but to faith in Christ. For many people he is hard to believe in now. Too good to be true! Too idealistic to fit this naughty world! So the idea creeps in that believers are credulous, gullible, softheaded, trusting this lovely Christ with his lovely ideas as "the way, the truth, and the life." Often on university campuses one runs upon this idea that to believe in Christ is comforting — yes! — but it takes a credulous mind to do it in a world like this. To which I say: Watch your step there! Again and again in history the shoe has been on the other foot. Not the believers in spiritual greatness but the unbelievers have proved to be mistaken.

I thought of that when recently in Washington I stood before the Lincoln Memorial, saw again that noble figure seated there, and read on the carved stone the immortal words of the Gettysburg Address. A newspaper editor in Harrisburg, thirty-five miles away from Gettysburg, heard Lincoln's Gettysburg Address. Fall for that kind of stuff? Not he! He was no sucker! He was a hardheaded realist, he was! So he wrote this in his paper: "We pass over the silly remarks of the President; for the credit of the nation, we are willing that the veil of oblivion shall be dropped over them and that they shall no more be repeated or thought of." Ah, you fool, you stood in the presence of greatness, and you disbelieved! It is you who were blind. It is you, the skeptic, at whom the centuries will laugh till the end of time. You doubted Lincoln. Why didn't you think twice, until you doubted your doubts?

The older I grow the more I ponder Judas Iscariot. He came so near to *not* betraying Jesus. He was a loyal disciple. It took courage to join that little band, and Judas had it. Then doubts began. What kind of Messiah was this who refused violent revolution and talked about loving one's enemies? Was not this idealistic Jesus letting them down? So the doubts grew, until in an explosive hour — oh, fifty-one votes against forty-nine — Judas sold his Lord. He came so near *not* doing it that when he saw what he had done he hanged himself in shame. Ah, Judas, if you had only doubted your doubts enough to wait until Easter, until Pentecost, until Paul came, you would not be the supreme traitor of the centuries. You stood in the presence of divine greatness, and you disbelieved.

You see what I am trying to say. Believers can be credulous, but disbelievers, too, can be gullible fools. Don't join their company! Take a long look at Christ! The world desperately needs him. He is the way and the truth and the life.

Let us apply our theme now to faith in man and his possibilities. Here especially the pessimists are having a field day now. The kingdom of God on earth — what a dream! What credulity it takes to believe that. On one of our campuses the college paper offered a prize for the best definition of life. Here are some that received honorable mention: "Life is a bad joke which isn't even funny." "Life is a disease for which the only cure is death." "Life is a jail sentence which we get for the crime of being born." My friends, when skepticism, not simply about religion but about human life, is thus carried to its logical conclusion, is it not about time to doubt our doubts?

You see, faith in God concerns something everlastingly so, whether we believe in it or not, but faith in man and his possibilities concerns something that may conceivably become so if we believe in it enough. Only if we have faith in human possibilities can they ever become real. If we all doubt them, they are dished. In this realm faith is creative; doubt is destructive.

Are the skeptics about human hopes the wise men they think they are? Some time since, I lectured at the University of Pittsburgh; and I recalled a man named Arthur Lee, who, in 1770, visited the present site of Pittsburgh and in his travel diary wrote this: "The place, I believe, will never be very considerable." There is the skeptic for you, multiplied millions of times in history, blind, blind as bats, to the possibilities that they lacked faith to see. Shakespeare was everlastingly right:

> Our doubts are traitors,
> And make us lose the good we oft might win,
> By fearing to attempt.

This truth that we are trying to make clear becomes most intimate when we apply it to our personal lives. God knows how many here today are burdened with the sense of failure — moral failure, it may be, so that they disbelieve in themselves and doubt that anything worthwhile can be made of their lives. Look at me, someone is saying, God would have to work a miracle to change me. Well, do you think that kind of miracle is incredible? Listen! I vividly recall the afternoon when I was well started on my radio sermon, when suddenly the man at the controls lifted his arms and stopped me. "It's all off," he said, "the Japanese are attacking Pearl Harbor." What a day! Who can put into words the outraged thoughts we had about those Japanese bombers? My friends, the pilot who led the attack on Pearl Harbor is in this country now training to be a Christian missionary. He is Captain Mitsuo Fuchida, and he is going back to preach the gospel to his people. Incredible! one would have thought. No! That kind of miracle has made Christian history for nearly two thousand years. And *you* think that *you* cannot be transformed by the renewing of *your* mind. In God's name, doubt your doubts!

I call you to witness that today I have given doubt fair play. I have said in its favor, I think, the best that can be said. But in this tremendous generation we need men and women who have won through doubt to faith — faith in the possibilities of world organization, faith in interracial brotherhood and the abolition of war, faith in the Christian church and its saving gospel, faith in what God can do in them and through them. I want someone here to come over now from skepticism to conviction. As John Masefield sang it:

> Oh yesterday our little troup was ridden through
>   and through,
> Our swaying, tattered pennons fled, a broken, beaten few,
> And all the summer afternoon they hunted us and slew;

But tomorrow
By the living God, we'll try the game anew.[1]

That is faith! May we all doubt our doubts until we get it!

1. John Masefield, "Tomorrow," in *Collected Poems* (New York: Macmillan, 1944).

JOHN CLAYPOOL

Life Is a Gift

Like God, Claypool's sermon brings good out of evil. Its author has no doubt that his daughter's leukemia was evil. He has a lot of doubt about "the will of God" in such evils. But Claypool, speaking while "still much in shock, much at sea, very much broken," nonetheless attempts to help others. He offers fellow travelers a map they may need one day. This is a map of the area of grief, revealing a couple of roads that end in a cul-de-sac, and one that leads on toward partial recovery.

Probing, asking, doubting, lamenting, Claypool enters the biblical wisdom tradition and also the lives of listeners and readers. Suppose you have pounded on the door of heaven till your knuckles are running with blood and all you hear on the other side of the door is a massive, emphatic silence. What then? Claypool's conclusion — all the more believable for being scarred and shaken — combines biblical wisdom, theological understanding, and pastoral care from the heart of one who both grieves and gives thanks.

John Claypool, "Life Is a Gift," from *Tracks of a Fellow Struggler* by John Claypool, pp. 67-83. Copyright 1974 Word, Inc., Dallas, Texas. Used with permission.

Life Is a Gift

After these things God tested Abraham, and said to him, "Abraham!" And he said, "Here am I." He said, "Take your son, your only son Isaac, whom you love, and go to the land of Moriah, and offer him there as a burnt offering upon one of the mountains of which I shall tell you." So Abraham rose early in the morning, saddled his ass, and took two of his young men with him, and his son Isaac; and he cut the wood for the burnt offering, and arose and went to the place of which God had told him. On the third day Abraham lifted up his eyes and saw the place afar off. Then Abraham said to his young men, "Stay here with the ass; I and the lad will go yonder and worship, and come again to you." And Abraham took the wood of the burnt offering, and laid it on Isaac his son; and he took in his hand the fire and the knife. So they went both of them together. And Isaac said to his father Abraham, "My father!" And he said, "Here I am, my son." He said, "Behold, the fire and the wood; but where is the lamb for a burnt offering?" Abraham said, "God will provide himself the lamb for a burnt offering, my son." So they went both of them together.

When they came to the place of which God had told him, Abraham built an altar there, and laid the wood in order, and bound Isaac his son, and laid him on the altar, upon the wood. Then Abraham put forth his hand, and took the knife to slay his son. But the angel of the LORD called to him from heaven, and said, "Abraham, Abraham!" And he said, "Here am I." He said, "Do not lay your hand on the lad or do anything to him; for now I know that you fear God, seeing you have not withheld your son, your only son, from me." And Abraham lifted up his eyes and looked, and behold, behind him was a ram, caught in a thicket by his horns;

and Abraham went and took the ram, and offered it up as a burnt offering instead of his son. So Abraham called the name of that place The LORD will provide; as it is said to this day, "On the mount of the LORD it shall be provided."

Genesis 22:1-14

For the last eighteen months now, this particular episode out of the life of Abraham has held a great fascination for me. As you might suspect, I can identify in large measure with much that took place there. For example, I know something of the overwhelming shock that Abraham must have experienced when he realized one night that God was demanding his son of him. I found myself engulfed in a torrent of emotions identical to that a year ago last June when I first heard the word "leukemia" spoken about my child. There is no way to describe the mixture of horror and bitterness and terror and fear that churns up within you at the advent of such a realization.

I can also identify with the way Abraham proceeded to respond to this eventuality. As I see him slowly setting out on this journey he had no desire to take, I can almost sense the double agenda that was going on within him. Though intellectually he realizes that the worst could very well happen, he does not try to run away but sets his face steadfastly for Moriah. Yet emotionally there is a hope within him that something will intervene even at the last moment to reverse the process.

Abraham gives expression to this residual hope there at the foot of the mountain when little Isaac asks about the lamb for the sacrifice, and I know exactly how he felt. I, too, have lived these last eighteen months with the same double agenda. Facing up with my mind to the fact that Laura Lue's situation was very serious, I did everything in my power to cope with it realistically. But at the feeling level, I had abounding hope. In fact, I did not realize just how hopeful I really was until that Saturday afternoon as I knelt by her bed and saw her stop breathing. You may find this incredible, but I was the most shocked man in all the world at that moment. You see, deep down, I did not believe she was going to die. In spite of all my mind told me, I found myself clinging to the hope that any day a cure would be found, or that God would see fit to heal her miraculously. I certainly did not demand this of God or feel that he owed it to us. I simply believed that what had happened for Abraham would happen for us, and that even if it came at the last moment, the knife would be stayed.

But, of course, that is not what happened four weeks ago last Saturday, and I am still in the process of trying to take in what did in fact occur. It is at this point that Abraham's experience and my own break off in different directions. He got to go down the mountain with his child by his side, and, oh, how his heart must have burst with joy at having come through so much so well.

But my situation is different. Here I am, left alone on that mountain, with my child and not a ram there on the altar, and the question is: how on earth do I get down and move back to the normalcy of life? I cannot learn from Abraham, lucky man that he is. I am left to grope through the darkness by myself, and to ask: "Where do I go from here? Is there a road out, and if so, which one?"

Let me hasten to admit that I am really in no position to speak with any finality to such a question this morning, for I am still much in shock, much at sea, very much broken, and by no means fully healed. What I have to share is of a highly provisional character, for as of now the light is very dim. However, if you will accept it as such, I do feel I have made a few discoveries in these last four weeks that may be of worth to some of you. To be very specific, now that I have looked down three alternative roads that seem to lead out of this darkness, I must report that two of them appear to be dead ends, while a third holds real promise.

The first of these routes comes highly recommended, and I would label it "the road of unquestioning resignation." If I have been told once, I have been told a hundred times: "We must not question God. We must not try to understand. We have no right to ask or to inquire into the ways of God with men. The way out is to submit. We must silently and totally surrender. We must accept what God does without a word or a murmur."

Now there is both ancient and practical wisdom in this approach to deep sorrow, and in one sense it is utterly realistic, for if I have learned anything in all of this, it is just how weak and ineffectual we humans are against the immensities of life and death. Since I was powerless a month ago to do anything to avert this agony, why bother now to try to struggle with it? I repeat, there is a wisdom of sorts down this road of unquestioning resignation. The only trouble is, it is not a Christian wisdom, and in fact it is a denial of the heart of our faith. I have been frankly dismayed at how many deeply devoted Christians have recommended this way to me, and I have wondered to myself: "Don't they realize what such an approach implies about the whole of existence?"

To put it bluntly, this sort of silent submission undermines the most precious dimension of our existence; namely, the personal dimension. It reduces all of life to a mechanical power transaction. To be sure, a leaf submits to the wind without saying a word, and a rock allows the floodwater to do whatever it pleases without murmur, but are these appropriate analogies for the relation of God and man?

According to the Bible they are not, for in this document the mystery of Godness is depicted as involving more than brute power. The One who moves through these pages is by nature a Being of love, "a Father who pitieth his children" rather than a Force who knocks about a lot of helpless objects. And, of course, words and questions and dialogue back and forth are at the heart of the way persons — especially fathers and children — ought to relate.

Where, then, did we Christians ever get the notion that we must not question God or that we have no right to pour out our souls to him and ask, Why? Did not Job in the Old Testament cry out to God in the midst of his agony and attempt to interrogate the Almighty? Did not Jesus himself agonize with God in Gethsemane, telling him how he felt and what he wanted, and then cry out from the cross: "My God, my God! Why? Why have you forsaken me?" Would the verse "Ask and it shall be given you, seek and you shall find, knock and it shall be opened unto you" ever have appeared in Holy Scripture if unquestioning acquiescence had been the way to meet tragedy?

I, for one, see nothing but a dead end down this road of silent resignation, for it is one of those medicines that cures at the expense of killing the organism it is supposed to heal. After all, my questions in the face of this event are a real part of me just now, and to deny them or to suppress them by bowing mechanically to a superior Force is an affront not only to God and to my own nature but to the kind of relation we are supposed to have.

There is more honest faith in an act of questioning than in the act of silent submission, for implicit in the very asking is the faith that some light can be given. This is why I found such help in a letter I received from Dr. Carlyle Marney just before Laura Lue died. He admitted that he had no word for the suffering of the innocent and never had had, but he said: "I fall back on the idea that our God has a lot to give an account for."

Now, to be honest, no one had ever said anything like that to me before, and at first it was a little shocking, but the more I thought about it, the truer it became to the faith of the Bible. At no point in its teaching is there ever an indication that God wants us to remain like rocks or even little infants in our relationship to him. He wants us to become mature sons and daughters, which means that he holds us responsible for our actions and expects us to hold him responsible for his!

I do not believe God wants me to hold in these questions that burn in my heart and soul — questions like: "Why is there leukemia? Why are children of promise cut down at the age of ten? Why did you let Laura Lue suffer so excruciatingly and then let her die?" I am really honoring God when I come clean and say, "You owe me an explanation." For you see, I believe he will be able to give such an accounting when all the facts are in, and until then, it is valid to ask.

It is not rebelliousness, then, but faith that keeps me from finding any promise down the road of unquestioning resignation. This approach is closer to pagan Stoicism than to Christian humility. I have no choice but to submit to this event of death. Still, the questions remain, and I believe I honor God by continuing to ask and seek and knock rather than resigning myself like a leaf or a rock.

Having said that, however, I need to hasten on to identify a second dead-end route, lest I badly confuse you. It is what I would call "the road of total intellectual understanding," the way of explaining everything completely or tying up all the loose ends in a tidy answer. To be sure, I have just said that I believe someday God will be able to give account for what he has done and show how it all fits together, but that eschaton is not now. Accordingly, any attempt at this moment to absolutize or to find an answer that will account for all the evidence will either end in failure or be a real distortion of reality.

I perhaps need to confess to you that at times in the last few months I have been tempted to conclude that our whole existence is utterly absurd. More than once I looked radical doubt full in the face and honestly wondered if all our talk about love and purpose and a fatherly God were not simply a veil of fantasy that we pathetic humans had projected against the void. For you see, in light of the evidence closest at hand, to have absolutized at all would have been to conclude that all was absurd and that there was no Ultimate Purpose. There were the times, for example, when Laura Lue was hurting so intensely that she had to bite on a rag and used to beg me to pray to God to take away that awful pain. I would kneel down beside her bed and pray with all the faith and conviction of my soul, and nothing would happen except the pain continuing to rage on. Or again, that same negative conclusion tempted when she asked me in the dark of the night: "When will this leukemia go away?" I answered: "I don't know, darling, but we are doing everything we know to make that happen." Then she said: "Have you asked God when it will go away?" And I said: "Yes, you have heard me pray to him many times." But she persisted: "What did he say? When did he say it would go away?" And I had to admit to myself he had not said a word! I had done a lot of talking and praying and pleading, but the response of the heavens had been silence.

But though in moments like that I was tempted to absolutize about life and arrange all existence around one explaining principle, clearer moments made me realize that such simplicity would not correspond to reality. For you see, alongside the utter absurdity of what was happening to this little girl were countless other experiences that were full of love and purpose and meaning. From people in the clinic and at the hospital, from unnumbered hosts of you in the church and the community, came evidences of goodness that were anything but absurd. And I realized that if I were going to judge it all fairly, this data had to be balanced in with equal weight alongside all the darkness.

I was reminded of a conclusion I came to a long time ago: that you do not solve all the intellectual problems by deciding that everything is absurd. To be sure, it is hard to account for evil on the assumption that God is all-good and all-powerful, but if you do away with that assumption and go to the other extreme, you are then left with the problem of how to account for all the goodness and purpose that most assuredly also exist. This leads me to conclude that expecting to find one total explanation or answer to this situation is futile.

Never has the stark paradox of real darkness alongside of real light been more apparent to me than in the last days, which means I shall continue to ask questions, but not expect, in history at least, to find any complete answer. George Buttrick is right in saying that life is essentially a series of events to be borne and lived through rather than intellectual riddles to be played with and solved. Courage is worth ten times more than any answer that claims to be total. We cannot absolutize in such a way that either the darkness swallows up the light or the light the darkness. To do so would be untrue to our human condition that "knows in part" and does all its seeing "as through a glass darkly."

For me, at least, then, the roads called unquestioning resignation and total understanding hold no promise of leading out of the darkness where I lost my child. But remember, I said in the beginning there was a third way, and what little I have learned of it I now want to share.

I call this one "the road of gratitude," and interestingly enough, it is basic to the story of Abraham and Isaac that serves as our text. Years ago, when I first started taking the Bible seriously, this whole episode used to bother me a good deal. What kind of jealous God is it, I wondered, who demands even a man's child as a sign of devotion? As I moved more deeply into the biblical revelation, however, I came to realize that the point at issue in this event was not that at all. What God was trying to teach Abraham here and throughout his whole existence was the basic understanding that life is gift — pure, simple, sheer gift — and that we here on earth are to relate to it accordingly.

The promise that came originally to Abraham from God was literally "out of the blue." Just as he had not been in on the creation of the world or his own birth, so Abraham had done nothing to earn the right of having a land of his own or descendants more numerous than the stars. Such a promise came as pure gift from God. Abraham was called on to receive it, to participate in it fully and joyfully, to handle it with the open hands of gratitude.

And this, of course, was a picture of how man was meant to relate to existence itself. Life, too, is a gift, and it is to be received and participated in and handled with gratitude.

But right here is the problem. God was having to start all over again with Abraham because mankind had lost this view of life and instead had tried to earn life by the ardors of legalism, or to possess it totally as if it belonged to them alone. And all these mistaken relations served only to curdle life and make of it a crushing burden or a prison of anxiety.

The whole point in the Abraham saga lies in God's effort to restore men to the right vision of life and a right relationship to it. Only when life is seen as a gift and received with the open hands of gratitude is it the joy God meant for it to be. And these were the truths God was seeking to emphasize as he waited so long to send Isaac and then asked for him back. Did Abraham realize that all was gift, and not something to be earned or to be possessed, but received, participated in, held freely in gratefulness?

This is the most helpful perspective I have found in the last weeks. And of all the roads to travel, it offers the best promise of being a way out.

A little something that happened to me years ago may help you to understand what I mean. When World War II started, my family did not have a washing machine. With gas rationed and the laundry several miles away, keeping our clothes clean became an intensely practical problem. One of my father's younger business associates was drafted, and his wife prepared to go with him, and we offered to let them store their furniture in our basement. Quite unexpectedly, they suggested that we use their washing machine while they were gone. "It would be better for it to be running," they said, "than sitting up rusting." So this is what we did, and it helped us a great deal.

Since I used to help with the washing, across the years I developed quite an affectionate relation for that old green Bendix. But eventually the war ended and our friends returned, and in the meantime I had forgotten how the machine had come to be in our basement in the first place. When they came and took it, I was terribly upset, and I said so quite openly.

But my mother, being the wise woman she is, sat me down and put things in perspective for me. She said, "Wait a minute, son. You must remember, that machine never belonged to us in the first place. That we ever got to use it at all was a gift. So, instead of being mad at its being taken away, let's use this occasion to be grateful that we had it at all."

Here, in a nutshell, is what it means to understand something as a gift and to handle it with gratitude, a perspective biblical religion puts around all of life. And I am here to testify that this is the only way down from the mountain of loss. I do not mean to say that such a perspective makes things easy, for it does not. But at least it makes things bearable when I remember that Laura Lue was a gift, pure and simple, something I neither earned nor deserved nor had a right to. And when I remember that the appropriate response to a gift, even when it is taken away, is gratitude, then I am better able to try and thank God that I was ever given her in the first place.

Even though it is very, very hard, I am doing my best to learn this discipline now. Everywhere I turn I am surrounded by reminders of her — things we did together, things she said, things she loved. And in the presence of the reminders, I have two alternatives: dwelling on the fact that she has been taken away, I can dissolve in remorse that all of this is gone forever; or, focusing on the wonder that she was given to us at all, I can learn to be grateful that we shared life, even for an all-too-short ten years. Only three choices, and believe me, the only way out is the way of gratitude. The way of remorse does not alter the stark reality one whit and only makes matters worse. The way of gratitude does not alleviate the pain, but it somehow puts some light around the darkness and builds strength to begin to move on.

Now, having gone full circle, I come back to caution you not to look to me this morning as any authority on how to conquer grief. Rather, I need you to help me on down the way, and this is how: do not counsel me not to question, and do not attempt to give me any total answer. Neither one of those ways works for me. The greatest thing you can do is to remind me that life is gift — every last particle of it, and that the way to handle a gift is to be grateful. You can really help me if you will never let me forget this fact, just as I hope maybe I may have helped this morning by reminding you of the same thing. As I see it now, there is only one way out of this darkness — the way of gratitude. Will you join me in trying to learn how to travel that way?

ALLAN BOESAK

The Reuben Option

Naturally enough, most prophetic biblical sermons develop texts found in Isaiah, Jeremiah, Amos, and the other prophetic books of the Old Testament. In this sermon, however, Allan Boesak draws a prophetic message from a Pentateuchal narrative, a portion of the Joseph story in Genesis. Boesak works up a single incident in this story — the attempt by Joseph's brother Reuben to find a reasonable compromise between actively supporting Joseph and joining the other brothers in their plot to murder him.

But the preacher is here to tell us that some reasonable moves are also contemptible. In fact, in an act of creative biblical interpretation, Boesak turns the Reuben option into a metaphor for all sorts of cowardly, face-saving maneuvers in the church and in society generally.

The Reuben Option

> But when Reuben heard it, he delivered him out of their
> hands, saying, "Let us not take his life." And Reuben
> said to them, "Shed no blood; cast him into this pit here
> in the wilderness, but lay no hand upon him" — that he
> might rescue him out of their hand, to restore him to
> his father.
>
> Genesis 37:21-22

Joseph was the favorite son of his father. He was, of course, the
son of Rachel, Jacob's first and real love. He was also the son of
his father's old age — not simply the son Rachel bore to him when
he was already well on in years, but also the son who was such a
comfort to him in his old age.

Joseph is special. All God's promises to Abraham and all the
hopes of Jacob are now centered in this favorite son. His name
means "add" — he is added, by the love and grace of God, a special
gift from God that reshapes everything.

Joseph's birth marks a decisive change in the life of Israel.
This son is a sign to Jacob that the promise of God still works in
his life and in his body. Joseph is the last, because little Benjamin
does not feature here. Once again we see the wonderful inversion
of life's order by Yahweh: the last becomes first. That is why Joseph
receives from his father the multicolored robe with the long sleeves,
a sure sign that he is the chosen one, the "crown prince," the one
who will lead the family.

Spoiled, too young to do hard work, Joseph easily becomes
a tattletale. Able to get away with things the older brothers are not
permitted, his actions elicit the chagrin of his brothers. But that
clearly is not the main reason for their hatred and jealousy. The real
reason is something else: Joseph dreams.

Joseph dreams, but in a real sense he is only the bearer of
dreams. The dream is Yahweh's dream, for Israel, for the world.

The dream is a vision of history being inverted, undermined, changed against all odds. Joseph's dream is a power that neither tradition nor force can resist. It is a dream in which the impossible happens, the weak becomes strong, the lowly is raised up, the powerless is crowned with glory.

The brothers hated him because the dream threatened them. "They hated him, and could not speak peaceably to him" (v. 4), a wonderfully loaded phrase. Not only were they "unkind" to him, they could never be *at peace* with him; he was no longer a brother, he became an enemy. The decision to kill him does not really surprise us; it is almost inevitable.

Jacob provides the opportunity by sending Joseph to his brothers as they were tending the flock near Shechem. "Here comes the dreamer," they say. Literally, here comes the lord, the master of dreams. A "master of dreams" is one who uses dreams to manipulate and intimidate others. The dreams now are not really visions, they are an instrument with which to gain control over others. As a sorcerer would use his powers, preying on superstition and the deep-seated fears of his victim, so Joseph is accused of using his dreams to intimidate and to control both his father and his brothers. They do not see his gift as a gift of God; for them it is not God's way of revealing the divine purposes for the chosen family and for the whole created world. They can only see Joseph's dream as a threat to the present order in which they have the upper hand. It is no longer a petty family quarrel — it is a life-and-death struggle. They simply *had* to kill him.

Reuben is not with his brothers in their strident demand that Joseph be put to death. He sounds so reasonable, so responsible — especially responsible. He emerges as Joseph's protector, saving him from certain death so that he could bring him back to Jacob.

Or so it seems. In reality, Reuben's role is much more ambiguous. He is the eldest, and therefore has special responsibilities. He is the one who must protect the family when the father is not present. He must also protect the family name and honor.

But Reuben's record is not all that clean. He seems to have shown little of the older brother's sense of responsibility as the tension builds up between Joseph and his brothers, and, by implication, the tension between the brothers and the father. There is no reconciling word, no attempt to mend the relations. No sign that he was trying to restrain his brothers as the grumbling grew more and more ominous. Even worse, Reuben has long since lost the confidence of his father, and his rightful place as the eldest, by sleeping with Bilhah, Jacob's concubine.

What made him commit this grievous sin, "shaming his father's bed"? Was it a calculated move to secure for himself the headship of the clan, a strategy that was not uncommon in the ancient East where the successor to the throne inherited also the harem? This act of Reuben's was probably more than passing passion; it was perhaps in the nature of the declaration of a takeover. For Reuben, Israel was no longer "father"; he was an old man, a rival who stood in his way to the top. With infinite sensitivity, in words pregnant with tragedy, the narrator simply notes: ". . . and Israel heard of it" (Gen. 35:22).

So now Reuben engages in deception to save his brother. More for his own sake than Joseph's. Is it meant to restore Joseph to his father, or to restore Israel's faith in his eldest son? "Let us not spill blood," Reuben says, "let us throw him into the pit. . . ." He appears to speculate on the effect of the superstitious fear over the spilling of blood, something we find expressed in Genesis 9:6 — as if murder would go unpunished as long as no blood is spilled.

But Reuben dares not choose openly for Joseph; he does not want to give up his popularity with his brothers now, and their support later, for his headship of the clan. So he sacrifices on two altars, as it were. He desperately wants to regain his father's favor, but he cannot risk alienation from his brothers. He knows what is right, he knows what he must do, but his hidden interests weigh too heavily on the other side. So Reuben opts for the feeble role of the "responsible" brother; his aim is to keep both sides happy, to do enough to salve his own conscience, but not enough to save the life of his brother.

Joseph is sold into slavery, and slavery is only a different kind of death. The fact that Joseph, many years later, can say that "it was not you who sent me here, but God" (45:8) does not alter this situation. Neither Joseph nor Reuben could have known this.

The grace of God that turns evil into good can never be an excuse for our continued sinfulness. Reuben is not presented here as an evil man. He is not a murderer. No, he is presented as concerned and responsible. As Walter Brueggemann says: "Reuben is presented as responsible, but cowardly, and the killers of the dream will not be restrained by a responsible coward."

This, I think, is the agony of the church: we know what we should be doing, but we lack the courage to do it. We feel we ought to do it and we cannot. We are afraid to make choices, so we are constantly on the lookout for compromises. We are paralyzed by the need to be all things to all people, to be a church where all feel welcome all the time, and so we sacrifice on both altars. We stand accused by a history of compromises always made for the sake of survival.

We have justified slavery, violence, and war; we have sanctified racism and split our churches on the issue of the preservation of white supremacy. We have discriminated against women and kept them servile whilst we hid our fear of them behind claims of "masculinity" and sanctimonious talk about Adam and Eve. We have grown rich and fat and powerful through the exploitation of the poor, which we deplored but never really tried to stop. All in the name of Jesus Christ and his gospel. Now this same gospel speaks to us, and we can no longer escape its demands. It calls us to love and justice and obedience. We would like to fulfill that calling, but we do not want to risk too much. The Reuben option.

The Reuben option: Take a stand, but always cover yourself. The problem cannot be ignored, so let us do something about it, but always in such a way that it does not hurt us too much. Take a stand; use the right words in the resolutions taken by the synod and the general assembly, but also make sure that you build into those resolutions all the necessary safeguards — just in case. Don't antagonize people too much, especially those in the church who have money. Opt for peace, but don't confuse that with justice.

The Reuben option: How often do we face it in my own country and in my own church! We know we have to say that we are against injustice, racism, and apartheid. We know that we must work for the kingdom of God, work in such a way that people's humanity will be restored, but we are afraid to join the struggle for liberation, to participate actively in that struggle. The risks are too many. Let us pass resolutions against apartheid, but let us frame them in such a way that we can defend ourselves when the white church threatens to withdraw its money.

The Reuben option: Opt for justice, work against racism, but in such a way that we will not cause too much tension in the church. Was that not how the world church functioned for many years? Think of all the controversy and the conflict over the World Council of Churches' Programme to Combat Racism. We came close to losing our unity on that issue; we almost jeopardized our whole Christian witness on it. So the churches went through agonizing times. How do we support the PCR and yet do it in such a way that no one (especially those conservatives who hold the purse strings) can accuse us of giving money to "terrorists"? To our shock we discover that we have to choose constantly between the interests of those who can afford to make television programs "exposing" the PCR and the interests of the oppressed, the poor, and the weak, the victims of exploitation and racism, who also happen to be our brothers and sisters in the Lord.

The Reuben option: Have a program for hungry children; collect millions and spend them on the poor. "Give and feel good!" is the legend on a poster from one charitable organization, with a picture of a little black child, arms grotesquely thin, protruding stomach, tears rolling down the cheeks. Yes, indeed. But to use all our energy, our resources, our ingenuity, to work honestly and openly to change an economic system that by its very nature cannot and will not give the poor a chance to become fully human? That we cannot do, because then we become "involved," and we have to look with new eyes at the systems on which our budgets are based.

The Reuben option: We face that ourselves. I know that we are called to serve God's kingdom in terms of peace and justice and human dignity. But how difficult it is when this call stands in the way of our ambition! When we live under the threat of death every day, when we are always only one step away from being "picked up," when they tell us that our name is "on the list" because we are a danger to "Christian civilization" — how difficult it is then to make that choice! And I have discovered that the choice for commitment and obedience is not made once for all. It is a choice that has to be made every day.

The Reuben option. And so we invent little excuses, and we dress them up as theological arguments about church and politics, violence and nonviolence, personal and public morality, and, above all, responsibility. We call ourselves evangelical and ecumenical and fight one another; in the meantime the poor continue to be exploited, the weak continue to be trampled upon, and the innocent continue to die. And we *know* we are being unworthy of the gospel.

"It is so difficult!" someone will say. Indeed it is. We are not "merely" human, we are *human!* But we are not the church of Reuben, we are the church of Jesus Christ. Are we not therefore able to do more than we think we can? Are we not those who will move mountains if we have faith "like a mustard seed"? Are we not those called by Jesus Christ to do his work in the world? Are we not those saved by him, and has he not made known to us "the mystery of his will" (Eph. 1:9)?

I know we sometimes say: the situation is more complex than we think; we have to be careful, because the most important thing is the survival of the church. I would, however, like to submit to you that the survival of the church is none of our business. It is God's business. We must simply learn to trust God to take care of it. Why should we be so worried about the survival of the church? Maybe because for us that often means: don't antagonize those who give the most money. Sometimes it means: don't antagonize the powers that be. But do we really believe that any earthly power can destroy the church of Jesus Christ? No, the survival of the church is *not* our main problem. Our main problem lies within ourselves, and with our difficulty to be faithful and to be obedient, to love justice and mercy and to walk humbly with our Lord.

Kaj Munk was a pastor of the church in Denmark. He became the spiritual force behind the Danish resistance to Hitler at the time of the Nazi occupation. In January 1944, they took him away one night and shot him like a dog in the field, but his life and death continued to inspire the Danes in their struggle for freedom. To me, Kaj Munk is one of the great men in the recent history of the Christian church. He reminded his fellow pastors of what they needed in a world where the choices were becoming more stark, more painful, more unavoidable day by day. "What is therefore the task of the preacher today? Shall I answer: faith, hope and love? That sounds beautiful. But I would rather say: courage. No, even that is not challenging enough to be the *whole* truth. . . . Our task today is recklessness. . . . For what we as (church) lack is most assuredly not psychology or literature. We lack a holy rage. . . ."

A holy rage. The recklessness that comes from the knowledge of God and humanity. The ability to rage when justice lies prostrate on the streets and when the lie rages across the face of the earth. A holy anger about things that are wrong in the world. To rage against the ravaging of God's earth and the destruction of God's world. To rage when little children must die of hunger while the tables of the rich are sagging with food. To rage at the senseless killing of so many and against the madness of militarism. To rage at the lie that calls the threat of death and the strategy of destruction "peace." To rage against the complacency of so many in the church who fail to see that we shall live only by the truth, and that our fear will be the death of us all. . . . To restlessly seek that recklessness which will challenge, and to seek to change human history until it conforms to the norms of the kingdom of God.

And remember, says Kaj Munk, "the signs of the Christian church have always been the lion, the lamb, the dove and the fish. But *never* the chameleon." And remember too: the church is the chosen people of God.

But the chosen shall be known by their choices.

JOHN R. FRY

Blindness

The best sermons are not timeless essays on eternal truths; they are attempts to speak the gospel at a particular historical moment to people of a particular place.

This prophetic sermon by John R. Fry was preached to a Chicago inner-city congregation in the 1960s, a time of deep social unrest, particularly in the heart of great American cities. The sermon reveals its time in a number of ways: it refers, for example, to a report of the Presidential Commission on Civil Disorders and to the testimony of the Welfare Tenants Union before the Illinois legislature. The sermon reveals its place by presenting the biblical character Bartimaeus as a savvy urban beggar — the sort of streetwise figure many in the congregation would have encountered daily, perhaps even on their way into the sanctuary.

Blindness

And they came to Jericho; and as he was leaving Jericho
with his disciples and a great multitude, Bartimaeus, a
blind begger, the son of Timaeus, was sitting by the
roadside. And when he heard that it was Jesus of
Nazareth, he began to cry out and say, "Jesus, Son of
David, have mercy on me!" And many rebuked him,
telling him to be silent; but he cried out all the more,
"Son of David, have mercy on me!" And Jesus stopped
and said, "Call him." And they called the blind man,
saying to him, "Take heart; rise, he is calling you." And
throwing off his mantle he sprang up and came to Jesus.
And Jesus said to him, "What do you want me to do for
you?" And the blind man said to him, "Master, let me
receive my sight." And Jesus said to him, "Go your way;
your faith has made you well." And immediately he
received his sight and followed him on the way.

                                     Mark 10:46-52;
                                see also Isaiah 40:1-8

Please ask no up-to-date questions of the great account of the
deliverance of Bartimaeus from his blindness, which is not an
up-to-date account. Do not say, "Was it a disease of the eye? Did
Jesus do the first corneal transplant? Was Bartimaeus psychosomati-
cally blind, perchance, his physical blindness caused by emotional
illness?" These are smart questions, all right, but the wrong questions, and questions the Mark account provides no answers for.
Instead, try to stand down nineteen centuries to another worldview
held by another people in another land. Listen to the story the way
the story was told.

    Jericho was a walled city. On a main road of Palestine. Barti-
maeus seated himself outside the gate of the city in order to present
himself in his afflicted condition to the numerous people using the

road, hence coming into or just leaving the city. He depended on pennies from travelers. Pitiful pennies. Pennies dropped because of pity. And he advertised his blindness by wailing. Poor blind man whose every day was spent in arousing token gifts from travelers. The people of the city, of course, who knew him, his history, his father, his family, did not pity him because they saw him every day and, as the residents of the city know, he could get around pretty well. He had memorized the streets, knew where to turn, could find his way. In the classic way of people who every day rub up against evil conditions, the citizens of Jericho ceased to care, to be horrified by blindness. He could die of hunger and they would accuse him of lack of initiative.

So there sat Bartimaeus, just outside the city, begging from travelers, wailing out, "Help the blind man." He sat with the other derelicts, the other beggars. Now, Bartimaeus had heard that the great healer was in Jericho and hoped that Jesus would come on the road out of Jericho because he would at least make a good hit on Jesus. Popular figure. Popular figures and candidates, then as now, are not able to afford to pass up beggars. They tend to have to perform generously. When, according to his estimation, the noise he heard just inside the city kept coming nearer him, and he got it confirmed by the nonblind derelicts that it was in fact Jesus, Bartimaeus set up a super-wailing. A tremendous racket. "Jesus, Son of David, have mercy on me!" Over and over again. At the top of his lungs. Over the wailing of the other beggars. Over the noise of the people around Jesus. Clear, unmistakably louder and more hearable than the noise. This was an impertinent wailing. Uppity. A breach of the unspoken contract between beggars and beggees: namely, that beggars be demure, their face to the ground, not overdoing it, otherwise beggees will be offended, stick their noses in the air and put their camels in low, and take off. So when Bartimaeus began his super-wailing, there were lots of people who started to shush him up. His fellow beggars, directly, and all of Israel, indirectly, who demand that beggars remain who they are and stay in the charity position, which is on their knees, quietly moaning. To all of these efforts to shush him up, to get him to remember who he was, for goodness' sake, Bartimaeus yelled louder, "Son of David, have mercy on me!" So what happened? Bartimaeus's bad tactics worked. Jesus did hear this one piercing voice over the general loud noise. Jesus instantly understood, as any Jew would, this breach of the charity situation. And maybe for a minute was stunned by that whole scene. These human wrecks. The legless, the diseased, the blind, absolutely depending for their very lives on the whimsical pennies of travelers because the people inside the city were too callous, too used to the obvious human suffering to care for them. The charity game. These misfits and maladepts, these wrecks having to prostrate themselves with quiet wailing before travelers in order merely and barely to survive. Thus half in anger he stopped and asked a disciple to produce the man. The bad tactic had worked. The beggars next to him told Bartimaeus the people were coming after him. He threw off his burnoose and met them halfway, with the dignity of the blind walking unassisted across well-known territory. Their one remaining dignity. Pay attention to this blind man as he rises up and walks toward the people coming after him. Across ground he has never seen, among voices coming from people he has never seen, under a sun he has never seen, outside a city he has never seen; he has since birth lived a private history. He has had to depend on others to tell him what has happened. He has had to depend on their eyes and yet has come to believe that these on whom he is dependent have not told him all that they see, but rather what they want him to know. If he depends on them alone, his view of the outside world, of life itself, will be warped, screened, censored, half a world, and that half the crazy half. Those who aid the blind tend to believe the blind are somehow also stupid since they accept any story. By his wits he has lived, by his sharpened wits. He would have to believe the world full of the hardhearted and the condescending. A true hustler, who, had he not been an expert, could not have survived. As he picks his way so carefully, with such exaggerated dignity, he represents all of the derelicts of the earth, turned into hustlers by the hard hearts of their fellows; and more, he represents all who cannot see, who live on the piecemeal reports of others, so biased, so screened and distorted, and as such live in private worlds instead of public worlds. He represents all who have blocked vision. They cannot see into things, or into people, or into the meaning of events. He becomes many people in those dramatic steps.

The blind Bartimaeus represented what the prophets called blindness, which had nothing to do with the physiological condition of the eyes but was, much more profoundly, a refusal to see, a stubbornness when it came to seeing. Blindness was hard eyes, evil eyes, which saw right through the plight of the poor as though they suddenly were invisible, which saw a representative of God as a troublemaker who should be killed. The blind Bartimaeus was blindness itself coming toward Jesus. He stopped. In those seconds it had taken him to come before Jesus, the entire human situation had been excavated, revealing the shape of charity, the dereliction in being blind and a beggar, and the blindness of everyone standing there watching Bartimaeus. So this representative from the side of blindness met this representative from the side of deliverance. Jesus did *not* first ask him how long he had been blind. Jesus did *not* reach into his purse and extract an especially large gift, which is the very thing he might have done. He instead asked simply, "What do you want me to do for you?" Bartimaeus could not see Jesus, his eyes. But Bartimaeus had grown skilled in listening to voice inflections. He heard no money in the voice, no condescension, no charity. So Bartimaeus lifted up the heaviest words in his vocabulary, trembling with the strain of hoping. The big super-wailer suddenly could do no more than mumble. He had no experience in hoping. He had never said these words to himself, much less out loud and to anyone. But out they came: "Teacher, let me receive my sight." Once said there was no waiting, no dramatic period when Jesus evaluated them, evaluated his worthiness. As soon said, it was done. With a mighty rush from the side of deliverance, the words were spoken with the laughter of pure ecstasy, as Bartimaeus began his laughing with ecstasy, his running around, and shouting, and jumping up into the air, not being able to believe that he could see. He looked, and pointed, and peered, and reveled in color, shapes, gradations, the slants, the roughs, his eyes trying to exhaust the infinite novelty of the total landscape, seeing more in ten seconds than most seeing people see in a lifetime.

And so a great and mighty deliverance took place outside the city of Jericho, which had consigned Bartimaeus to everlasting blindness. Please do not single out this one deliverance. It fits within a pattern of accounts. Jesus had delivered people from insanity, paralysis, leprosy, suppurating wounds, deformity, and muteness. Each act of deliverance was symbolic because it demonstrated his sad cry for the plight of all permanently hopeless people in Palestine, and like bolts of lightning these acts of deliverance illuminated the ugliness of man to man. And these mighty acts of deliverance reveal the divine repugnance with the way things are. Every deliverance at the same time a judgment on the hard hearts of Israel. Every deliverance at the same time an excavation of Israel. Every deliverance at the same time an excavation of the human plight.

This Jesus, this King Jesus, this Lord Jesus, this Jesus Christ whose name we use to adorn our prayers, was a mighty man. His might lay in being able to see the textures of misery that everyone else passed right over. The miracle was that he looked across a beggar and was stunned into outrage at the sight, while the rest of mankind passed over such sights or began searching around for a suitably small coin to give the man — if, of course, he was clever in begging for it.

It is in just such a context we ought to read the commission report on civil disorders. It highlights more than all else the inability of America to conceive, even, the plight of the urban poor. America cannot see the charity situation for what it is. The situation of police brutality for what it is. The story of the deliverance of Bartimaeus should be required reading before you read the commission report. Then you have background to understand its insistence that there is a fundamental blindness in the land. Not merely an unwillingness but an inability to see the rank disparity in the living situations of the poor to the rich. Especially the black poor. All that can be said about the plight of Bartimaeus can be transferred exactly and said exactly of the members of the Welfare Tenants Unions who spoke with such eloquence yesterday as they testified before Illinois lawmakers down in Springfield. They talked about the enforced patterns and degradation built into our charity system.

These derelicts were accepted by Jesus, therefore, as models of the deeper misery that afflicts mankind; in the instance of Bartimaeus, the deeper blindness. Our deeper blindness: an affliction of the spirit, some deformity of affection, some crippled courage, hidden agonies, all of them, hidden behind our flashing eyes and brilliant talk. But I hope you have understood, all along, that this description of blindness can go very far toward describing the fundamental blindness of all those who do not see the plight of the actually blind and who invent these charity situations. Blindness is fundamentally reciprocal.

Forever seeking Jesus in the religious places and then missing him and his mighty deliverance. Seeking him among the crosses and candles. Not there. On the road with Bartimaeus, and if we cry hard enough and assault him with sufficient impertinence there, and these great blindnesses of ours are brought before him and we are actually delivered from their clutching power. Then be prepared to meet him at this communion table. Amen.

WILLIAM MUEHL

The Cult of the Publican

In a deep and discerning survey of those who linger too long "on the border between judgment and mercy," William Muehl goes after one of our favorite biblical characters. The publican looks good, says Muehl, largely because he is in a two-person lineup and the other person is one of our stock villains.

But has the parable of the pharisee and the publican become too familiar to us? Has it lost its bite? Have preachers rigged this little lineup so often and so predictably that we no longer really *engage* the text that presents it?

Answering in the affirmative, Muehl offers an intelligent and, in some ways, disturbing antidote. He aims not so much to preach a famous parable as to deconstruct listeners' shopworn and traditional understanding of it, to preach not *for* a text, but *against* a particular misuse of it. In so doing he addresses all who are too aware of their despair, all who are tempted to make themselves "heirs by adoption not of Christ but of the penitent publican."

William Muehl, "The Cult of the Publican," in William Muehl, *All the Damned Angels* (Philadelphia: Pilgrim Press, 1972), pp. 25-31. Reprinted with permission of the Pilgrim Press, Cleveland, Ohio.

The Cult of the Publican

There are people in this world who do not wear well. Men and women who impress us favorably upon first meeting, but prove disappointing upon repeated contact and closer scrutiny.

Sometimes our disenchantment results from the discovery of character traits that did not appear in the original encounter. We conclude that so-and-so appeared to be a charming fellow and undoubtedly has many splendid qualities, but . . . At other times our change of mind arises not from the appearance of new data so much as from the too-frequent appearance of the same old data. A different perspective upon qualities that had once seemed appealing. The chap who was terribly funny with a lampshade on his head or impressively profound with his quotations from Camus and Sartre upon the occasion of our first contact is often less amusing under the third and fourth lampshade and something short of profound as we hear the same lines from the same authors repeated for the tenth time. Some people do not wear well.

For me this has long been true of the publican who upstages the Pharisee and makes himself the star of the eighteenth chapter of the book of Luke. His psychological welcome wears thin with amazing speed. Oh, there is something impressive about him at first reading. We see him enter the temple bowed down under a sense of his own unworthiness. He fears to approach the altar and stands at a distance, not even daring to lift his eyes to heaven. He asks nothing of God but forgiveness for his sinful life. Viewed for the first time, especially in contrast to the self-righteous Pharisee in a single vignette, he makes a winsome picture. And on the basis of this original good impression he is able to score his point in repeated readings of the familiar story.

But if we are able to react honestly to the Bible and admit such reactions to ourselves, we must confess, I think, that after a while, perhaps after the fortieth or fiftieth recitation of the incident, our feelings for the publican undergo a change.

Nathaniel Hawthorne in his novel *The Marble Faun* has one of his characters complain about a bit of statuary that catches the human figure in a transitional posture. The living form, he objects, should never be frozen by the artist in such a halfway position that one viewing it for the second or third time longs to cry out, "Well, get on with it. Throw it or drop it. Stand or fall. Live or die. But don't just hang there in between!"

Isn't this something of what we all feel about the *moral* posture of the penitent publican? As we encounter him going through his ritual of self-abnegation for the fifty-first time, we may be forgiven for supposing that this thing has turned into a career, or at least an avocation. Sometimes in my mind's eye I can see him raising his children to follow in his footsteps: "Now, kiddies, when you enter the temple you must on no account approach the altar. Stand at a humble distance, and for pity's sake, don't raise your eyes. Bring your arm up in a full swing and strike the breast just below the collarbone. Now all together. Let's take it once more from the top. And this time make your daddy proud of you."

Well, you will perceive, I trust, that I am trying in a fanciful way to approach the problem of divine grace and human responsibility. I mean to suggest that the publican's terrified humility has salutary power *only so long as he does not know that he is being observed and approved*. Only so long as his abject confession is a spontaneous reaction to the presence of God. The moment this fellow reads the book of Luke or even a good review of it and begins to realize that there is saving power in his sense of personal depravity, the well of his naive piety will have been poisoned. Then his allegations of unworthiness become not an honest response to the holiness of the Almighty but mere liturgical exercises, more obnoxious than the self-congratulations of the Pharisee. For if there is anything worse than pride in one's righteousness, it must be pride in one's corruption.

Now admittedly there is great moral power and splendid redeeming force in moments of genuine self-discovery, in the kind of personal recognition in which we catch the publican upon first meeting. But by their very nature such moments are rare and brief. They are like the quick, unexpected glimpses of ourselves that we get from misplaced mirrors or slanted store windows on a commercial street. Glimpses that take us off guard, before we have had time to compose our features and adjust our attire. When without any warning we see briefly what the rest of the world views more often. The anxious squint. The vacuous stare. The glazed indifference or petulant anger. Just a fleeting moment of truth before self-consciousness takes over to remind us who and where we are.

When one is given the opportunity to see himself with this sudden clarity, we might say that he is standing on the border between judgment and mercy. In such a moment he is the naive publican, artless and open. Humility wells up without guile and mingles with the compassion of God in what is surely the essence of grace.

But in that very moment, the publican inevitably loses his innocence. He becomes the sophisticated sinner, reveling in divine love and tempted to make a ritual of self-discovery. Like the disciple Peter in the presence of the transfiguration of Christ, he longs to build a tabernacle and dwell in the midst of this splendid experience.

This is a powerful temptation for all men, is it not? The longing to preserve the first dawn of redemption, the yearning to make the sense of guilt the single active ingredient of piety, the will to define a kind of stylized despair as the most robust spiritual health. It is what Paul Tillich once called man's "last and most intellectual defense against God," the offering not of his whole self but of his sense of unworthiness. Or in the words of Karl Barth, we offer "our little bit of despair" as the currency with which to bargain for salvation.

The tendency is hard to resist and reflects itself in many ways in the life of modern man. The late George Jean Nathan once wrote that he was getting tired of plays in which the leading character was a philosophical bartender, a bank robber who loved canaries, or a prostitute with a heart of gold. (This last he named the "Cosmic Tart.") We are, I think, familiar with the dramatic phenomena of which Nathan spoke. Here is a drama in which the "hero" makes his living selling "rotgut"; but every time he serves a shot he adds a chaser of homely counsel. Or another in which the star is a man who cracks safes. But who, when he learns that his rooming house is on fire, rushes into the flames to save his canary. Or the proverbial woman of the streets. She sells herself over and over again in rituals of commercial love. However, over her bed she keeps a picture of Albert Schweitzer, and she reads the poems of Santayana in her spare time.

These, you see, are people who *have* read the book of Luke. They have made themselves heirs by adoption not of Christ but of the penitent publican. Their hope of salvation lies not in the transformation of life but in isolated, insulated acts of virtue, by which they are not rescued from their depravity but only made more acutely aware of how total that depravity has become. They have chosen to dwell perpetually on the border between judgment and mercy, offering up their "little bit of despair" as a kind of spiritual bribe.

Nathan misdirected his indignation, however, when he blamed the playwrights who created such characters. The fault lies not with the dramatist, who merely holds the mirror up to nature, but with the moral temper of our whole age. A temper to which an important strain in Christian theology has contributed generously. If the Cosmic Tart has become Broadway's symbol of human hope, it is in large part because the penitent publican has become religion's symbol of God's demand.

One who needs more evidence to support this charge than is afforded by the legitimate theater will find it in abundance on the movie screen and television tube. Both of these media of entertainment repeat many times weekly the same liturgies of pious despair that Nathan condemned in the serious drama. In one story after another the same lesson is pounded home. The only dependable source of moral power is the sinner's moment of self-discovery.

In the classical western *High Noon,* the beleaguered town marshall is deserted in his time of trial by everyone except the local drunk who sobers up and offers his assistance. In *The Magnificent Seven* a Mexican town is saved from bandits by a group of vicious killers whose hearts are mysteriously touched by the people's plight. *The Music Man* tells the tale of River City, Iowa, suffocating in self-righteousness, until redeemed by a confidence trickster who falls in love with one of the fairest of its daughters. And when *Lawman*'s Dan Troop sets out to recruit jurors in the trial of a notorious outlaw, only one citizen has the courage to volunteer:

Miss Lily, proprietress of the town dance hall, saloon, and God-knows-and-we-can-guess-what-else.

Thus does the popular culture confirm the darkest suspicions of the serious commentator. Life's vitalities are seen to be the energies generated by sin. Virtue is almost by definition static. It may be the legalistic moralism of the Pharisee or the muscle-bound irrelevance of a Hollywood preacher. But whatever its form, virtue is without strength, zeal, or hope. Where moral force appears in history it is almost invariably depicted as the momentum left over when the sinner, recognizing his guilt, dedicates what is left of his glands to the service of the community. For a brief period he possesses both the energies of sin and the posture of prayer. We must use him quickly, as does the dramatist, before his energies run down and his posture congeals into hypocrisy.

If one accepts this view of things, Augustine's prayer, "Lord, make me chaste, but not yet," may have been more honorably motivated than we have been led to believe.

I suppose that I resent the penitent publican because he is, with that "still unravished bride of quietness," another "foster child of silence and slow time." He is made able to stand forever on the border between judgment and mercy without ever going forward or sliding back. No one can break in upon his moment of self-discovery to ask what he intends to do about what he has so lately learned. None can intrude upon his privacy to speak of implications and consistency. The maiden on the Grecian urn may be frigid, sterile, or a nymphomaniac with a sound sense of strategy. But no one will ever put her to the test. We are only left to wonder whether she will skip so lightly in the eighth month of a difficult pregnancy.

So the philosophical bartender can allow himself the luxury of giving sermons to his clientele, because the play ends before he must choose between preaching and paying the rent. But I had a grandfather who ran a saloon. He was saved by Billy Sunday five times, and until the day of his death he loved to speak of those conversion experiences. His eyes would light up as he talked of the sense of sin, the awareness of his separation from God, the broken spirit, and the contrite heart. Sometimes he even wept a little as he told me of the joy of knowing that no matter how low the sinner,

Jesus was always waiting to receive him into grace. Then with an almost ritualistic gesture he would rise from his chair, brush one arthritic palm against another, and say with a wry grin, "But every Monday morning there was that damned saloon."

You see, no one ever rang down the curtain at the right moment for my grandfather. No one ever said, "Here endeth the lesson," and closed the book. He was not permitted to stand forever at the juncture of self-awareness and divine compassion, possessor in perpetuity of sin's vitalities and faith's assurances. There was always Monday morning and that "damned saloon."

Billy Sunday himself seemed to recognize the problem with an almost cynical clarity. He is reported to have said once that the best thing that could happen to any man would be to accept Jesus Christ as his personal Savior, walk out of the tent, be hit by a truck, and killed instantly. Well, that would be grand, wouldn't it? To be taken at the peak of freshness, like the tomatoes in the television commercial, and popped into the bottle in the first flush of grace; kept forever fair.

Men linger on the border between judgment and mercy, I suspect, hoping that something will happen to end the drama before they have to move forward or slide back. We cultivate the fine edge of guilt much as an alcoholic cultivates the fine edge of intoxication. And for the same reason. So our literature abounds in images of despair. Our dramatists celebrate the villain whose only redeeming feature is his consciousness of corruption. With pardonable pride we tell ourselves that no age has faced its depravity more candidly than our own. The penitent publican has become our patron saint; and in his ritual self-abasement, we profess to see the outlines of the truest piety.

Well, it is an easy thing to condemn this religious charade. However, to indict it honestly is to indict a major aspect of Christian faith itself. The penitent publican does not stand alone in the New Testament. He is one of a large company, those who are glimpsed only briefly and in the moment of self-discovery. These are the people in whom the normal continuities of faith have been ruthlessly abrogated so that they might witness to one thing, the breadth and abundance of divine grace. The prodigal son, the woman taken in adultery, the one at the well in Samaria, Zacchaeus, the repenting thief on the cross, and a host of others. They appear before Christ, confess their sins, receive salvation, and disappear into the wings until the table of scripture readings or a preacher's whim brings them forth to go through the same ritual another Sunday.

It is the message of Christian faith that Jesus Christ came into the world to save sinners. We believe that God was in him reconciling the world unto himself. But precisely because of this conviction we often seem to limit the Almighty to this single manifestation of his love. We sometimes speak as though God is *only* in Christ and doing nothing but *reconciling*. In a significant sense we have made the Mighty One of Israel the prisoner of the incarnation. From Catholic high mass to Baptist revival meeting, the great moments of the faith are those of penitence and forgiveness. And in its most radical form this suggests, in the language of Billy Sunday, that nothing in the life of faith can ever come up to its beginning. Once you have risen from the dead, what can you do for an encore?

Men linger on the border between judgment and mercy, because that is where the action is. If the primary spiritual force of Christian faith is generated in the conjunction of penitence and compassion, man can never again be as close to God, as plugged in, as it were, to divine power, as in the moment of conversion. And so there are people who linger on the border between judgment and mercy, even though it puts them at the edge of the abyss. Because the edge of the abyss is where they have been taught to expect to see God most clearly.

Our age is, I am sure, growing tired of the gospel of guilt. It has confessed its shame and admitted its corruption. And now it challenges Christian theology to speak of what lies beyond repentance. It is asking urgent questions about the content of salvation, the style of the Christian life. The noble prostitute has learned that she cannot be saved in her spare time and begins to mourn her lost virtue. And this is as it should be. For Jesus did not tell the parable of the publican and the Pharisee to publicans in order to show them the inherent value of their guilt. He told it to Pharisees to warn them of the danger of pride. The story was intended to chasten the proud, not exalt penitent depravity.

The distortion of the parable that has given birth to the cult of the publican must be attributed in part, of course, to the sinfulness of man. But this catchall is not the full explanation. A part of the blame, and a large part at that, attaches to the Christian theologian himself and his own best intentions. In our eagerness to make God simple and religion easy to understand we have tried to say all that must be said of ultimate things in the redemptive assurances of the New Testament. We have lifted the truth made manifest in Jesus Christ out of the context of the whole Bible. And it has become in consequence a half-truth, with all the power of the half-truth to condemn what it is meant to serve.

When the word of God's undemanding forgiveness stands apart from the proclamation of God's full nature, that word can undermine man's sense of the meaning and value of his own life. It drains history of its purpose and turns the tumult of our days into "sound and fury, signifying nothing." If the Christian gospel is to be more than a counsel of pious despair, it must be preached and understood in the context of a creative and demanding doctrine of God's purpose for the world.

I hope that someday the penitent publican will read a *good* review of the book of Luke and discover for all our sakes that he must either move toward the altar in commitment or go down to his house, not justified, but condemned.

LEWIS B. SMEDES

The Power of Promises

Lewis B. Smedes — pastor, theologian, ethicist, professor — has written scholarly books, popular books, and some that are both scholarly and popular. Smedes's sermons belong in this last category. "The Power of Promises" is typical. Here Smedes analyzes a single concept with intellectual vigor, but also with the humane understanding of a pastoral care provider. Add passion and colloquial eloquence (in our culture, "what passes as a promise reads like a deal") and you have an offering that is both classic and contemporary — a new navy blazer of a sermon.

This sermon achieves multiple aims. While retrieving the biblical significance of a seemingly ordinary activity, Smedes also carries on cultural criticism, shores up the faithful, and highlights a much-neglected feature of the image of God.

The four introductory paragraphs climax with a sentence that at once summarizes the sermon and sticks in one's memory like a triumph.

Lewis B. Smedes, "Promises: The Power to Control the Future." Used with permission of the author.

The Power of Promises

God said to Moses, "I AM WHO I AM."

Exodus 3:14

He said. . . "I will be with you."

Exodus 3:12

Somewhere today a woman is saying, "I would like to chuck this marriage and start over with somebody who knows how to love me; God knows the clod I married has not given me the love I need." But then she remembers a promise that she made and decides to stick with her marriage and try to make it work.

Somewhere today a father is saying to himself, "I want my impossible daughter to get out of the house and never come back; God knows she has driven me out of my mind." But he remembers a promise he made to her when she was born, and he decides to hang in with her in hurting love.

Somewhere today a minister is thinking, "I am going to give up my calling and find a line of work that pays off in a little more appreciation; God knows this congregation has given me third-degree burnout." But he remembers a promise he made to God when he was ordained, and he decides to renew his spirit and stick with his vocation.

Yes, somewhere people still make and still keep promises. They choose not to quit when the going gets rough because they promised once to see it through. They stick to lost causes. They hold on to a love grown cold. They stay with people who have become pains in the neck. They still dare to make promises and care enough to keep the promises they make. I want to say to you that if you have a ship you will not desert, if you have people you will not forsake, if you have causes you will not abandon, then *you are like God*.

What a marvelous thing a promise is! When a person makes a promise, she reaches out into an unpredictable future and makes one thing predictable: she will be there even when being there costs her more than she wants to pay. When a person makes a promise, he stretches himself out into circumstances that no one can control and controls at least one thing: he will be there no matter what the circumstances turn out to be. With one simple word of promise, a person creates an island of certainty in a sea of uncertainty.

When a person makes a promise, she stakes a claim on her personal freedom and power.

When you make a promise, you take a hand in creating your own future. When I make a promise to you, I am acting on the assumption that my future is not locked on some bionic beam; I am not totally bound to the fateful combination of x's and y's in my genetic code. When I make a promise I refuse to surrender my relationships with people I love to the wayward drives of my subconscious. When I make a promise I act in freedom. I am not a cigar butt thrown out into the cosmos. I am not a hunk of clay waiting to be shaped by my culture. I am free to create a future of my own.

And an identity of my own. I create my identity as this woman's husband and that child's father and that man's friend. Our culture tries to tell us we can be real selves only if we claim our right to self-satisfaction and self-fulfillment. A free self knows he becomes a genuine self by making commitments to other people — promises that he intends to keep even when keeping them exacts a price.

Some people ask, "Who am I?" and expect an answer to come from their feelings. Some people ask, "Who am I?" and expect the answer to come from their accomplishments. Other people ask, "Who am I?" and expect the answer to come from what other people think about them. A person who dares to make and keep promises discovers who she is by the promises she has made and kept to other people.

What you feel is not what you are. Feelings are flickering flames that fade with every fitful breeze. What you desire is not what you are. Desires rise and fall and change so fast that they can only tell you what you want at any trembling moment; knowing what you want is not the same as knowing what you are.

It is the power of promise-making that creates a lasting and genuine identity for us. Listen to the Jewish philosopher, Hannah Arendt: "Without being bound to the fulfillment of our promises we would never be able to keep our identities; we would be condemned to wander helplessly and without direction in the darkness of every person's lonely heart, caught in its contradictions and equivocalities."

To wander in the darkness of our lonely hearts — this is the fate of a person who does not know who he is. To be caught in our own contradictions — this is the sadness of a person who cannot find her identity.

Do you remember *A Man for All Seasons,* that brilliant play about Sir Thomas More? His daughter Meg begged him to save his skin by going back on a promise that he had made. His answer tells us how dangerous it is to make light of a promise, no matter how risky it is to keep it: "Ah, Meg, when a man takes an oath he holds his own self in his hands, like water, and when he opens his hands he need not hope to find himself again."

We are our promises, and we lose hold of ourselves when we take no pains to keep them.

There is a paradox here. The freedom we demonstrate in making commitments is the freedom to limit our freedom. When you make a promise you limit your freedom so that you can be there with the person who trusts you to keep your promise. "The person who makes a vow," said Chesterton, "makes an appointment with himself at some distant time and place and he gives up his freedom in order to keep the appointment." You freely tie yourself down so that other persons can be free to trust that you will keep your promise to them.

On this sort of trust, the whole human family depends.

The future of the human race hangs on a promise. Is there a happy ending to the human romance? It depends completely on a word spoken, a promise made. One thing can assure us that the story of mankind will not end in global disaster. One thing can assure us that this shining globe will not turn into a global garbage heap. One thing gives us hope that one day the world will finally work right for everyone and that the human family will discover peace and love and justice and freedom together. That one thing is a promise made and a promise kept.

It began, you remember, when a common Chaldean named Abraham burned his bridges and gambled his destiny on the reliability of a promise he heard from a stranger in the wilderness.

Stopped in his tracks by a flaming clump of chaparral that did not want to stop burning, Moses came to attention at the voice of an invisible, ineffable Someone calling him to lead his neglected people out of slavery.

Moses was skeptical. "What is your name?" he asked the invisible Stranger. "The people will need some identification." The name came from behind the flame; it came in a word of four cryptic Hebrew consonants that have defied confident translation. "I am who I am," the metaphysically bent scholars have rendered it. But Moses was not a metaphysician. He was a level-headed Hebrew who knew that everything depended on whether this Stranger God could be trusted.

What Moses needed to know was whether he could depend on the Stranger. And what the Stranger God wanted to tell Moses was that he was a God who made promises and kept the promises he made. So the most likely translation of his name goes something like this: "I Am the One Who Will Be There With You." This is God's identity, this is who and what God is: a promise-maker and a promise-keeper.

No one on earth at that moment could have predicted the rises and falls of the people who heard and believed the promise. Moses led them out of Egypt, but once in the land of promise, they acted like a people with a national death wish.

One thing kept them going — the promise of the Stranger in the wilderness, the "One who will be there with you." And one day, in a most unpromising time, when it seemed as if the Stranger had surely forgotten who he was and what he promised, a man came out of Judea saying strange and wonderful things about being Immanuel. In the end he let his blood flow over God's good earth, and with that shedding of blood sealed again the ancient promise: "I am the One who will be there with you."

Will he be? This is the peg on which the future hangs. What will come of it all in the end? A global garbage heap? Or a new earth that finally works right?

Early followers of the Risen One asked the same question in their fashion: "Whatever happened to the promise? What have we got to look forward to?"

Their question is our question: What will it all come to? And where can we get a clear answer?

The data from our natural environment is ambiguous. The evidence from history is discouraging. In the first volume of his great work on ethics, James Gustafson shares his melancholy judgment that nothing in natural history can assure us that nature is basically friendly to the human species. And nothing in the human story gives us a hint that the human species is wise and good enough to make the world work right. There is very little to convince us that the odds of the cosmic game are tilted in our favor.

But then those early Christians did not put their question about the future to natural scientists and historians. They put their question to a fisherman. A man called Peter. And this was the answer they got: "According to his promise, we look forward to a new heaven and a new earth where everything will work right" (2 Pet. 3:13). There it is again: a promise, the promise of the One whose name is "I will be there with you."

Will there be a happy ending? It depends on a promise. Everything hangs on a promise made and a promise kept.

And what comes of our own communities, too, is settled by the power of our own all-too-human promises. Our friendships. Our marriages. Our families. Our neighborhoods. These are the communities that matter to us now. And every community we live in is born and bred by promises made and promises kept.

What else keeps a marriage together? When two people get married, they take on two new identities. Each of them says to the other what God said to Moses: "I am the one who will be there for you."

This sort of promise is countercultural these days. We have, in our culture, decided to make contracts instead of promises. What passes as a promise reads like a deal: "I will be there for you as long as you provide me with all the satisfaction I have coming." This is not a promise; it is a contract. The difference is this: we keep promises even when we are not getting what we have coming. The power of a promise is — in Stanley Hauerwas's words — the power to stick with what we are stuck with.

Nobody knows what she is getting into when she gets married. Nobody knows for sure what sort of person she will become. A man or woman can become several different persons before a marriage is finished. My own wife has slept with at least six different men since she married me, and each of them has been me. But in one most important sense, we can stay the same person we were when we first got married: the person who makes and keeps the promise is always "the one who will be there" with the other.

Take the family for another instance. What is a family but a community of promises made and promises kept — no matter what? A family is not just two or more people related by blood who happen to live under one roof. A family is not a management device by which two adults shuffle children around to the various experts who do the real rearing. A family is a community of people who dare to make a promise and care enough to keep it — no matter what. A real parent has the same name as God does: "the one who will be there with you."

A family is held together by promises: where promises fail, families fail. The rebirth of the family can begin only in the rebirth of promise keeping.

When you get right down to it, everything we do together, from a nation conceived and born in liberty to a family reunion, from a successful political campaign to a winning baseball season, from a United Nations Organization to a church picnic — everything hangs on the thin thread of promises made and promises kept.

Toward the end of his three volumes on the history of the French Revolution, Thomas Carlyle concluded that the revolution failed, not because of corruption in high places, but because ordinary people in their ordinary places neglected to keep their promises.

If we do not keep our promises, what once was a human

community turns into a combat zone of competitive self-maximizers. We are at sea, loose-jointed, uncertain, leery of each other, untrusting. Nobody can trust her neighbors. And without trust, no law, no police force, no legal contracts can keep a community human. The fact is that we are a people who can join together in a permanently free society only if we are a people who can keep promises together.

Let me conclude by repeating what I have been trying to say here.

Our human destiny hangs totally on whether God will retain his identity as the One who will be there with us.

You and I can create an identity for ourselves in the promises we keep to each other.

You and I will experience genuine human community only if we keep our promises to each other.

In short, life begins and ends with those who dare to make a promise and care enough to keep the promise they make.

THE FORMS
AND DYNAMICS
OF THE SERMON

Suppose a preacher has a text, a theme, and a worthy reason for bringing them to a congregation. How shall the preacher deliver these goods? After all, as Fred Craddock says in *Preaching,* "that the preacher has a message does not mean that the listeners will get the message."

Assuming, with Craddock, that all good sermons hold a tight focus, tap Christian tradition, invite listeners into the world of the sermon so that they feel both curious and at home in it, and establish intimacy between preacher and hearers — assuming that all effective sermons offer some blend of these qualities, how do they do it?

The sermons that follow have been chosen especially for their technique along these lines: for the way they live and move and shape themselves; for the way they lure listeners into them; in short, for the form and dynamics they employ in order to achieve their aim. Beginning with a well-cut three-point sermon of Ernest Campbell, this section includes sermons that splay out from a central image, or adopt a novel point of view, or deliberately move in "waves." Some use language uncommonly well. One of them is a prayer. All show their author's awareness that where the use of sermon forms and dynamics is concerned, the idea is not merely to deliver the freight, but also to move listeners to sign for it.

163

ERNEST T. CAMPBELL

Follow Me

Although more than one contemporary homiletician has danced on the grave of the three-point sermon, that form is in fact remarkably hard to kill. We should be glad; it is an excellent teaching instrument, as is clear from Campbell's fine use of it.

Captivated by a stark and seemingly simple command of Jesus, Campbell wonders about its meaning and contemporary force. Probably he could have listed twelve implications of following Jesus. But Campbell is wise: he knows that everything important, everything that rests on the pillars of the earth, and — more to the point — everything memorable is grouped in twos and threes.

So Campbell tells us that to follow Jesus means three things. He explains and develops these things. Then, as a faithful and adroit teacher, he packs them up, hands us the package in the last two paragraphs, and sends us home.

Follow Me

When a minister has a keynote message in his bones, Homecoming Sunday is surely the time to turn it loose. The summer is past. A new season beckons. Anticipation runs high.

But what can a man say to a troubled church, in a troubled city, in a troubled world. Pep rally rhetoric is for university campuses. Crash programs and the promise of instant cures belong to Batten, Barton, Durstin, and Osborne — not to Matthew, Mark, Luke, and John.

Thick volumes of social analysis are the province of research fellows who have lucked into a foundation grant. Throwing in the towel is no possibility for those who have been given a towel and commissioned to serve.

What can a man say? He can lift up and commend two words of Jesus that resonate with relevance for men today: "Follow me."

Jesus uttered these words not once but many times: to Peter and Andrew by the Sea of Galilee; to Levi, the son of Alphaeus at the seat of customs. To a balking inquirer Jesus' words were, "Let the dead bury their dead, and come, follow me"; to the rich young ruler, "Sell what you have, give to the poor, and come, follow me." And to all in his time and in succeeding times, "If any man would come after me, let him deny himself and take up his cross and follow me."

These words of entreaty and command are plain and disconcertingly personal. They cut through a maze of theology. They are no respecter of denominational ties or ecclesiastical lines. They do not bow to rank or privilege. They are tall enough and deep enough to guide a church in the most ambiguous of times.

There are several considerations that have moved me in recent months to a new appreciation of these words. First, anyone who says "Follow me" is going someplace — and we need direction. These words strike us initially as unwelcome and intrusive. They threaten to dislocate us. But ponder them longer and find that part of their appeal lies in the fact that *they promise to connect us with one who is going someplace.*

The therapy of hibernation, so widely practiced by so many in our time, cannot really heal what hurts us deep inside. Yet leadership that knows where it is going is hard to come by in our society, and so we hibernate. There was more truth than humor to the legend I spotted on a T-shirt in Hew Hampshire a few summers back: "Don't follow me, I'm lost!" One of our more vocal public leaders was criticized the other day by a veteran politician who spoke his mind frankly: "I don't take him seriously because I don't think he is going anyplace."

Jesus has a plan, a work to do, a purpose to achieve in history and beyond. And he deigns to cut us in. The word that is translated *follow* in most instances in the gospel is rooted in the Greek word for road. To follow is to share the same road. The Christian's prayer is not for a longer stay with God but for a closer walk with God.

Moreover, anyone who says "Follow me" is obviously more interested in the future than in the past — and we need a loyalty to the future. With Jesus it's not where you've been that matters, but where you're going; not whether you have fallen, but whether you will get up; not whom you've hurt in the past, but whom you will help in the future.

A relatively new approach to psychiatry has been abroad for a few years now under the name reality therapy. Its founding mentor was William Glasser. The approach makes sense to me. Reality therapists insist that it is futile to keep on rummaging around in someone's past, getting people to articulate and amplify yesterday's failures and to recall how the world has mistreated them. The important thing is to get them to face their needs and prepare for a future worth living.

This approach may err a bit on the side of oversimplification, but I find myself saying "Amen" when Glasser writes: "Without denying that the patient had an unsatisfactory past, we find that to look for what went wrong does not help him. What good comes from discovering that you are afraid to assert yourself because you had a domineering father? Both patient and therapist can be aware of this historical occurrence; they can discuss it in all of its ramifications for years, but the knowledge will not help the patient assert himself now."

Fan through the pages of the gospel record and you will be startled to discover how little time Jesus spent allowing people to expand on a burdened past. When the woman taken in adultery was thrust into his presence he did not try to explore the circumstances that had pushed her to her fall. He simply took her by the hand and said, "Go thy way and sin no more" (John 8:11). When Nicodemus came to him under the cover of night, shackled by an impossible legalism, Jesus didn't ask him how he got that way but said simply, "You must be born again" (John 3:3).

The story of the prodigal son may indeed be the paradigm that indicates how God deals with men and women who have failed. The younger brother in the far country never got to recite before his father the speech that he had so carefully learned and memorized. Instead, his words were smothered in his father's love. He was given a ring for his finger, a robe for his back, and shoes for his feet, and restored to full status as a son. For to be penitent is to be forgiven, and to be forgiven is to rise up and follow.

Yes, we might fall again. We do not move on brashly, for our failures are still very much in our minds. But we know that we are being led by light and love. This is what the eminent New Testament scholar T. W. Manson was testifying to when he said: "The living Christ still has two hands, one to point the way, and the other held out to help us along. So the Christian ideal lies before us, not as a remote and austere mountain peak, an ethical Everest which we must scale by our own skill and endurance; but as a road on which we may walk with Christ as guide and friend. And we are assured, as we set out on the journey, that he is with us always, 'even unto the end of the world'" (Matt. 28:20).

Finally, consider the fact that whoever commands us to follow and wins our allegiance has given us a norm by which to test our living. Christ does not absorb us or intend to absorb us. There is a distance between the Lord and the servant, so that our selfhood, integrity, and individuality might be preserved. Moreover, he calls us not to slavish imitation but to follow — each of us in the context of his time and place. There is no time or place or circumstance where one cannot follow.

What Christian living is all about, singly or corporately, is following Christ — an important thing for us to see at this particular time in the life of our nation and church when we are being prodded by the living Lord to move with history. "Follow me" — this is the word that ought to monitor what we do and say and think as trustees, deacons, committee members, council members, ministers, and members of the congregation. Is this action, this decision, this policy, this attitude of such a quality that it is moving our church in the direction Jesus is going? We may not always agree on what it means to follow Jesus, but we cannot question the fundamental presumption that we are here to follow Jesus. This is the acid test stripped of its theological decor.

It's safe to tell it now. A few days after John F. Kennedy was assassinated, a member of the church I was serving in Ann Arbor called and suggested that the one thing we might do to partially redeem the tragedy would be to provide Marina Oswald with an opportunity to improve her English. Mrs. Oswald had expressed a desire to stay in the United States and learn its language better. Because it would have been unwise to bring this before the entire congregation, a few of us who represented the executive committee of that church got in touch with Marina Oswald.

To make a long story short, in due time and in cooperation with the FBI and others, Marina Oswald came to Ann Arbor. She slipped into our community at night by train while a battery of reporters were waiting hawkishly at the airport. She lived with a modest family that takes seriously its devotion to God and its love for people. When we were finally pressed to do so, we joined the University of Michigan in issuing a modest press release. The mail began to come in. There were some who were quick and hot to say that what we did was unpatriotic. Others told us that our action was unwise, still others that it was unfair. (One woman said that she had belonged to a church for forty years and what it had done for her in all that time she could write on the back of a postage stamp.) Others were prompted to say that what we did was grossly un-American. I answered every letter, rightly or wrongly feeling it the obligation of my ministry to do so. I said in effect to each person who criticized, "The one thing you haven't shown us is that what we have done is unlike Christ."

It doesn't really matter whether an action is profitable or popular, whether it is practical or realistic, whether it wins a salute from a city or nation. What matters only and always is whether it can be understood as following Jesus Christ.

As a Presbyterian, I stood a few inches taller in the fall of 1970 when I read what the General Assembly of the Presbyterian Church of South Africa said to the prime minister of that country. The World Council of Churches had decided to give financial aid to several black African liberation movements, including some listed in South Africa as terrorist organizations. Because of this stand, the government asked the churches of South Africa to pull out of the World Council of Churches. The answer of the General Assembly was: "The Assembly reminds the prime minister that its only Lord and master is Jesus Christ and it may not serve other masters and that its task is not necessarily to support the government in power but to be faithful to the gospel."

"Follow me." To follow Jesus is to have a plan. To follow Jesus is to face and embrace the future. To follow Jesus is to have a star by which to steer. Every time he comes across our way and bids us follow, he creates a crisis. And we can never be the same again. For when that command registers on our souls, we can choose to die to God and live to self, or to die to self and live to God.

The kind of loyalty I should like to command of myself and see congregations offer up to God can be summed up in the words of an obscure figure in the Old Testament by the name of Ittai, who belonged to a foreign country. On a dark day when many of David's troops were choosing to desert their chief, David turned to Ittai and said, in effect: "You've got it made at home. Why don't you go back? You've served us well." But Ittai answered: "As the Lord liveth, and as my lord the king liveth, surely in what place my lord the king shall be, whether in death or life, even there also will thy servant be" (2 Sam. 15:21).

ANNA CARTER FLORENCE

At the River's Edge

Some sermons are straight-shot arrows — swift, efficient, direct. They hit the bull's-eye, quiver for a second, and stop.

But this sermon by Anna Carter Florence flows across hearers' minds like the deep-current river that serves as its central image — sometimes surging, sometimes slowing, occasionally doubling back in wide loops to irrigate previously crossed land. The sermon carries us along the Nile of Moses' peril, spills over into the floodwaters of the California depression, merges with the Ganges, and finally courses through our hometown, where a crisis must be faced and decisions made.

Anna Carter Florence, "At the River's Edge," in *Sacred Strands: Sermons by Minnesota Women,* edited by Barbara Mraz, pp. 31-37 (Rochester, MN: Lone Oak Press, 1991). Used by permission.

At the River's Edge

Now a man from the house of Levi went and married a Levite woman. The woman conceived and bore a son; and when she saw that he was a fine baby, she hid him three months. When she could hide him no longer she got a papyrus basket for him, and plastered it with bitumen and pitch; she put the child in it and placed it among the reeds on the bank of the river. His sister stood at a distance, to see what would happen to him.

The daughter of Pharaoh came down to bathe at the river, while her attendants walked beside the river. She saw the basket among the reeds and sent her maid to bring it. When she opened it, she saw the child. He was crying, and she took pity on him, "This must be one of the Hebrews' children," she said. Then his sister said to Pharaoh's daughter, "Shall I go and get you a nurse from the Hebrew women to nurse the child for you?" Pharaoh's daughter said to her, "Yes." So the girl went and called the child's mother. Pharaoh's daughter said to her, "Take this child and nurse it for me, and I will give you your wages." So the woman took the child and nursed it. When the child grew up, she brought him to Pharaoh's daughter, and she took him as her son. She named him Moses, "because," she said, "I drew him out of the water."

Exodus 2:1-10, NRSV;
see also Exodus 1:8-22
and Romans 8:22-25

You can tell a lot about a society by looking at its children. Take the United States, for example. These days, we have daycare, *Sesame Street*, Nintendo, and Bart Simpson. We also have crack, street gangs, homeless children, and babies with AIDS. One out of four children in our country lives below the poverty line, and for African-American families that number increases to one out of two. In 1989, fifty-three percent of our tax dollars went to military defense instead of to education for our children. That tells you a lot about us, doesn't it?

Children are more than wet cement; they are spokespeople for our values, our choices, our circumstances, and our life-styles.

By all rights of the law, baby Moses should have been dead. That tells you a lot about Egypt. Moses didn't start life with many advantages. He was born in the equivalent of a Hebrew refugee camp, or the Hebrew slave quarters on an Egyptian plantation. He was a boy baby, and the Pharaoh, sounding a lot like King Herod in Jerusalem two thousand years later, had ordered that all male infants were to be thrown into the Nile River to drown. That tells you a lot about the Pharaoh. He'd even gone so far as to instruct the midwives and anyone else who might happen upon a woman in labor to kill the boy babies as soon as they appeared. If things had gone as the Pharaoh had ordered, that ought to have taken care of Moses.

But in baby Moses' case, there were three other people the Pharaoh didn't count on: the midwife, the mother of Moses, and the daughter of Pharaoh. They wouldn't play ball. The midwife feared God, the mother loved her baby, and the Pharaoh's own daughter had compassion on the abandoned child. They each had to break the law to save the life of that baby. That tells you a lot about them. And they weren't saints. They were ordinary people acting under extraordinary circumstances, whose faith, love, and compassion made them more than they were.

There are theologians who will argue that this story is just a legend about a national hero, just a parallel version of a tale that exists in many other cultures. There are other theologians who insist that it was the providence of God, not a handful of scared human beings, that saved baby Moses from the fate of a thousand other Hebrew boy babies. But what interests me about this passage is the action of the story itself, the characters who labor between right and wrong at the river's edge. That's what interests me, because I know that I've been down at the river's edge almost every day of my life, sitting on the bank, watching stuff pass: the boats, the dead logs, and sometimes the babies in a basket. You can learn a lot about a culture by watching what floats by on a river, because some of it belongs there and some of it doesn't. This is a story about our ability as human beings to know the difference between those two things, or between what is kind and just and merciful, and what is cruel and unjust and abominable in the eyes of God. It's a story about breaking down stereotypes, and we can learn a lot from it.

When I was in New York last month, I went to see the new production of *The Grapes of Wrath*, John Steinbeck's classic novel of the Great Depression. It's a story about an Oklahoma sharecropper family, driven off their land by big agricultural interests and, like thousands of other desperate families, lured to the promised land of California in hope of finding work. Of course there isn't anything there but dirt-poor wages and strikes and corruption and starvation. They lose everything except their dignity and the will to survive.

In one of the last scenes of the play — and the novel, too — the daughter, who has been pregnant throughout the story, goes into labor in the middle of a flood and delivers a stillborn baby. Her Uncle John is sent out to somehow bury the baby in spite of the rising waters of the river. Listen to what Steinbeck writes:

> Uncle John . . . put his shovel down, and holding the box in front of him, he edged through the brush until he came to the edge of the swift stream. . . . He held the apple box against his chest. And then he leaned over and set the box in the stream and steadied it with his hand. He said fiercely, "Go down an' tell 'em. Go down in the street, an' rot an' tell 'em that way. That's the way you can talk. Don' even know if you was a boy or a girl. Ain't gonna find out. Go on down now, an' lay in the street. Maybe they'll know then."

You can learn a lot about the Great Depression from that scene. I know we all have stories about that period; my own family lost everything and went to California on a hoax, too. Migrant workers, farmers, factory workers, and so many others suffered without a voice then, and no one seemed to hear.

Steinbeck's grim scene makes a strong statement: What does it take for us to realize that things are skewed and wrong? What does it take for us to realize that we can do better, we can BE better? If a starving migrant worker doesn't spark compassion in us, then will a baby in a box, or a basket, floating down the river? If a statistic won't do it, a statistic that tells us that one out of every two black children we meet in this country doesn't get enough to eat, then what will? We need to know what our breaking point is, don't we? — especially when we're at the river's edge. What does it take?

The Pharaoh's daughter came down to the river with her entourage of servants for a swim. Who knows what she'd been brought up to believe about the Hebrews, those coarse foreigners who multiplied like rabbits in their filthy ghettoes? Presumably, she'd seen them working at a distance on yet another enormous building project. But it's hard to imagine that she'd ever actually had a conversation with a Hebrew girl her age, or broken bread with a Hebrew family.

So here she is, the princess of Egypt, taking her daily dip at the river's edge, when she sees a basket floating in the reeds, and hears something that sounds like a faint cry. One of her maids goes to fetch it, and what should be inside but a real, live baby, a squalling, hungry, frightened infant. Her first thought must have been, whose baby is this? And then: why would any mother put her baby in the river in such a carefully constructed little ark if she wasn't desperate for it to live? She looks to see if it's a boy or a girl; it's a boy, all right. And then it dawns on her: "This must be one of the Hebrew's children," she says.

Her mind must have been racing. "One of *them*," she thinks. "An actual Hebrew baby, who's going to grow up to be huge and ugly and a threat to my life, according to my father! What am I going to do? I'm supposed to kill it; I can't do that. What if I just leave it here? But then it will die anyway; how long can a baby go without milk?" And before she can decide what to do, a young girl comes bounding out of the bullrushes, saying, "Shall I go and get you a nurse from the Hebrew women to nurse that baby for you?" Obviously this is more than a coincidence; the girl means the baby's mother; she's probably his sister. And she's talking as if the baby now belonged to the Pharaoh's daughter, as if the princess, not the mother or the sister, were responsible for it! The girl is talking as if they have a connection beyond the fact that they all just happen to be there together down at the river's edge: the baby, his sister, the princess and her maids. And everyone is waiting for the princess to make a decision — everyone, that is, but the baby, who just wants to be held, and fed, and given a warm place to sleep.

We know how the story ends. The princess has compassion on the baby, and probably on his family, too, and decides to save the child. She tells them that she will pay them to take care of him, and when he is older, that they should bring him back to the palace so that she can raise him as her own son. It's a huge risk for her to take, to disobey her father's law, but I think what happened is this: when she actually saw this Hebrew baby at the river's edge, and stepped into the shoes of that mother, all the things she'd been taught to believe since childhood, and all her fear and ignorance about this other group of people, just evaporated. She had a connection with someone, a relationship. No law was more important than that.

What does it take for us to realize that things have to change? What does it take for us to meet our prejudices head-on? It takes a connection, a relationship. Sometimes I think it takes a baby in a basket floating at the river's edge. But it also takes an awareness that we're laboring at something that isn't finished yet. Learning to be truly open to people who are different than we are takes time, and unlearning our prejudices and fears can be painful. But when we stand at the river's edge, God gives us the strength to do what we have to do. God gives us the gifts of compassion and love to overcome our fears and pull that baby out of the water.

There is a scene from the film *Gandhi* that I will never forget. India is groaning in its labor pains to be an independent nation, and once again it is the tragic conflict between Hindus and Muslims that is tearing things apart. The slaughter goes against everything that Gandhi, their beloved leader and the promoter of nonviolence, has worked for. And so, despite the great risks to his health, he goes on another hunger strike, vowing not to eat until the violence between Hindus and Muslims ceases. Many days go by; the fighting rages on, and Gandhi's physicians tell him that, given his frail state of health, if he does not eat soon he will die. One morning, a ragged Muslim man makes his way into Gandhi's bedroom, hurls a piece of bread at him, and says, "Here, eat this! I'm already going to hell, but I don't want your death on my conscience too!" Gandhi asks him quietly, "What do you want?" And the man says, "Last night, my only son was killed in the riots by a Hindu. And I was so full of grief and rage that I went out and took a baby Hindu boy, and I smashed him against a wall until his head broke open. I know I'm going to hell. But you mustn't die for us, or we will have twice the torment." Gandhi thinks a moment, and then asks him, "You are a Muslim?" "Yes," the man says, "I am." "Then what you must do," Gandhi tells him, "is to go out and find a Hindu boy whose father was killed last night. Take him home and adopt him to be your only son, and raise him to be a good Hindu."

The Hebrew people couldn't soften the hearts of the Pharaoh and his daughter. But a mother who couldn't keep her own baby put him in a basket at the river's edge, hoping that someone would see him and have pity on him. And someone did. The Pharaoh's own daughter came down to the banks of the Nile and got her first real look at a Hebrew family, her first real taste of the miserable dilemma they were in, and she did what she could. She said, enough. Enough fear. Enough hatred. Enough ignorance. This baby is laboring to be somebody, and I've got to labor at it, too. I've got to realize that the water has broken, and nothing can hold this baby back from coming; not the law, not the Pharaoh, nothing. I've got a connection with this baby because we're both here at the river's edge, and I can do something to help it. And then I'll never be able to look at another Hebrew without seeing my own son.

What are we laboring for down at the river's edge? What old fears and stereotypes and worn-out ways are we clinging to down in the bullrushes? Well, stand guard, because God is breaking the waters around us, the labor pains are fierce, and the baby in the basket is on its way. Nothing we can do to stop the pain, nothing we can do to push the baby back. We've got to reach in there and pick it up and say,

> "Yes, you're my son. You're my daughter. Doesn't matter what color you are; you're my sister. Doesn't matter what religion you are; you're my brother. I don't care what I used to believe, you can love anyone you want to, male or female. You don't have to grow up to be smart, or pretty, or strong, or perfect, because I don't care. It's all right. Don't you cry anymore. We'll just sit here together, down at the river's edge. We'll just sit here."

EUGENE H. PETERSON

My Eyes Are Not
Raised Too High

This sermon is a skillful textual/topical sermon, in which the text controls the sermon but also lets it breathe. Peterson exposes the heart of an eloquent psalm and then, in its terms, analyzes two spiritual virtues. He moves this project forward by the use of a controlling image and also by means of apt literary allusions and cultural critique. Throughout, the sermon exhibits a winning way with the English language — a Peterson trademark.

Eugene H. Peterson, "My Eyes Are Not Raised Too High," reprinted from *A Long Obedience in the Same Direction: Discipleship in an Instant Society* by Eugene H. Peterson, pp. 145-54. © 1980 by InterVarsity Christian Fellowship of the USA. Used by permission of InterVarsity Press, P.O. Box 1400, Downers Grove, IL 60515.

My Eyes Are Not Raised Too High

O LORD, my heart is not lifted up,
    my eyes are not raised too high;
I do not occupy myself with things
    too great and too marvelous for me.
But I have calmed and quieted my soul,
    like a child quieted at its mother's breast;
    like a child that is quieted is my soul.

O Israel, hope in the LORD
    from this time forth and for evermore.

                                    Psalm 131

Humility is the obverse side of confidence in God,
whereas pride is the obverse side of confidence in self.

                                    John Baillie

Christian faith needs continuous maintenance. It requires attending
to. "If you leave a thing alone you leave it to a torrent of change.
If you leave a white post alone it will soon be a black post."[1]
    Every spring in my neighborhood a number of people prune
their bushes and trees. It is an annual practice with people who
care about growing things. It is also one of those acts that an
outsider, one who does not understand how growth works, almost
always misunderstands, for it always looks like an act of mutilation.
It appears that you are ruining the plant, when, in fact, you are
helping it. We have a rosebush that hasn't been pruned for several
years. When it first bloomed the roses were full and vigorous. Last

1. Gilbert Keith Chesterton, *Orthodoxy* (New York: John Lane, 1909),
p. 212.

summer the plant was larger than ever. The vines ranged up to the roof on a trellis I had made. I anticipated more roses than ever. But I was disappointed. The blossoms were small and scrawny. The branches had gotten too far from their roots. The plant couldn't grow a good blossom. It needed a good pruning.

Psalm 131 is a maintenance psalm. It is functional to the person of faith as pruning is functional to the gardener: it gets rid of that which looks good to those who don't know any better and reduces the distance between our hearts and their roots in God.

The two things that Psalm 131 prunes away are unruly ambition and infantile dependency, what we might call getting too big for our breeches and refusing to cut the apron strings. Both of these tendencies can easily be supposed to be virtues, especially by those who are not conversant with Christian ways. If we are not careful, we will be encouraging the very things that will ruin us. We are in special and constant need of expert correction. We need pruning. Jesus said, "Every branch of mine that bears no fruit, he takes away, and every branch that does bear fruit he prunes, that it may bear more fruit" (John 15:2). More than once our Lord the Spirit has used Psalm 131 to do this important work among his people. As we gain a familiarity with and an understanding of the psalm, he will be able to use it that way with us "that we may bear more fruit."

"O LORD, my heart is not lifted up, my eyes are not raised too high; I do not occupy myself with things too great and too marvelous for me. But I have calmed and quieted my soul."

These lines are enormously difficult for us to comprehend — not that they are difficult to understand with our minds, for the words are all plain, but difficult to grasp with our emotions, feeling their truth. All cultures throw certain stumbling blocks in the way of those who pursue gospel realities. It is sheerest fantasy to suppose that we would have had an easier time of it as Christian believers if we were in another land or another time. It is no easier to be a Chinese Christian than to be a Spanish Christian than to be a Russian Christian than to be a Brazilian Christian than to be an American Christian — nor more difficult. The way of faith deals with realities in whatever time or whatever culture.

But there are differences from time to time and from place to place that cause special problems. For instance, when an ancient temptation or trial becomes an approved feature in the culture, a way of life that is expected and encouraged, Christians have a stumbling block put before them that is hard to recognize for what it is, for it has been made into a monument, gilded with bronze and bathed in decorative lights. It has become an object of veneration. But the plain fact is that it is right in the middle of the road of faith, obstructing discipleship. For all its fancy dress and honored position it is still a stumbling block.

One temptation that has received this treatment in Western civilization, with some special flourishes in America, is ambition. Our culture encourages and rewards ambition without qualification. We are surrounded by a way of life in which betterment is understood as expansion, as acquisition, as fame. Everyone wants to get more. To be on top, no matter what it is the top of, is admired. There is nothing recent about the temptation. It is the oldest sin in the book, the one that got Adam thrown out of the garden and Lucifer tossed out of heaven. What is fairly new about it is the general admiration and approval that it receives.

The old story of Doctor Faustus used to be well known and appreciated as a warning. John Faustus became impatient with the limitations placed upon him in his study of law, of medicine, of theology. No matter how much he learned in these fields he found he was always in the service of something greater than he was — of justice, of healing, of God. He chafed in the service and wanted out: he wanted to be in control, to break out of the limits of the finite. So he became an adept in magic, by which he was able to defy the laws of physics, the restrictions of morality, and relations with God and use his knowledge in these fields for his own pleasures and purposes. In order to bring it off, though, he had to make a pact with the devil, which permitted him to act for the next twenty-four years in a godlike way — living without limits, being in control instead of being in relationship, exercising power instead of practicing love. But at the end of the twenty-four years was damnation.

For generations this story has been told and retold by poets and playwrights and novelists (Goethe, Marlowe, Mann), warning people against abandoning the glorious position of being a person created in the image of God and attempting the foolhardy adventure of trying to be a god on our own. But now something alarming has happened. There have always been Faustian characters, people in the community who embarked on a way of arrogance and power; now our entire culture is Faustian. We are caught up in a way of life that, instead of delighting in finding out the meaning of God and searching out the conditions in which human qualities can best be realized, recklessly seeks ways to circumvent nature, arrogantly defies personal relationships, and names God only in curses. The legend of Faustus, useful for so long in pointing out the folly of a God-defying pride, now is practically unrecognizable because the assumptions of our whole society (our educational models, our economic expectations, even our popular religion) are Faustian.

It is difficult to recognize pride as a sin when it is held up on every side as a virtue, urged as profitable, and rewarded as an achievement. What is described in Scripture as the basic sin — the sin of taking things into your own hands, being your own god, grabbing what is there while you can get it — is now described as basic wisdom: improve yourself by whatever means you are able; get ahead regardless of the price; take care of me first. For a limited time it works. But at the end the devil has his due. There is damnation.

It is additionally difficult to recognize unruly ambition as a sin because it has a kind of superficial relationship to the virtue of aspiration — an impatience with mediocrity, and a dissatisfaction with all things created until we are at home with the Creator, the hopeful striving for the best God has for us — the kind of thing Paul expressed: "I press on toward the goal for the prize of the upward call of God in Christ Jesus" (Phil. 3:14). But if we take the energies that make for aspiration and remove God from the picture, replacing him with our own crudely sketched self-portrait, we end up with ugly arrogance. Robert Browning's fine line on aspiration, "A man's reach should exceed his grasp, or what's a heaven for?" has been distorted to "Reach for the skies and grab everything that isn't nailed down." Ambition is aspiration gone crazy. Aspiration is the channeled, creative energy that moves us to growth in Christ, shaping goals in the Spirit. Ambition takes these same energies for growth and development and uses them to make something tawdry and cheap, sweatily knocking together a Babel when we could be vacationing in Eden. Calvin comments, "Those who yield themselves up to the influence of ambition will soon lose themselves in a labyrinth of perplexity."

Our lives are only lived well when they are lived in terms of their creation, with God loving and we being loved, with God making and we being made, with God revealing and we understanding, with God commanding and we responding. Being a Christian means accepting the terms of creation, accepting God as our maker and redeemer, and growing day by day into an increasingly glorious creature in Christ, developing joy, experiencing love, maturing in peace. By the grace of Christ we experience the marvel of being made in the image of God. If we reject this way the only alternative is to attempt the hopelessly fourth-rate, embarrassingly awkward imitation of God made in the image of man.

Both revelation and experience (Genesis and Goethe) show it to be the wrong way, and so the psalmist is wise to see it and sing, "O LORD, my heart is not lifted up, my eyes are not raised too high; I do not occupy myself with things too great and too marvelous for me. But I have calmed and quieted my soul." I will not try to run my own life or the lives of others; that is God's business. I will not pretend to invent the meaning of the universe; I will accept what God has shown its meaning to be. I will not noisily strut about demanding that I be treated as the center of my family or my neighborhood or my work, but I will seek to discover where I fit and do what I am good at. The soul, clamorously crying out for attention and arrogantly parading its importance, is calmed and quieted so that it can be itself, truly.

But if we are not to be proud, clamorous, arrogant persons, what are we to be? Mousy, cringing, insecure ones? Well, not quite. Having realized the dangers of pride, the sin of thinking too much of ourselves, we are suddenly in danger of another mistake, that of thinking too little of ourselves. There are some who conclude that since the great Christian temptation is to try to be everything, the perfect Christian solution is to be nothing. And so we have the problem of the doormat Christian and the dishrag saint: the person upon whom everyone walks and wipes their feet, the person who is used by others to clean up the mess of everyday living and then discarded. These people then compensate for their poor lives by weepily clinging to God, hoping to make up for the miseries of everyday life by dreaming of luxuries in heaven.

Christian faith is not neurotic dependency but childlike trust. We do not have a God who forever indulges our whims but a God whom we trust with our destinies. The Christian is not a naive, innocent infant who has no identity apart from a feeling of being comforted and protected and catered to but a person who has discovered an identity that is given by God which can be enjoyed best and fully in a voluntary trust in God. We do not cling to God desperately out of fear and the panic of insecurity; we come to him freely in faith and love.

Our Lord gave us the picture of the child as a model for Christian faith (Mark 10:14-16) not because of the child's helplessness but because of the child's willingness to be led, to be taught, to be blessed. God does not reduce us to a set of Pavlovian reflexes in which we mindlessly worship and pray and obey on signal; he establishes us with a dignity in which we are free to receive his word, his gifts, his grace.

The psalm shows great genius at this point and describes a relationship that is completely attractive. The translators of the Jerusalem Bible have retained the literalism of the Hebrew metaphor: "Enough for me to keep my soul tranquil and quiet like a child in its mother's arms, as content as a child that has been weaned." The last phrase, "as a child that has been weaned," creates a completely new, unguessed reality. The Christian is "not like an infant crying loudly for his mother's breast, but like a weaned child that quietly rests by his mother's side, happy in being with her. . . . No desire now comes between him and his God; for he is sure that God knows what he needs before he asks him. And just as the child gradually breaks off the habit of regarding his mother only as a means of satisfying his own desires and learns to love her for her own sake, so the worshipper after a struggle has reached an attitude of mind in which he desires God for himself and not as a means of fulfillment of his own wishes. His life's centre of gravity has shifted. He now rests no longer in himself but in God."[2]

The transition from a sucking infant to a weaned child, from squalling baby to quiet son or daughter, is not smooth. It is stormy and noisy. It is no easy thing to quiet yourself: sooner may a person calm the sea or rule the wind or tame a tiger than quiet oneself. It is pitched battle. The baby is denied expected comforts and flies into rages or sinks into sulks. There are sobs and struggles. The infant is facing its first great sorrow, and it is in sore distress. But, as Spurgeon put it, "to the weaned child his mother is his comfort though she has denied him comfort. It is a blessed mark of growth out of spiritual infancy when we can forego the joys which once appeared to be essential, and can find our solace in him who denies them to us."

Many who have traveled this way of faith have described the transition from an infantile faith that grabs at God out of desperation to a mature faith that responds to God out of love . . . "as content as a child that has been weaned." Often our conscious Christian lives do begin at points of desperation, and God, of course, does not refuse to meet our needs. There are heavenly comforts that break through our despair and persuade us that "all will be well and all manner of things will be well." The early stages of Christian belief are not infrequently marked with miraculous signs and exhilarations of spirit. But as discipleship continues the sensible comforts gradually disappear. For God does not want us neurotically dependent upon him but willingly trustful in him. And so he weans us. The period of infancy will not be sentimentally extended beyond what is necessary. The time of weaning is very often noisy and marked with misunderstandings: "I no longer feel like I did when I was first a Christian. Does that mean I am no longer a Christian? Has God abandoned me? Have I done something terribly wrong?"

The answer is, "Neither: God hasn't abandoned you, and you haven't done anything wrong. You are being weaned. The apron

2. Artur Weiser, *The Psalms* (Philadelphia: Westminster Press, 1962), p. 777.

strings have been cut. You are free to come to God or not come to him. You are, in a sense, on your own with an open invitation to listen and receive and enjoy our Lord."

The last line of the psalm addresses this quality of newly acquired freedom: "O Israel, hope in the LORD from this time forth and for evermore." Choose to be with him; elect his presence; aspire to his ways; respond to his love.

When Charles Spurgeon preached this psalm he said that it "is one of the shortest Psalms to read, but one of the longest to learn." We are always, it seems, reeling from one side of the road to the other as we travel in the way of faith. At one turning of the road we are presented with awesome problems and terrifying emergencies. We rise to the challenge, take things into our own hands to become master of the situation, telling God, "Thank you, but get lost. We'll take care of this one ourselves." At the next turning we are overwhelmed and run in a panic to some kind of infantile religion that will solve all our problems for us, freeing us of the burden of thinking and the difficulty of choosing. We are, alternately, rebellious runaways and whining babies. Worse, we have numerous experts, so-called, encouraging us to pursue one or the other of these ways.

The experts in our society who offer to help us have a kind of general-staff mentality, from which massive, topdown solutions are issued to solve our problems. Then when the solutions don't work, we get mired in the nothing-can-be-done swamp. We are first incited into being grandiose and then intimidated into being infantile. But there is another way, the plain way of quiet, Christian humility. We need pruning. Cut back to our roots, we then learn this psalm and discover the quietness of the weaned child, the tranquillity of maturing trust. It is such a minute psalm that many have overlooked it, but for all its brevity and lack of pretense it is essential. For every Christian encounters problems of growth and difficulties of development.

A number of years ago Peter Marin made an incisive observation that was very much in the spirit of Psalm 131. "There are cultural conditions," he wrote, for which there are no solutions, turnings of the soul so profound and complex that no system can absorb or contain them. How could one have "solved" the Reformation? Or first-century Rome? One makes accommodations and adjustments, one dreams about the future and makes plans to save us all, but in spite of all that, because of it, what seems more important are the private independent acts that become more necessary every day: the ways we find as private persons to restore to one another the strengths we should have now — whether to make the kind of revolution we need or to survive the repression that seems likely . . . what saves us as men and women is always a kind of witness: the quality of our own acts and lives.

And that is what Psalm 131 nurtures: a quality of calm confidence and quiet strength that knows the difference between unruly arrogance and faithful aspiration, knows how to discriminate between infantile dependency and childlike trust, and chooses to aspire and to trust — and to sing, "Enough for me to keep my soul tranquil and quiet like a child in its mother's arms, as content as a child that has been weaned."

GEORGE A. BUTTRICK

God and Laughter

George Buttrick's Harvard sermons are typically wise, suggestive, and wide-ranging in both formal and anecdotal learning. "God and Laughter" displays these excellences and more in a classic Buttrick pattern. Framed by an overture and a recapitulation, this sermon runs laughter like a musical theme through the three great movements of creation, sin, and redemption. By the time the music stops, we are left to wonder whether the sermon really was about laughter, or rather about the movements themselves, and especially about redemption — the last laugh of God.

God and Laughter

He that sitteth in the heavens shall laugh:
the Lord shall have them in derision.

Psalm 2:4, KJV

When the Lord turned again the captivity of Zion,
we were like them that dream.
Then was our mouth filled with laughter,
and our tongue with singing.

Psalm 126:1-2, KJV

"Just so, I tell you, there is joy before the angels of God
over one sinner who repents."

Luke 15:10

Laughter is a strange portent. In a world held in mystery, in seeming nothingness, a world in which we can neither prove God nor escape him, our faces pucker in smiles. In a generation that competes in destructive weapons until final destruction looms, a cartoon appears in *The Boston Globe* showing Uncle Sam as a hitchhiker while two Russian sputniks flash past him, one of them with a little grinning dog on board. We laugh at our own predicament. We joke even about death. A friend of mine, a bishop, is still chuckling over a pompous, humorless mortician who congratulated him on "your *graveside* manner." We can quip even in the act or moment of death, as when the not-so-saintly Charles II apologized for being "so unconscionable a time in dying." In a world dark with griefs and hollow with graves we laugh. Even in war and sorrow we pity the man who cannot laugh. Why? Here are some comments that you can use to better purpose than I.

I

There seems to be laughter in creation itself, and if so, that is the basic laughter. On the first day of history, so the Bible tells us, "the morning stars sang together." Every new springtime breaks into the gaiety of flowering meadows and purling streams. "The trees . . . clap their hands"; the little hills skip like lambs. These phrases come, of course, from our minds, but not without beckonings from nature. This laughter of creation may seem to us to be mockery when sorrow strikes, but it accords with our joyous moods. There is even a comic side to nature. A row of penguins looks for all the world like the speakers' table at the annual banquet of the National Association of Manufacturers. The small boy rightly exclaimed on first sight of a camel, "I don't believe it." Children's books, which are quite as important as our philosophies, feature this comic side of animal life. No somber God could ever have made a bullfrog or a giraffe.

This creation-laughter we see in little children. Nietzsche said gloomily: "Man . . . alone suffers so excruciatingly that he was compelled to invent laughter." But man did not invent laughter, or anything else, except from materials given to his hand. Who taught a child to laugh? Who needs to do any such teaching? You say that they imitate the chuckling of their parents? That only presses the question further back, even supposing it to be a valid question. Children laugh as birds sing: because they are made that way. We listen to a child's laughter, listen guiltily, and wish that our laughter were as unspoiled.

Theologians and preachers sometimes discuss the "duty of cheerfulness." It is a contradiction in terms and a horrible phrase in any event. Say, rather, that laughter is native and that our world has times and occasions that provoke it and that if we do not then laugh, we stultify ourselves. The Harvard man who placed an advertisement in *The Crimson* for the sale of a bike, offering as inducement for the bike that it "knows its own way to Wellesley," is a benefactor in our community. The Anglican hymnbook has a hymn that should be in every hymnbook, "Glad that I live am I." The Bible says again with deep wisdom: "There is . . . a time to weep and a time to laugh." We should not choke the laughter because tears sometimes stain our days. The laughter has its own rightful time and place. If people laugh even on the way home from a funeral (as they do, as any wise pastor can tell you), perhaps they should: that release is given in our pent-up sorrow. We believe despite our morbid moods that creation-laughter *is* basic. There remains for us what Browning called "the wild joys of living."

II

There is also the laughter of man's dilemma. We quip by nature at our own predicament. Because the dilemma is a dilemma, because the predicament is always mixed with human guilt, this laughter has elements of derision, and it is never far from tears. Nature has cancer as well as flowering fields, death as well as birth; and human nature has monumental self-idolatries as well as neighborly kindness. Who can doubt this ambiguity in nature? It confronts us wherever we walk and wherever we stay. Who can doubt this ambiguity in human nature? Think of Hitler dancing a jig when France surrendered, and think of the long failure of statesmanship that was left with no better expedient than to fight his fire with fire. In "this ambiguous earth" we can still laugh, but the laughter is now inevitably "mixed." It has undertones of self-condemnation and overtones of irony. In bad men it becomes a bitter trampling sarcasm; in good men, a rueful smile.

We should examine with more care this typical laughter of our adult life, for laughter also has gifts of wisdom. When are we ourselves comic? Whenever we try to live beyond the bounds of our ordained nature. And these bounds? We are in the material order and cannot escape it, even though we are never content with it; at the same time we see ourselves in the natural order, from a stance above our earthborn life, which we still cannot escape. The bounds of our nature are those of a precarious line between time — which does not content us — and eternity — into which we cannot lift ourselves. Whenever we leave that line, we become comic. Henri Bergson argues that man becomes comic when he acts like a thing, that is, when he sinks below the ordained line of creaturehood; Alexander Bain likewise proposes that humor is always the humor of man's "degradation." Both are right, but both perhaps fail to see that man is comic when he tries to live above the line, when he poses as an angel or as his own god, as well as when he seeks a lower order of life.

Consider instances of a man becoming laughable because he is posing as a wiser or holier man than human nature grants — the comedy of his trying vainly to live above the line of precarious creaturehood. Ashes from a man's pipe on an upper balcony are carried by a whimsical wind into the dinner of a man eating on a lower balcony. Says the one: "Why do you knock your ashes on to my terrace?" Says the other: "Why do you place your terrace underneath my pipe?" Neither man has power to control even the minor forces and vicissitudes of life, and both are angry in consequence because they are not gods or angels. Thus our "calculated risks" in statesmanship or in the building of apartment-house balconies are always miscalculated. Our terrifying defenses do not defend, for our adversary tries to outdo us in terror. Thus comedy, and irony, and guilt and tears. To take another instance: a hobo falling on a winter slide that boys are using would not be funny, for we would be sorry for him as victim of new misfortune piled on old misfortune; but if a bishop thus fell while wearing full regalia, or a professor dressed for a graduation ceremony, he would definitely be comic; for nobody can be as good as a bishop is supposed to be, or as wise as a professor sometimes thinks he is. We try to live above the line, and become comic.

Now take an instance of comedy and laughter that comes of life below the line of creaturehood. Two men imitating a horse, the one providing the forequarters and the other the hindquarters, with a horseskin thrown over them to complete the disguise, always bring merriment, especially in an ice show; for the men are acting as less than men by sinking into horse nature (what Bain calls "degradation"), and the pseudo-horse is trying to be more than a horse since horses do not skate. Similarly with the cartoon showing a man in the subway, with a pigeon on each shoulder. "Where are you taking them?" he was asked; and he answered, "Don't ask me: they got on at Fifty-ninth Street." The man was less than a man, for he had become a perch for pigeons; the pigeons were more than pigeons, for they were imitating foolish humans who bedevil themselves with subways. Naturalism merits no rebuttal, for men have always laughed it out of court. A man sinking into the natural order is tragically comic (for example, the red nose of a drunkard: wood is painted red, not noses); and that laughter against naturalism is a stronger retort than any argument.

But mark the tragedy of our thus leaving the line of our ordained nature. We know in these instances that we are neither animals nor angels. So we become self-estranged, and estranged from the true ground of our nature in God. In that self-estrangement we imagine that God is laughing at us: "He that sitteth in the heavens shall laugh: the Lord shall have them in derision." Perhaps God *is* laughing, perhaps he does hold us in derision, if there is that in God which in the deeps of his mystery answers to these human terms. There is "wrath" in God — the indignation of his "love." There is "derision" in God — the protest of his "pity." Always men have dimly sensed that derision. It is in *The Iliad*: "And unextinguishable laughter rose among the gods." Heaven laughs, with tears, at our foolish attempts to be more than men or less than men. That our boasted defenses should now darken over us as a final threat, that our refusal to confront the real problem (our constitutional anxiety and pride) should lead us into a frenetic competition in sputniks, that our science should become instrument of our suicide, that our wealth should by our pursuit of it become taxed poverty, that our victories should reappear as defeat — this is the irony of history: "He that sitteth in the heavens shall laugh." Creation's laughter is sheer joy, but adult laughter in man's dilemma is close to tears and shame. A certain story tells of a doctor's impatience when he could find nothing wrong with his patient: "Why don't you forget yourself? Go see the clown Grumaldi, and laugh." Said the patient: "I am Grumaldi."

III

But there is another kind of laughter, the healing laughter of redemption. It is not a child's laughter, and it is not man's dilemma-laughter. It is the joy of a new birth. Francis knew child's laughter in his earliest years in Assisi; and he knew adult laughter when as an unruly youth in that city he was the "life of the party," not without knowing and giving some real happiness; but the third laughter he did not know until with vows of poverty he gave himself to God before a high altar. Then and there joy was born in him by which he preached to the sparrows and danced in the village square. This laughter is the laughter of childlikeness beyond childishness. Perhaps our life is a pilgrimage from childish laughter through the laughter of our guilty dilemma, to the childlike laughter that comes of God's forgiving and renewing grace. Many a man lives and dies only in the ruefulness of that middle term.

Can we find any parable of this best laughter? The small boy decided to run away from home: "I do not like this nasty house." Always we rebel against the walls of creaturehood. His mother told him that she was sorry for his desire but that she would help him pack. The lad was plucky: he left, scarcely able to lift the luggage. Where to go? When he reached the sidewalk, he sat there on the step between the garden path and the sidewalk. Where *shall* we go, where *can* we go, when we try to leave our humanness? His parents watched from behind window curtains. Soon he returned, saving face cheerfully: "I've been away a long time." They agreed: "Was it a nice journey?" But, oh, the joy of the homecoming for them and for him! "Even so, I tell you, there is joy before the angels of God over one sinner who repents." This is the word of Christ. This is the joy that he revealed to our world. The bells of heaven ring whenever a man turns from his perverted skills and his insensate pride, from his poor attempts to live an animal life, to trust in the Power and the Love — the God who can lift him when he cannot lift himself.

Another parable, since here story is better far than argument? In the sequel to *The Pilgrim's Progress*, Christiana (Pilgrim's wife), her children, and a friend called Mercy follow him to the Celestial

City. Christiana asks Mercy: "What was the matter that you did laugh in your sleep to-night? I suppose you was in a dream." Yes, Mercy had dreamed. She saw herself bemoaning the hardness of her heart, with people about her who were impatient of her complaint: "At this, some laughed at me, some called me fool, and some began to thrust me about" — the earthy answer to those ill-content with merely an earthy life. Then an angel came: "Mercy, what aileth thee?" As if she knew! Only angels know! "Peace be to thee!" Then she saw herself clothed in silver and gold, led by the angel through the skies to a throne, which was not "derision," for he who sat there said gently: "Welcome, daughter." Said Mercy: "So I woke . . . but did I laugh?" She laughed and cried, with tears no longer bitter but rather childlike and at peace. "When the Lord turned again the captivity of Zion, we were like them that dream. Then was our mouth filled with laughter, and our tongue with singing."

IV

Even the laughter of our dilemma is still laughter, as if we knew unawares that the dilemma is always held in light. To the portent of laughter Christian faith gives the Christ-event, the historical drama of uncoercive love. So we may now choose how to laugh. We can laugh because life despite its darkness is good: "Glad that I live am I." That is basic laughter, and sadness may wait its turn. We can laugh too loud: that is dilemma-laughter, its loudness confessing its insecurity. We can laugh ruefully, with realism for man's failures, yet with kindly judgment since we also are "in the same condemnation," well knowing that adult laughter is never far from tears. Are there not two faces over the proscenium arch of the theater, which portray our mortal life — a laughing face and a weeping face?

But if we will, we may laugh in the midst of the storm in "unmixed" laughter. We can "become as little children," in a new childlikeness, beyond childishness and beyond the adulthood that has known too many roads and too many doors. We can laugh even in an atomic age, even in the storm that we have raised by our own unruliness:

> Well roars the storm to those that hear
> A deeper voice across the storm.[1]

"Be of good cheer, I have overcome the world." "Be of good cheer": laugh! Beyond the clinging doubt and beyond the unruly deed — God. Has he not "found" us in Jesus Christ? So *that* door is always open — into laughter.

---

1. Tennyson, *In Memoriam*, sec. cxxvi, st. 1.

HERBERT O. EDWARDS, SR.

Things Are Not Always
What They Seem

Sodom's final evening was lovely. Cool air carried the perfume of flowers, and the starry curtain of night hung over the sleeping world. But things are not always what they seem. The city of this lovely night is doomed. Soon, fountains of fire will burst up from the deep, and Sodom will be gone.

Edwards's language is sensuously rich in its appeal to sight, smell, and sound — an excellence that Edwards paradoxically employs in service of the theological claim that the deepest truth lies beyond the senses.

Things Are Not Always What They Seem

> The sun was risen upon the earth when Lot entered into Zoar. Then the LORD rained upon Sodom and upon Gomorrah brimstone and fire from the LORD out of heaven.
>
> Genesis 19:23-24, KJV;
> see also Genesis 19:1-22

Our text is the story of Sodom and Gomorrah, and of how Lot was saved from their awful destruction (Gen. 19:1-26).

The first scene that arrests our attention is one of quietness and peace. It is evening. A fair city lies upon the border of a plain that looks like a garden in beauty and fertility. Laborers are coming in from the vineyards and fields nearby, and shepherds are settling down with their flocks on the distant hills for another peaceful night. There are no signs of trouble in the air, no indication that the wrath of God might fast be approaching. And yet the last night is casting its long shadows upon the walls of the doomed city. Things are not always what they seem. Appearances can be deceiving.

According to the custom of the land and of the time, the chief men are sitting in the gate. Old and young are abroad in the open air. The idle multitude are coming and going to gather the gossip of the day and enjoy the cool wind that comes up from the lake beyond the walls.

The people of this city have a reputation for going to every excess in indulgence. They have everything that the sensual can desire, and their only study is to find new ways of gratifying their passions.

Two strangers are seen approaching the city. They seem to be only common travelers coming down from the hill country and turning in for shelter for the night, that they may rise up early in the morning to go on their journey refreshed. Only one man paid attention to them. Lot did not know who they were, nor did he suspect the awful errand upon which they had come. But he treated them with courtesy and respect: "Behold now, my lords, turn in, I pray you, into your servant's house, and tarry all night, and wash your feet, and ye shall rise up early, and go on your ways."

The idle throng in the streets deride the hospitable old man for taking the two strangers home to his own house. The masses are much more ready to treat the pair with rudeness and contempt. A crowd gathers outside Lot's house, demanding that he send the strangers out so that they might have some sport with them. The people themselves did not think this unusual; apparently they had done as much many times before. But there is a point beyond which the patience of God cannot go. Lot refused their request, and when the mob clamored outside Lot's door a sudden blindness fell upon them, and they did not realize that they had already passed "the hidden boundary between God's patience and his wrath."

This night seemed no different from any other. No trumpet of wrath has shattered the stillness; no earthquake has shaken the hills; no threatening wave has rolled upon the shore of the peaceful lake; no cloud of vengeance darkens the coming day. But things are not always what they seem.

Nations and individuals tend to believe that they see no evidence of approaching doom, that because God does not seem to be doing any more today than he did on days and weeks gone by they can continue in the old way. So often we fail to see the gathering clouds of disaster until they are overhead ready to rain down trouble.

The history of our country is a case in point. Thomas Jefferson once said, in commenting on the slavery in which he was also heavily involved: "I tremble for my country when I recall that God is just." But neither he nor the country was sufficiently impressed with the justice of God to do anything about slavery. So President Abraham Lincoln was to say some sixty years later: "Fondly do we hope, fervently do we pray, that this mighty scourge of war may speedily pass away. Yet, if God wills that it continue until all the wealth piled by the bondsman's two hundred and fifty years of unrequited toil shall be sunk, and until every drop of blood drawn with the lash shall be paid by another drawn with the sword, as was said three thousand years ago, so still it must be said, The judgments of the Lord are true and righteous altogether."

How often we go on our way ignoring God because he does not seem to be interfering with our activities. "Why sayest thou, O Jacob, and speakest, O Israel, My way is hid from the Lord, and my judgment is passed over from my God? Hast thou not known? hast thou not heard, that the everlasting God, the Lord, the Creator of the ends of the earth, fainteth not, neither is weary? there is no searching of his understanding."

In the winter of 1955, an insignificant and unimportant woman took a seat on a city bus in Montgomery, Alabama. Rosa Parks was not known beyond her immediate circle of family and friends, and her continued insignificance was assured by the color of her skin. When the bus driver asked her to give up her seat to a white man, the bus driver never dreamed that something was about to happen that would change the course of this nation's history. He was only doing what he had done on so many previous occasions. Why should this time be any different? But things are not always what they seem.

What happened in Montgomery, Alabama, on that fateful day in 1955 might well have been God's way of giving this country another chance to redeem itself and purge itself, to repent, to make amends, and to be saved. But few were sensitive enough to receive and understand the message, and subsequent opportunities, too, have been largely ignored.

The messengers to Sodom give Lot the privilege of going out and urging his sons-in-law to flee from the doomed city. He makes his way to their houses through the blinded rabble in the streets and gives the warning. But he seems to them as one that is a madman. They cannot think it possible that he is in his right mind, to be coming to them at that late hour of the night with such an alarming message. They will sleep on till morning, and tomorrow they will laugh at the kindhearted old father about his midnight call.

Dawn begins to break for the doomed city. The morning star shines with its customary brightness over the mountains of Moab. The cool air, mingled with the perfume of flowers, comes up like refreshing incense from the placid sea, and the song of birds welcomes the returning light. There is nothing to fear except that one word of the angels: "The Lord will destroy this city." The beautiful skies speak peace and safety. The sleeping city dreams of long life and continued pleasure. The coming day looks down from the eastern hills with a smile. But the angels have said: "The Lord will destroy this city!" All seems the same as the day before. But the hour of doom has come; desolation befalls a city . . .

And God made this great desolation in his own beautiful and glorious work because the sin of Sodom was great and the cry of its iniquity had come up to heaven. The last night, as serene and beautiful as ever, hung its starry curtain over a sleeping world. And when the golden dawn broke into day the rising sun had not seen in all the gorgeous East a fairer city than Sodom. Then suddenly, in one moment, her last cry went up to heaven amid tempests of fire that rained down from above and fountains of fire that burst up from the deep, and Sodom was gone. Sodom — its name had become a symbol of infamy for all generations, and now its awful doom stands forth as a perpetual sign that God's patience with sin has a point beyond which it will not go.

Every nation, every group, every individual is ever listening to two words; one is from man and the other is from God. One says: "Tarry, be at ease, enjoy yourself while you can." The other says: "Escape for your life." The one says: "Wait, be not alarmed." The other says: "Make haste, look not behind thee, flee to the mountain lest thou be consumed." One says: "Soul, take thine ease, eat, drink, and be merry." The other says: "Thou fool, this night thy soul may be required of thee." Things are not always what they seem.

There is another side of the coin. There is a tendency to lose faith in God and to despair of hope for change when it seems that all the power is on the side of wrong and injustice, when it seems that all is lost.

Peter and the apostles had left their occupations, given up their normal pursuits, and placed their faith and hope in the teachings and promises of Jesus of Nazareth. He had told them many times that he had to leave them, that the Son of man must suffer many things. But they would not hear of it. Now on this fateful evening, with his disciples gathered around the table, Jesus' words fall like a trip-hammer on their spirits, crushing their dreams, challenging again their commitment to him: "One of you is going to betray me!"

The act is done. The guards have taken him away, the court is convened, the decision rendered. The sentence is pronounced: "Crucify him!" Now all is surely lost. The disciples scatter, propelled by their fear, overwhelmed by their grief, distraught in their disappointment: "We had thought that he was the one to redeem Israel!"

All appears to be over: the broken body is buried. The tomb is securely sealed. The guards are posted. And faith and hope are buried with the corpse. But God, who always reserves the last word unto himself, immobilizes the guards, breaks the seal, removes the stone, relativizes the finality of death, and raises Jesus from the dead.

Things are not always what they seem. . . .

JOHN VANNORSDALL

The Elder Son's Defense

Vannorsdall's sermon is full of wonderful touches of irony, humane sympathy, and biblical wisdom. But, of course, what immediately gets our attention is the sermon's novel point of view.

First-person character sketches are risky business. The preacher who attempts one needs a big technique, good judgment, and, as always, thorough knowledge of the text so that the sermon trajectory follows biblical tracers.

Vannorsdall disappoints on none of these scores. Readers who let him lead them into the sermon's parable may find that, while elder brothers cannot dance very well, they can sin and repent and crave the grace of God as well as any prodigal.

The Elder Son's Defense

"Now his elder son was in the field; and as he came and drew near to the house, he heard music and dancing. And he called one of the servants and asked what this meant. And he said to him, 'Your brother has come, and your father has killed the fatted calf, because he has received him safe and sound.' But he was angry and refused to go in. His father came out and entreated him, but he answered his father, 'Lo, these many years I have served you, and I never disobeyed your command; yet you never gave me a kid, that I might make merry with my friends. But when this son of yours came, who has devoured your living with harlots, you killed for him the fatted calf!' And he said to him, 'Son, you are always with me, and all that is mine is yours. It was fitting to make merry and be glad, for this your brother was dead, and is alive; he was lost, and is found.'"

Luke 15:25-32

To All Concerned for Justice:
Greetings!

Year after year preachers great and small, in a hundred languages, lead you from the bathos of my younger brother's self-imposed exile to the sounds of dancing and leave you staring at me, disgusted because I will not share the celebration for the prodigal's return. It's time that you heard my side of the story, what it's like to be an elder brother and why I reacted as I did.

I should, I suppose, enlist the aid of a panel of experts. My brother has, after all, turned his case over to the worthy clergy who have so embroidered their bias in his favor that I can never hope to balance the facts by myself. It occurs to me, however, that many of the people of the world are themselves elder brothers, and, I hasten to add, elder sisters, and that our common status will facilitate a larger understanding. So I make my own defense in the hope that a simple, honest statement is all that's needed.

I cannot deny that one unlovely moment in my life to which the clergy point. I had come from the fields at evening, as has been reported, and when I heard the sound of dancing and smelled the roasting meat I was surprised and asked a servant what was happening. I cannot deny the jealousy and hurt that rose within me when I learned that it was a party for my wayward brother. I make no defense for my behavior. I cannot even say that I would behave differently should history repeat itself. But I want you to understand that I will regret it for the rest of my life. I hate the feeling in myself. I know that jealousy is the worst of me.

Without in any way defending my reaction, I do want to say what it's like to be an elder brother. I think you'll understand, and I need that understanding.

Let me say first of all that being an elder brother has something to do with being responsible. I'm not referring to chronological age, but about an elder brother syndrome that can occur in the life of anyone. And the most significant element in the elder brother syndrome is a sense of responsibility.

I was responsible for a large farm. We had servants, of course, lots of them, but there is a difference between being a servant and being an owner. Servants take orders, but owners are the ones who take responsibility. We are the ones who must decide when the fields are ready to plow and plant. We select the seed. Owners decide how many sheep the land can support. We decide when to shear the sheep. And since there will inevitably be bad years when the crops fail and the sheep die, it is our responsibility to see that enough food and money has been set aside so that the farm can continue and the servants be fed.

Do you think that I had no moments — even days, weeks, months — when I wanted to leave? That I have no hunger for wine, women, and song? Do you think l was born a drudge? No, I was born an elder brother, son of aging parents who looked to me to share the responsibility of being an owner. From the day I was born I was reared to be accountable, as though my parents, the servants, and all the generations to follow were dependent upon me. I was reared to be responsible. I say this with only a touch of pride, certainly not with regret. I say it only in the hope that you will understand me.

There are those who come to a party, and there are those who work to prepare for that party, who see to it that the house is clean, that there is enough wine, that the fire is well built, and that the musicians are ready. There are those who go home from the party singing their happy songs, and there are those of us who clean up after them, who sweep the cracker crumbs and bits of smoked fish from the floor and wipe the white circles left by the mugs on the polished wood. There are those who come as guests and go home carefree, and there are those who prepare for the party and clean up when the revelry is over. I am one of the latter, you see. Usually, I am not unhappy about this, nor offensively proud of it either. It's one of the roles in the human family, and I play it well. I am marked with the elder brother syndrome.

Let me say also that elder brothers are harder to love. I wonder sometimes why it is that people find it so easy to love people like my younger brother. (Notice that now I call him my brother. It was only in that awful moment of jealousy when the worst of me came out that I called him my father's younger son.) His offenses were so clear. He had wasted money that had come from generations of work on the farm. He had lived with harlots. He came home with nothing. Why is it so easy to accept the wayward? Perhaps they are so vulnerable that it's easy to accept them. They are so obviously in trouble that they pose no threat. Perhaps it's easiest to love people who are no threat — the fools, those who write their sinning large.

I have been pictured as self-righteous, the hardest of all to love. I know that. But look into your own hearts, you elder brothers and sisters, those of you who, like me, are responsible. You know that we are sinners, too. I work with the servants in the field, and as the sun grows unbearably hot, my anger rises and I find myself beating the ground so hard with the hoe that the handle breaks. The other day the goat kicked over the pail of milk again and, in anger, I kicked the goat. You laugh, perhaps, but it is of the nature of elder brothers and sisters to carry their anger, their sins, hidden within their hearts. What did you expect? Should I go home and say to my father, "Father, I have sinned against heaven and against you. Today I was angry and broke another hoe, and yesterday I kicked a goat?"

No, elder brothers and sisters are the responsible kind, and our sins are not obvious — nor easily shared. Therefore, we are harder to love.

I want also to acknowledge that being responsible has its rewards. I do understand that my father was right when he said, "You are always with me, and all that is mine is yours." I know that, I really do. My satisfaction, the reward for my being responsible, is to look out over a field sprouting green and to take in the beauty of it and, in the harvest, to gather in the sheaves, exulting in the weight of the sacks of grain filled from the threshing floor. My reward is that of a job well done, of a household running smoothly with people fed and with provision against the times of famine, and the taxes paid. My satisfaction is in the respect of those around me, in being able to give to those in need. I am a gold watch person. We elder brothers and sisters, we are the ninety and nine who take care of ourselves, the ones whom the shepherd can leave to look for the lost.

As you can tell, I write these words easily. I know what our rewards are, coming quietly every day of our lives. But it is so hard to see that no-good son of my father. . . . Excuse me. It is so hard to see my younger brother come home empty-handed and receive the ring, the robe, and the shoes, to smell the roasting meat and hear the music for his dancing. Ah, the anger is not all gone, is it? I understand it with my mind, and I know how to say it with words, that elder brothers are responsible and sinners like everyone else, the harder to love, whose rewards come quietly day by day. Gold watch people. I understand it. It's harder to make my emotions behave.

Well, that's my side of the story. But I leave you with a question. How shall we be saved, we elder brothers and sisters? How can we go home when we are already home? How can we confess the squandering of resources, the harlots, the months and years of neglect, when in fact we have built and not squandered, not gone with harlots, and been responsible for preserving the family fortunes? How shall we be helped: those of us with our secret anger and the harlotry that stays in our hearts; those of us who are hard to love because we show so little need, who show only on rare occasions the jealousy that made me turn away from the dancing to become forever the ill-reputed elder brother? How shall we be saved?

I'll tell you what I think, and you may have some insight too. It would probably help if we shared with others some of the responsibilities that make our lives such a burden. Do we have to be owners in the sense that we make all of the decisions? Wouldn't it make for a less lonely and isolated life if we invited our servants to be partners in the productive process? Teachers and students could become collaborators in the process of gaining and sharing knowledge. Managers and those they now manage could become partners in a common enterprise. Children could share more of the responsibilities for creating a family, and by that I mean that children could help to make decisions and not simply respond to shouted orders. Do we not, by the very way in which we structure our relationships, create the burdens under which we chafe and grow angry? To become less owner-like, to enter into partnerships and to be collaborators — that could be a part of our salvation.

I suppose that this could be said in a less pompous way. (It has probably not escaped your attention that self-importance is one of the more obvious manifestations of the elder brother syndrome.) You'll remember that, among other things, I said to my father, "You never gave me a kid, that I might make merry with my friends." The truth of the matter is that I never asked my father if I could have a party. I wonder about that. Somehow it didn't seem appropriate. There was always so much to do, not just with my hands — that's the easy part — but so much thinking to be done, so many problems to be solved. Thinking and problem solving don't mix with parties. Actually, I think I was concerned about the appearance of things. Would the servants and the neighbors look up to a person, depend upon a person who throws a party, drinks wine, and dances? A cocktail before dinner is one thing, but a party?

To be perfectly honest, I don't have many friends. I'm respected, you understand. When I go to the bank, the teller calls me sir and my check is never refused. I like that. But there is a difference between respect and friendship. So you see, by assuming authority and by refusing to share it, I have set myself apart. I have fit myself into a total model of human interaction in which I have isolated myself and must behave according to the model. I never asked my father for a kid so that I might make merry with my friends. Servants and prodigals dance. I have a drink before dinner. Servants and prodigals have friends. I have respect. Isn't there some other model for elder brothers? That's my question, and a larger sharing of responsibility could well be a part of the answer.

Another part of our salvation could be a fuller recognition of the gifts that come to us day by day as a consequence of our being responsible. If we could see more often the greening fields that we have planted and know our partnership with God; if we could see our growing children fed and clothed and rejoice in our partnership with them and with God; if we could rejoice to feed the hungry, to set some tangled person free — then we would probably find in these things a quiet joy, which is both our reward and a replacement for our anger. This would be a part of our salvation. My father said it well, "Son, you are always with me, and all that is mine is yours." And will our heavenly Father deny us this healing sense of partnership with him if we ask that he renew a right spirit within us?

The other part of our salvation must be the same as that experienced by our younger brothers and sisters, the prodigals. Our sins are not flamboyant; in many ways they are a little boring, but no less damaging. In fact, our hidden anger may be more damaging than their more flagrant sins, at least to those around us. In some ways it would be easier to repent of what is obvious, the extravagant sins of the far country, than to speak the pain of our jealousy and self-righteousness, the hidden anger and dark fantasies that come as we pursue our more ordered lives.

God knows these hidden sins, of course. Erect, we stand as solid citizens before the cross, but our hearts are bowed; he embraces us with his eyes, and not just those who are bent with weeping. There may be no turning spit and no music for dancing. We elder brothers are not the best of dancers anyway. But we go down the hill from Golgotha knowing that he died for us, too. We go down to our green valley to see the field of sprouting seed, knowing that all that he has is ours, and we are his.

> O God, creator of the elder brothers and sisters
>   of the world,
>   have mercy on us.
> O God, redeemer of those unmasked by a moment
>   of jealousy,
>   have mercy on us.
> O God, sustainer of those who receive gold watches,
>   grant us your peace.

WALTER J. BURGHARDT, S.J.

Do We Deserve Peace?

Like other good sermons, "Do We Deserve Peace?" was preached to a particular audience on a particular occasion. The audience for this sermon was God, with worshipers at St. Patrick's Cathedral, New York, invited to listen in. The occasion was a special Mass for Peace, November 13, 1969, at the height of the war in Vietnam.

A sermon in the form of a prayer may strike us as ambitious and theatrical. In addition, the form raises an old problem familiar to every congregation that has had to sit through a prayer littered with news items that missed the deadline for the weekly church bulletin. How can the preacher inform his or her real audience, the worshiping congregation, without slipping into an annoying "You know, O Lord" form of redundancy?

Walter Burghardt knows the problems that come with a prayed sermon, and he finds deft ways of handling them. Indeed, he carefully preserves the integrity of his offering, both as a sermon and as a prayer. In so doing, he follows excellent precedent: the Scriptures are full of homilies in the form of prayers, most notably in the Psalms.

Walter J. Burghardt, "Do We Deserve Peace?" reprinted from *Tell the Next Generation* by Walter J. Burghardt, S.J., pp. 20-25. © 1980 by Walter J. Burghardt, S.J. Used by permission of Paulist Press.

Do We Deserve Peace?

When [Jesus] drew near and saw the city, he wept over it, saying, "Would that even today you knew the things that make for peace! But now they are hid from your eyes."

Luke 19:41-42

I

Lord, we come before you a motley lot. We are wonderfully and dreadfully different. Some of us are violent in our convictions; others could not hurt a fly. Some of us have years behind us; the lives of others lie ahead. Some of us are knowledgeable, others quite ignorant. Some of us are happy people; others have forgotten how to laugh. Some of us have money; others must pinch and squeeze, beg and borrow. Most of us are white; only a few, I'm afraid, are black or yellow or brown. Some of us are settled, have it made; others are restless, trying to make it. Some of us have killed; others have seen death only on TV.

Some of us are awfully sure — about the war, about its morality or immorality, about ROTC and Dow Chemical, about American idealism or imperialism, about napalm and defoliation; others are confused, uncertain, torn this way and that, even anxious about our own uncertainty. Some of us think your church is "out of it," a slave to the status quo, hidebound and a straddler; others feel she has gone too far too fast, runs after the latest fashion, is even heretical. Some of us have tasks that excite us; others go through motions from nine to five. Some of us have stored up hate in our hearts; others thrill with love. Some of us are neat and clean; others could not care less for middle-class hygiene. Some of us have come to terms with society; others have fled it or vowed to destroy it. Most of us are here because we still believe in you; some surely have come from curiosity, or custom, or even despair. A few of us may even be "effete snobs."[1]

Lord, we *are* a motley lot, aren't we?

II

Only one thing unites us at this moment, Lord: we all want peace. We are *all* convinced that war is hell. We *all* feel that there is something tragically wrong when the governments of the world spend 120 billion dollars a year to kill, to threaten, to deter, to keep peace. When a B-52 sets fire to fifty square miles so that nothing therein can live. When homes of the innocent are converted into incinerators. When the ratio of civilian-to-military casualties is three or five to one. When three million refugees water the roads and rice paddies with their tears. When human beings are tortured by other "human" beings.

We *all* weep for it, Lord — even those of us who feel that it cannot be otherwise, that it is not Christian, is not human, but must be. Even those who are soldiers or sailors or marines — who are trained to kill and to destroy — even they are nauseated at what they must do.

We all want life, Lord, and not death. We know the love and the anguish and the pain and the joy that goes into fashioning a single child. Many of us have shared with you the creation of life. We sense how precious each life is to you. And so we weep for each life that is snuffed out. We cannot rejoice when a headline proclaims that *only* two hundred Americans were killed this week; we cannot be glad when five thousand Viet Cong are flushed out and massacred. For these are not statistics, Lord; these are persons. And when even one shrieks to heaven with his flesh in flames — friend or enemy — we all weep, we are all ashamed, we all want peace.

---

1. A caustic characterization of some adversaries by a high-ranking official in the Nixon administration around that time.

III

We all want peace, Lord. The problem is, we are not agreed on how to get peace; we do not know "the things that make for peace." Oh yes, we have our convictions. There are those of us who "know" that the first step to peace is for us to get out, leave Southeast Asia. There are those who "know" that only all-out war will bring peace. And there are those silent millions somewhere in between who don't want us to stay and don't see how we can go. And there are *all* of us who sense that, even if Southeast Asia is pacified, there is still the Middle East, there is Czechoslovakia, there are Libya and Bolivia, there is the whole vast continent of Africa.

We do not know, save superficially, "the things that make for peace." For some reason — perhaps for our sin — "they are hid from [our] eyes." If, as your prophet proclaimed, "peace is the fruit of righteousness" (Isa. 32:17), and if, as your Council taught, "peace is likewise the fruit of love,"[2] then war is the fruit of unrighteousness, of hate. But I dare not lay that unrighteousness, that hate, solely at the feet of the enemy, only in the heart of the politician — in Hanoi or Washington or Saigon. If I am as honest as I want my neighbor to be, I must look within, to see if the seeds of war are planted in my heart.

IV

And as we look, Lord, we must be distressed. Our love for human beings, we were told by your Son, our love would be the sacrament, the visible sign, that he is among us. This is how the world would recognize him. And the world does not see him, because the world does not see him in our love. Whole cities could live on the garbage from our dumps, on the clothes we wear once, on the luxuries we have made necessities. Black and white are threatened with bloody combat because we have been as color-conscious as our unbelieving neighbors. For so many of us, a court of law is more effective than

2. Vatican II, Constitution on the Church in the Modern World, no. 78.

the Sermon on the Mount. There is no evidence that we Catholics drink less, lust less, hate less than the men and women who never eat the flesh of your Christ or drink his blood. I am afraid we are what Paul called the pagans of his time: we are "faithless, ruthless, pitiless" (Rom. 1:31).

For all its own tyranny, what does Hanoi find in America, in us, to shake it, to make it marvel and cry, "Look how they love"? The seeds of war are within us, from the jealousy of Cain to the hate in my own heart, from the commerce that makes a jungle of the world to the ghettos we have structured for the Jew and the black, from the dishonesty of the little clerk to the tyranny of the big cleric.

A horrifying thought has just struck me, Lord: perhaps we do not deserve peace. Perhaps war is the logical fruit of our unrighteousness, of our personal hate, of our lack of love. It may be that what is happening in Southeast Asia began in our hearts, in my heart, not too long ago. No wonder your Son weeps over *our* city, saying: "Would that even today you knew the things that make for peace! But now they are hid from your eyes."

V

When we first came to you this evening, Lord, I think we came for a miracle, for your special intervention in the world, for a breakthrough that would change the heart of Hanoi, inspire our president, make the lamb and the lion lie down in Paris. I rather think now it is a different miracle we are asking. Just as you do not make wars, Lord, so neither do you end them. We make them, Lord, and so we have to end them. With your grace, of course; but unless *we* do it, it will not be done.

The miracle we ask, each of us, is a conversion. Change *us,* Lord. If we are unshakable on Vietnam, keep us from being unloving. If we are uncertain, let it not make us cowards. Take bitterness from us, even if we have cause to be bitter. Take hate from us, for we have never just cause for hatred. If we have bled, let the blood we shed be redemptive like your Son's. If we have grown fat — by our own honest industry or over the bodies of others — scourge us till we cry out. Each of us knows what it is within us that makes for war. Prick all our hearts with a sense of guilt; for we have sinned, Lord, all of us — we have sinned against peace.

VI

We are a motley lot, Lord; but do not let difference destroy love. Two days ago, in our Woodstock College community, two young guests threw from our dining room a large bowl of fruit, because it included some grapes, and the grapes might be from California. A young friend, also a guest, was asked by a Jesuit in the community if *he* had done this. He replied: "In the sense that the hands that did this were the hands of my brother, yes, I did it." He was pressed: "But aren't we your brothers too?" His answer, slow and serious: "I'm afraid I must say no."

Dear Lord, if this is the way we are, I weep, for we do not deserve peace. If we can love (as indeed we should) a hostile soldier on the other side of the Pacific, call him brother, can we not open our hearts to the human being next to us, despite our deep divisions?

That is why, Lord, in much hope and some fear, I am asking the men and women in front of me to take a first step toward peace. I am asking each to clasp the hand of the person next to him or her, the person on each side — whoever that person is, whatever he or she looks like — without even looking. I want them, by this act of faith and trust and love, to cry out to you that we do want peace, that we want to begin it here and now, that we see in each human being a brother or sister and the image of your Christ, that our hearts are open to them as never before, that we are ashamed and weep for our crimes against them. And I am asking them to sit like that, hands clasped, for one minute — all of us . . . for one minute . . . at peace.

DAVID G. BUTTRICK

Up Against the Powers
That Be

David Buttrick is not only an accomplished preacher but also a leading theorist of preaching. In Buttrick's view, ideal sermon structure resembles theories of the physics of light: it comprises both particles and waves. Sermon "particles" are the major divisions of the sermon (what older homiletics called "points"); sermon "waves" develop when the particles work together to create movement and progression.

"Up Against the Powers That Be" nicely serves as a lab demonstration of Buttrick's theory. To see the "particles," note how a major division of the sermon begins with a strong topic sentence that names the theme of that division, and how, after developing its theme, the division ends crisply with a sentence similar to the one with which it began. (See, for example, the division that begins, "Well, if you're going to live for God in the twentieth century, you're in for a fight.")

Placed in linear sequence, the particles form waves of motion, each surge carrying sermon and listeners alike toward their destination.

"Up Against the Powers That Be" is a call to do battle with culture in the name of faith. When the sermon begins, we are only vaguely aware that a fight is brewing. When it ends, we are at the front lines, dressed and ready for combat.

Up Against the Powers That Be

Finally, be strong in the Lord and in the strength of his might. Put on the whole armor of God, that you may be able to stand against the wiles of the devil. For we are not contending against flesh and blood, but against the principalities, against the powers, against the world rulers of this present darkness, against the spiritual hosts of wickedness in the heavenly places. Therefore take the whole armor of God, that you may be able to withstand in the evil day, and having done all, to stand. Stand therefore, having girded your loins with truth, and having put on the breastplate of righteousness, and having shod your feet with the equipment of the gospel of peace; besides all these, taking the shield of faith, with which you can quench all the flaming darts of the evil one. And take the helmet of salvation, and the sword of the Spirit, which is the word of God. Pray at all times in the Spirit, with all prayer and supplication. To that end keep alert with all perseverance, making supplication for all the saints, and also for me, that utterance may be given me in opening my mouth boldly to proclaim the mystery of the gospel.

Ephesians 6:10-19

Some years ago, one of the Protestant denominations was putting together a hymnbook. A committee had to decide which hymns to keep and which to discard. Well, the committee got into an awful fight over "Onward Christian Soldiers." Some said the hymn was loved and had to be included, while others claimed it was militaristic and ought to be dumped. If we have trouble with our hymns, what on earth are we going to do with the Bible? The Bible is filled with warfare. Almost every book of the Old Testament tells of battles, and the New Testament is not much better. Listen: "Put on the whole armor of God," cries Ephesians, and then goes on to talk of shield and buckler, helmet and sword. Why is it that whenever we want to describe the Christian life, we end up using military metaphors? "Put on," says Ephesians, "Put on the whole armor of God!"

I

Well, if you're going to live for God in the twentieth century, you're in for a fight. Living for God these days is nothing less than combat. Oh, we're not involved in a little arm wrestling; no, our warfare is something straight out of Starship *Galactica*. The forces we're up against are huge: "We wrestle not against blood and flesh, but principalities and powers and world rulers." Think of it, a handful of believers up against General Motors, the Pentagon, an American eagle, a Russian bear, and in the words of a famous senator, "the best congress money can buy!" Do you remember the story of John Steinbeck's sharecropper? He wanted to know who had foreclosed his farm. It wasn't the local banker because he was responsible to a home office; and it wasn't the home office because they had a board of directors; and it wasn't the board of directors because after all there were thousands of stockholders. Conclusion: nobody was guilty, because everybody was guilty. The system was guilty. "We wrestle not against flesh and blood, but principalities and powers and rulers of the world." Fact is, if you want to keep faith in the twentieth century, you're in for a fight.

Of course, the actual enemy is unseen. The actual enemy is invisible, and bigger than we know. For the real enemy is in our minds, in the common mind of our age. We've all been brainwashed, haven't we? We can't seem to think without a twist in our thinking. Suppose you want to urge folk to live lives of simple poverty in a needy world; can they hear you? Not a chance. They've seen too many pictures of Volvos and stereos, of stainless steel kitchens and firelit family rooms. Or suppose you want to stand up for "peace on earth" in a nuclear age, how can you cut through the slogans? "Keep America strong." "Never bargain from weakness." "Winning isn't everything; it's the only thing!" The real enemy is ideas, ideas that invade our minds and subtly take over. There was a wonderful cartoon in *The New Yorker.* It showed a plump housewife talking to her four-star-general husband: "Tell me again, dear," she asked, "how big an army will we need to live at peace with the whole world?" We laugh, but not loudly, for we know that mind-set writes our defense budgets and, incidentally, elects presidents. "Principalities and powers": the real enemy is unseen and bigger than we know. Listen, if you want to live for God in the twentieth century, you're in for a fight.

II

Now it's time to be honest. Our cause, the Christian cause, is absolutely hopeless. We are too few and the enemy too great. So almost anyone who dares wait for kingdom come in our kind of world is bound to be filled with exotic despair; the situation is hopeless. We Christians are outnumbered and, almost always, out-maneuvered. Did you see the poster that showed up in some churches a few years ago? It showed a tiny little clapboard church surrounded: an X-rated drive-in theater, a munitions factory across the street, and miles of concrete freeway crammed with cars. Two church members stand on the front steps, one saying to the other: "Do you ever get the feeling that we're losing ground?" Well, it's more than a feeling, isn't it? Here we Christians are, less than forty-five percent of the nation, less than ten percent of the world, dropping pennies in a mission basket, up against The System! You don't have to be Jimmy the Greek to figure the odds. A Bible study circle up against the corporate wealth of Wall Street; a sweet sermon on sacrifice versus a million-dollar advertising campaign bought and paid for by the Mobil Oil Company. "Do you ever get the feeling that we're losing ground?" Good heavens, by all odds, we haven't got a chance! Be honest; our Christian cause *is* absolutely hopeless.

Except. Except that it happens to be God's cause. "Shalom," peace, is God's cause; reconciliation is God's cause; justice is God's cause. Contrary to public opinion, God is not on the side of the bigger battalions; God is on the side of the poor, of pennies in a mission basket; God on the side of those who long with longing lives for freedom. And in the Bible, God's cause triumphs! Remember old Isaiah's vision: the swords will be beaten into plowshares, and the lion will bed down with the lamb. Perhaps someday in God's good purpose the eagle will waltz with the bear, and fat-cat Americans share holy bread with skeletal kids of Biafra. It shall be! For who can withstand the will of our God? Not armies that once clanked around the cross on Calvary, nor public opinion that cried, "Crucify him!" nor frightened religion that, to protect its hold on human minds, branded Jesus Christ a heretic. But if Christ was raised by the power of God, will not peace and justice be raised? It's guaranteed by the promise of God. This conversation was overheard in a supermarket: a woman, pointing to a book rack, said, "I couldn't finish the book; it was too depressing." The reply was: "Gee, you should always turn to the end of the story." What's the end of God's story? A world where everyone lolls at peace in their own vineyard, a fine, free world where folk can party together — "The song of them that triumph, the shout of them that feast." God's world doesn't end with a whimper, but with choiring angels and the Lamb upon the throne. God's cause will be!

III

Well, meanwhile back here on the battlefield, how do we fight? How can we take on the "powers that be"? We are given one weapon, only one. "Take up the sword," says Ephesians, "which is the word of God." Think of it, we are to go up against the powers that be with nothing more than a word. Doesn't sound like much, does it, in a world where words are tarnished? After all, advertisements use words, and party platforms use words, and it was an American president who labeled the MX missile system "the peacekeeper." There's a euphemism for you! What good is a word when words are so easily twisted around? No good at all, unless it is the impudent, guileless Word of our God! Do you know the wonderful story that came out of the Czech underground after the

Russian takeover? To tout their victory, the Communist Party scheduled a great parade — lumbering tanks, trucked-in missiles, battalions of lockstepped soldiers. Suddenly, in the midst of the parade, there was a little blue pickup truck weaving in and out, disrupting the parade, with a six-foot sign on it reading, "For God's sake, why?" Perhaps that's a clue. God's word in all its impudent glory must be spoken to the powers that be, asking, Why? Why? to a bulging defense budget when there are street people huddled in doorways. Why? to our high standard of living when most of the world has a mighty high standard of dying. Why? to the stainless steel kitchen and the firelit family room. Why? The impudent Word of God questions our world and can pierce its heart. Think of it, our only weapon, the sword of the Spirit, which is the Word of God.

Time for confession: we have been silent. The pulpit has been tame and the pew timid. We Christians have been speechless. Perhaps the Catholic Church is still trying to prove it's an all-American option, while the Protestants are trying to hold onto the cash. Perhaps. So in our century, a Catholic cardinal blessed a battleship, while a Protestant evangelist crisscrossed Alabama six times during the height of the civil rights controversy and never once mentioned the subject of race — there's discreet Christianity for you! Fact is, nowadays, the church is running flat-out scared, trying to hold onto public approval in a crumbling age. Think of a Christian community whose bravest utterance during the past few years has been a bumper sticker, reading, "I found it!" Look, is there anything worse than the strange strangulated sense of "I should have spoken"? To live on, knowing that we missed the moment when we should have spoken. So, can we confess? We have been silent, a "silent majority" church. We should have spoken.

Now, guess what: maybe it is time to speak to our churches. Maybe it is time for *us* to speak with our churches, to stab away the slumbering Christian conscience of the land with the sharp Word of God. Oh, there's no room for self-righteousness: we speak as people who should have spoken to a people who should have listened. But maybe now's the time to speak out, like Amos standing in front of the suburban church in Bethel, or Jeremiah bumbling up the Temple steps in Jerusalem to meet churchgoers face to face. A few years ago a multimillion-dollar church was built in an eastern city, "New England Colonial" of course. The day of dedication had been set, but not all the furnishings had arrived. The chancel was empty: no pulpit or table, no tapestry for the back wall. When worshipers gathered for the dedication, they found that someone had snuck into the building at night and, with a wide brush, had painted in big black letters on the bare wall, "Stop the killing, Feed the poor, Sincerely yours, Jesus Christ." Well, do you sense our strange calling in a blasé world, in a world that will go along with anything for a tank full of gas and an I.R.A.? Somehow we are called to speak, to shake awake God's people with the strong word of Christ. Now, now it is time for us to speak to the churches.

Here we are, 1987. Do you ever get the feeling we're losing ground? Not against blood and flesh, but against principalities and powers and the rulers of our age. Listen, all you need tucked in your arsenal is a word. "The Prince of Darkness grim, we'll tremble not for him, one little word will slay him." Dear friends, the word is Jesus Christ. There is no other word worth speaking. The word is Jesus Christ.

FREDERICK BUECHNER

A Sprig of Hope

Like other Buechner sermons, "A Sprig of Hope" uses an array of masterfully drawn images to move us through a biblical narrative (in this case, "as dark a tale as there is in the Bible"). The sermon is impressionistic, but not wispy. The images — Noah's vacant face, flickering with bewilderment; his dusty feet, dragging a little as they turn toward the lumberyard; the ark, staggering like a drunk; the heart of the dove, thrumming in her breast; and, above all, the face of one who weeps like a clown or a fool over the world's darkness and light — these images come together to form a portrait of hope as vital and painful as a successful birth.

The paragraph in which Buechner describes the return of the dove has become famous in contemporary homiletic literature.

Frederick Buechner, "A Sprig of Hope," from *The Hungering Dark* by Frederick Buechner, pp. 34-44. Copyright © 1969 by The Seabury Press, Inc. Reprinted by permission of HarperCollins, Publishers, Inc.

A Sprig of Hope

Now the earth was corrupt in God's sight, and the earth was filled with violence. And God saw the earth, and behold, it was corrupt; for all flesh had corrupted their way upon the earth. And God said to Noah, "I have determined to make an end of all flesh; for the earth is filled with violence through them. . . . Make yourself an ark of gopher wood; make rooms in the ark, and cover it inside and out with pitch. . . . For behold, I will bring a flood of waters upon the earth, to destroy all flesh in which is the breath of life. . . . And of every living thing of all flesh, you shall bring two of every sort into the ark, to keep them alive with you; they shall be male and female. . . . For in seven days I will send rain upon the earth forty days and forty nights; and every living thing that I have made I will blot out from the face of the ground." And Noah did all that the LORD had commanded him. . . .

In the six hundredth year of Noah's life, in the second month, on the seventeenth day of the month, on that day all the fountains of the great deep burst forth, and the windows of the heavens were opened. . . .

The flood continued forty days upon the earth; and the waters increased, and bore up the ark, and it rose high above the earth. The waters prevailed and increased greatly upon the earth; and the ark floated on the face of the waters. And the waters prevailed so mightily upon the earth that all the high mountains under the whole heaven were covered . . . fifteen cubits deep. . . . Only Noah was left, and those that were with him in the ark. . . .

At the end of forty days Noah opened the window of the ark which he had made. . . . Then he sent forth a dove from him, to see if the waters had subsided from the face of the ground; but the dove found no place to

set her foot, and she returned to him to the ark, for the
waters were still on the face of the whole earth. So he
put forth his hand . . . and brought her into the ark with
him. He waited another seven days, and again he sent
forth the dove out of the ark; and the dove came back
to him in the evening, and lo, in her mouth a freshly
plucked olive leaf.

Genesis 6:11–8:11, passim

It is an ironic fact that this ancient legend about Noah survives in
our age mainly as a children's story. When I was a child, I had a
Noah's ark made of wood with a roof that came off so you could
take the animals out and put them in again, and my children have
one too; yet if you stop to look at it at all, this is really as dark a
tale as there is in the Bible, which is full of dark tales. It is a tale
of God's terrible despair over the human race and his decision to
visit them with a great flood that would destroy them all except
for this one old man, Noah, and his family. Only now we give it
to children to read. One wonders why.

Not, I suspect, because children particularly want to read it,
but more because their elders particularly do not want to read it
or at least do not want to read it for what it actually says and so
make it instead into a fairy tale, which no one has to take seriously
— just the way we make black jokes about disease and death so
that we can laugh instead of weep at them; just the way we translate
murder and lust into sixth-rate television melodramas, which is to
reduce them to a size that anybody can cope with; just the way we
take the nightmares of our age, the sinister, brutal forces that dwell
in the human heart threatening always to overwhelm us, and present
them as the Addams family or the monster dolls that we give, again,
to children. *Gulliver's Travels* is too bitter about man, so we make
it into an animated cartoon; *Moby Dick* is too bitter about God, so
we make it into an adventure story for boys; Noah's ark is too
something-or-other else, so it becomes a toy with a roof that comes
off so you can take the little animals out. This is one way of dealing

with the harsher realities of our existence, and since the alternative is, by facing them head-on, to risk adding more to our burden of anxiety than we are able to bear, it may not be such a bad way at that. But for all our stratagems, the legends, the myths, persist among us, and even in the guise of fairy tales for the young they continue to embody truths or intuitions that in the long run it is perhaps more dangerous to evade than to confront.

So, what then are the truths embodied in this tale of Noah and his ark? Let us start with the story itself; more particularly, let us start with the moment when God first spoke to Noah; more particularly, let us start with Noah's face at that moment when God first spoke to him.

When somebody speaks to you, you turn your face to look in the direction that the voice comes from; but if the voice comes from no direction at all, or the voice comes from within and comes wordlessly, and more powerfully for being wordless, then in a sense you stop looking at anything at all. Your eyes become unseeing, and if someone were to pass his hand in front of them, you would hardly notice the hand. If you can be said to be looking at anything then, you are probably looking at, without really seeing, something of no importance whatever, like the branch of a tree stirring in the wind or the frayed cuff of your shirt where your arm rests on the windowsill. Your face goes vacant because for the moment you have vacated it and are living somewhere beneath your face, wherever it is that the voice comes from. So it was maybe with Noah's face when he heard the words that he heard, or when he heard what he heard translated clumsily into words: that the earth was corrupt in God's sight, filled with violence and pain and unlove — that the earth was doomed.

It was presumably nothing that Noah had not known already, nothing that any man who has ever lived on this earth with his eyes open has not known. But because it came upon him, sudden and strong, he had to face it more squarely than people usually do, and it rose up in him like a pain in his own belly. And then maybe, like Kierkegaard's Abraham, Noah asked whether it was God who was speaking or only the pain in his belly; whether it was a vision of the glory of the world as it first emerged from the hand of the

Creator that led him to the knowledge of how far the world had fallen, or whether it was just his pathetic human longing for a glory that had never been and would never be. If that was his question, perhaps a flicker of bewilderment passed across his vacant face — the lines between his eyes deepening, his mouth going loose, a little stupid. A penny for your thoughts, old Noah.

But then came the crux of the thing, because the voice that was either God's voice or an undigested matzoh ball shifted from the indicative of doom to the imperative of command, and it told him that although the world was doomed, he, Noah, had a commission to perform that would have much to do with the saving of the world. "Make yourself an ark of gopher wood," the voice said, "and behold, I will bring a flood of waters upon the earth to destroy all flesh in which is the breath of life." So Noah had to decide, and the decision was not just a theological one — yes, it is God; no, it is not; and you live your life the same way in either case — because if the voice proceeded not from the mystery of the human belly but from the mystery and depth of life itself, then Noah had to obey, and Noah knew it; and out of common humanity, this is the point to shift our gaze from his face, because things are happening there that no stranger should be allowed to see, and to look instead at his feet, because when a man has to decide which way he is going to bet his entire life, it is very often the feet that finally tell the tale.

There are Noah's feet — dusty, a little slew-footed, Chaplinesque, stock still. You watch them. Even the birds in the trees watch. Which direction will the feet move, or will they move at all? It comes down to that with every man finally. And finally they do move. Maybe with no spring in the step, maybe dragging a little, but they move nevertheless. And they move in the direction of . . . the lumber yard . . . as he bets his life on his voice.

There are so many things to say about Noah, whoever he was, if ever he was, the old landlubber with the watery, watery eyes; but the one thing that is certain is that he must have looked like an awful fool for a while, for all those days it took him to knock together the great and ponderous craft. Three hundred cubits long and fifty cubits wide and thirty cubits high, all three decks of it covered inside and out with pitch, and he had nothing more plausible in the way of an explanation than that he was building it — and building it many a mile from the nearest port — because a voice had told him to, which was maybe God's voice or maybe hardening of the arteries. Only a fool would heed such a voice at all when every other voice for miles around could tell him, and probably did, that the proper business of a man is to keep busy: to work, to play, to make love, to watch out for his own interests as all men watch out for theirs, and to leave the whole shadowy business of God to those who have a taste for shadows. So Noah building his ark becomes the bearded joke draped in a sheet who walks down Broadway with his sandwich board inscribed REPENT; and Noah's face becomes the great white moonface of the clown looking up with anguish at the ones who act out their dance of death on the high-wire. A penny for your thoughts, old Noah, as you pound together your zany craft while the world goes about its business as usual and there is not a cloud in the sky.

His thoughts, one imagines, were of water, and as the windows of heaven were opened and all the fountains of the great deep burst forth so that the sea crept in over the earth, and where there had been dry land and order all was disorder and violence, perhaps Noah knew that it had always been so. Perhaps Noah knew that all the order and busy-ness of men had been at best an illusion and that, left to himself, man had always been doomed. The waters came scudding in over forest and field, sliding in across kitchen floors and down cellar stairs, rising high above television aerials and the steeples of churches, and death was everywhere as death is always everywhere, men trapped alone as they are always trapped, always alone, in office or locker room, bedroom or bar, men grasping out for something solid and sure to keep themselves from drowning, brother fighting brother for the few remaining pieces of dry ground. Maybe the chaos was no greater than it has ever been. Only wetter.

The ark rose free from its moorings, cumbersome old tub creaking and pitching in the wilderness of waves, with the two of everything down below and a clown for a captain who did not know his port from his starboard. But it stayed afloat, by God, this

Toonerville trolley of vessels, clouted from side to side by the waves and staggering like a drunk. It was not much, God knows, but it was enough, and it stayed afloat, and granted that it was noisy as Hell and stank to Heaven, creatures took comfort from each other's creatureliness, and the wolf lay down with the lamb, and the lion ate straw like the ox, and life lived on in the ark while all around there was only chaos and death.

Then finally, after many days, Noah sent forth a dove from the ark to see if the waters had subsided from the earth, and that evening she returned, and lo, in her mouth a freshly plucked olive leaf. Once again, for the last time, the place to look, I think, is Noah's face. The dove stands there with her delicate, scarlet feet on the calluses of his upturned palm. His cheek just touches her breast so that he can feel the tiny panic of her heart. His eyes are closed, the lashes watery wet. Only what he weeps with now, the old clown, is no longer anguish but wild and irrepressible hope. That is not the end of the story in Genesis, but maybe that is the end of it for most of us — just a little sprig of hope held up against the end of the world.

All these old tales are about us, of course, and I suppose that is why we can never altogether forget them; that is why, even if we do not read them anymore ourselves, we give them to children to read so that they will never be entirely lost, because if they were, part of the truth about us would be lost too. The truth, for instance, that, left to ourselves, as a race we are doomed — what else can we conclude? — doomed if only by our own insatiable lust for doom. Despair and destruction and death are the ancient enemies, and yet we are always so helplessly drawn to them that it is as if we are more than half in love with our enemies. Even our noblest impulses and purest dreams get all tangled up with them, just as in Vietnam, in the name of human dignity and freedom, the bombs are falling on both the just and the unjust, and we recoil at the horror of little children with their faces burned off, except that somehow that is the way the world has always been and is, with nightmare and noble dream all tangled up together. That is the way we are doomed — doomed to be what we are, doomed to seek our own doom. And the turbulent waters of chaos and nightmare

are always threatening to burst forth and flood the earth. We hardly need the tale of Noah to tell us that. *The New York Times* tells us just as well, and our own hearts tell us well, too, because chaos and nightmare have their little days there also. But the tale of Noah tells other truths as well.

It tells about the ark, for one, which somehow managed to ride out the storm. God knows the ark is not much — if anybody knows it is not much, God knows — and the old joke seems true that if it were not for the storm without, you could never stand the stench within. But the ark was enough, is enough. Because the ark is wherever human beings come together as human beings in such a way that the differences between them stop being barriers — the way, if people meet at the wedding, say, of someone they both love, all the differences of age between them, all the real and imagined differences of color, of wealth, of education no longer divide them but become for each a source of strength and delight, and although they may go right on looking at each other as very odd fish indeed, it becomes an oddness to gladden the heart, and there is no shyness anymore, no awkwardness or fear of each other. Sometimes even in a church we can look into each other's faces and see that, beneath the differences, we are all of us outward bound on a voyage for parts unknown.

The ark is wherever people come together because this is a stormy world where nothing stays put for long among the crazy waves and where at the end of every voyage there is a burial at sea. The ark is where, just because it is such a world, we really need each other and know very well that we do. The ark is wherever human beings come together because in their heart of hearts all of them — white and black, Russian and American, hippie and square — dream the same dream, which is a dream of peace, peace between the nations, between the races, between the brothers, and thus ultimately a dream of love. Love, not as an excuse for the mushy and innocuous, but love as a summons to battle against all that is unlovely and unloving in the world. The ark, in other words, is where we have each other and where we have hope.

Noah looked like a fool in his faith, but he saved the world from drowning, and we must not forget the one whom Noah foreshadows and who also looked like a fool spread-eagled up there, cross-eyed with pain, but who also saved the world from drowning. We must not forget him because he saves the world still, and wherever the ark is, wherever we meet and touch in something like love, it is because he also is there, brother and father of us all. So into his gracious and puzzling hands we must commend ourselves through all the days of our voyaging wherever it takes us, and at the end of all our voyages. We must build our arks with love and ride out the storm with courage and know that the little sprig of green in the dove's mouth betokens a reality beyond the storm more precious than the likes of us can imagine.

THE OCCASIONS
OF THE SERMON

Philosophers who write about "performative utterances" sometimes conduct thought experiments designed to show that certain words need a particular setting in order to do their job. Suppose, for example, that you travel to New York harbor, walk out onto pier 17, and try to christen a ship. You might say, "I dub thee Queen Kathleen." You might dub away all day, smashing one bottle of champagne after another, and never get the job done. The reason, of course, is that for the words to take, for the utterance "I dub thee" to have performative power, you need authorization and an official context. You need a particular occasion. It is the same with the words "I do." You want to be sure of your context.

The word of God is occasional: it is a word to particular people gathered at a particular time and place, usually under disciplined auspices. The setting matters. For example, the old question of Ecclesiastes, "Is there anything of which it is said, 'See, this is new?'" strikes us one way on the Sunday we hear the golden calf story and quite another way on Christmas Eve.

This final section presents a number of occasional sermons, sermons that take much of their force from their setting. These are sermons for Christmas, and Good Friday, and Easter; for the height of controversy and the depth of grief; sermons for the celebration of holy baptism and of holy communion — sermons, in other words, whose preachers have learned to tell time.

EDMUND A. STEIMLE

The Eye of the Storm

Edmund Steimle had a keen sense of the theological meaning of ordinary experience. A chance conversation in a tailor's shop, the nostalgic revival of a sentimental Broadway musical, somebody's fuss over lamb and rice for a homey meal, a breakaway touchdown in a college football game on a golden autumn afternoon, the hum of a lathe in a basement workshop, a police officer's delivery of a baby in a tenement stairwell — these are the kinds of knobbly, particular events that stand up from the surface of a Steimle sermon and give it texture.

"The Eye of the Storm" is a Christmas triptych. The first panel vividly depicts the preacher's experience of a hurricane, focusing on the strangeness of the calm at its eye. The second panel turns this experience into a metaphor of the deceptive peace at Bethlehem on one silent, holy night. In the final panel, Steimle plots our own Christmas Eves on the weather map, finding them where his title tells us to look.

E. A. Steimle, "The Eye of the Storm," reprinted from *Preaching the Story* by E. A. Steimle, M. J. Niedanthal, and C. L. Rice, pp. 121-25. Copyright © 1980 by Fortress Press. Used by permission of Augsburg Press.

237

The Eye of the Storm

In those days a decree went out from Caesar Augustus that all the world should be enrolled. This was the first enrollment, when Quirinius was governor of Syria. And all went to be enrolled, each to his own city. And Joseph also went up from Galilee, from the city of Nazareth, to Judea, to the city of David, which is called Bethlehem, because he was of the house and lineage of David, to be enrolled with Mary, his betrothed, who was with child. And while they were there, the time came for her to be delivered. And she gave birth to her first-born son and wrapped him in swaddling cloths, and laid him in a manger, because there was no place for them at the inn.

And in that region there were shepherds out in the field, keeping watch over their flock by night. And an angel of the Lord appeared to them, and the glory of the Lord shone around them, and they were filled with fear. And the angel said to them, "Be not afraid; for behold, I bring you good news of a great joy which will come to all the people; for to you is born this day in the city of David a Savior, who is Christ the Lord. And this will be a sign for you: you will find a babe wrapped in swaddling cloths and lying in a manger." And suddenly there was with the angel a multitude of the heavenly host praising God and saying,

> "Glory to God in the highest,
> and on earth peace among men with whom
> he is pleased!"

When the angels went away from them into heaven, the shepherds said to one another, "Let us go over to Bethlehem and see this thing that has happened, which the Lord has made known to us." And they went with haste, and found Mary and Joseph, and the babe lying in a manger. And when they saw it they made known the saying which had been told them concerning this child; and all who heard it wondered at what the shepherds told them. But Mary kept all these things, pondering them in her heart. And the shepherds returned, glorifying and praising God for all they had heard and seen, as it had been told them.

Luke 2:1-20

I think I shall never forget the time when hurricane Hazel, back in the fifties, was sweeping through eastern Pennsylvania and hit Philadelphia, where we were living at the time, head-on. Unlike most hurricanes, which lose much of their force when they turn inland, this one hit with all the fury of a hurricane at sea: drenching rains, screaming winds, trees uprooted, branches flying through the air, broken power lines crackling on the pavements. It was frightening. Then suddenly there was a letup, a lull. Shortly all was still. Not a leaf quivered. The sun even broke through briefly. It was the eye of the storm. "All was calm, all was bright." And then all hell broke loose again: branches and trees crashing down, the screaming winds, the torrential rain, the power lines throwing out sparks on the pavement. But that was a breathless moment — when we experienced the eye of the storm.

Christmas Eve is something like that, like the experience of the eye of the storm. At least the first Christmas night. So Luke reports: "And she gave birth to her first-born son and wrapped him in swaddling cloths, and laid him in a manger, because there was no place for them in the inn." The Christmas crèche and the Christmas pageantry picture it so today: "All was calm, all was bright."

Mary . . . resting now, after the pain of the contractions and the delivery without benefit of anesthetic.

The child . . . sleeping peacefully in the swaddling cloths and the straw. At least we like to think him so. "Silent night, holy night." Of course, maybe his face was all contorted reds and purples with the frantic bleating of a newborn child, fists clenched, striking out at this new and strange environment after nine months in the warmth and security of the womb. But no. Let's picture him sleeping, exhausted perhaps from his frantic protests. "All is calm, all is bright. . . . Silent night, holy night." The eye of the storm.

For make no mistake, he comes at the center of a storm — both before and after the birth. The storm before: From devastation of a flood expressing the anger of God with a people whose every thought and imagination was evil, to his anger at the golden calf, to the destruction of Jerusalem and the Exile in Babylon, to Jonah desperately trying to run away from this God, to the narrow legalism of the Pharisees, to the oppression of the Roman occupation. He comes at the eye of the storm before.

And what followed this "silent night, holy night"? The storm after: The massacre of the innocent male children two years old and under by Herod in his frantic effort to deal with the threat of this child sleeping in the manger. And as he grew up, his family thought him a little bit nuts, his hometown neighbors threw him out of the synagogue when first he tried to preach. Then the sinister plots to do away with him, the angry mob crying for his blood on that first Good Friday, and the end? Death to the child.

What we tend to forget on Christmas is that these lovely stories of the birth — the manger, the shepherds, the angel chorus in the night sky, the wise men following the star and presenting their rare and expensive gifts — are not children's stories. If you think it takes children to make a Christmas, then you don't belong in church tonight. These are adult stories for adult Christians. Oh, let the children delight in them, of course — and get out of them what they may. But they were written down by adult members of the early Christian community for other adult members of the Christian community.

Moreover, they are postresurrection stories — that is, they grew up in the tradition after the resurrection. Who knows where they came from? They came into being in the years following the resurrection as Negro spirituals came into being, as mature Christians pondered the mystery of the beginnings of this life whom they had seen die and rise again from the dead. They knew about the storm that preceded the birth. And they knew even more —

firsthand — about the storm that followed. They were not carried away by "the romantic fantasies of infancy." Like one standing in the eye of a hurricane, they were aware of the storm that went before and that followed.

And so tonight you and I come here, not wanting, I hope, to block out or forget the storms around us. Because if we do, we miss the whole point. We, too, are aware tonight of the storms that surround this "silent night, holy night."

We are aware of the confusion and destruction around us in the world. The violence in the Middle East, southern Africa, and Northern Ireland, the hunger in the Third World. Or closer to home, the muggings on the streets, the unemployment (a grim and passive kind of violence), the ghettos, the injustice to the blacks, the inner cities gutted by poverty and inflation amid the massive indifference — sloth is the old-fashioned word for it — on the part of so many of us who do not live in the gutted inner cities. Moreover, we are aware of the precarious future that haunts all of us. People are dying this Christmas night as people die on every night. As one day, one night, you will die and I will die. And before that the inner loneliness which no one of us can entirely shake, and the specter of hopelessness which haunts us — for peace in the world, for the end of inflation, for families breaking up, for our nations as they drift along often so aimlessly, and for ourselves and our future.

The point is, we don't forget all this on Christmas Eve — or block it out. Like a person standing in the eye of a hurricane, we are aware of it all. If you want to forget it all tonight — OK! Go home and listen to Bing Crosby dreaming of a white Christmas. And there's a place for that — but not here!

For what other message on Christmas Eve is worth listening to? What peace? What hope? If it is simply a forgetting — when we can't forget, really — then we're reducing the Christmas story to a bit of nostalgia and indulging ourselves in the sentimental orgy that Christmas has become for so many, or we are reduced to the deep depression that grips so many others on Christmas Eve.

No. The Bible — praise God — tells it like it is. They saw the birth of the child as the eye of the storm — a peace that passes all understanding because it is not a peace apart from conflict, pain, suffering, violence, and confusion; that's the kind of peace we can understand all too well. But it's a peace like the peace in the eye of a hurricane, a peace smack in the middle of it all, a peace that indeed passes all understanding.

So in this hour, this night, worshiping at the manger of the child when "all is calm, all is bright," we rejoice in the hope born of the conviction that the storm, the destruction, the violence, the hopelessness, does not have the last word. But God — who gives us this "silent night" in the middle of the storm — he has the last word.

So rejoice . . . and sing the carols . . . and listen to the ancient story and light the candles . . . and be glad — with your families, your friends, with the God who is above all and through all and in you all, who comes to us miraculously in this child, this night when "all is calm, all is bright."

HARRY EMERSON FOSDICK

Shall the Fundamentalists Win?

The following sermon, preached in New York City's First Presbyterian Church in May 1922 and subsequently published in *Christian Century*, remains one of the most important documents in what is usually called the fundamentalist controversy among American Protestants in the 1920s. From then on, readers of the sermon have taken theological sides with or against Fosdick's "evangelical liberalism," but even some of Fosdick's opponents admitted that he fought fair. Sometimes he fought lovely: of belief in the virgin birth, for example, Fosdick says, "many are the gracious and beautiful souls who hold it."

At the core of "Shall the Fundamentalists Win?" is a gentlemanly plea to fundamentalists — and to young liberals. Get acquainted with Gamaliel, says Fosdick, and learn "magnanimity and liberality and tolerance of spirit."

The plea and the rest of the sermon are put in stout and enduring pulpit prose.

Harry Emerson Fosdick, "Shall the Fundamentalists Win?" in *The Riverside Preachers,* edited by Paul H. Sherry (New York: Pilgrim Press, 1978), pp. 27-38. Reprinted with permission of the Pilgrim Press, Cleveland, Ohio.

Shall the Fundamentalists Win?

This morning we are to think of the fundamentalist controversy that threatens to divide the American churches, as though already they were not sufficiently split and riven. A scene, suggestive for our thought, is depicted in the fifth chapter of the book of the Acts, where the Jewish leaders hale before them Peter and other of the apostles because they have been preaching Jesus as the Messiah. Moreover, the Jewish leaders propose to slay them, when in opposition Gamaliel speaks: "Refrain from these men, and let them alone: for if this counsel or this work be of men, it will come to nought: but if it be of God, ye cannot overthrow it; lest haply ye be found even to fight against God."

One could easily let his imagination play over this scene and could wonder how history would have come out if Gamaliel's wise tolerance could have controlled the situation. For though the Jewish leaders seemed superficially to concur in Gamaliel's judgment, they nevertheless kept up their bitter antagonism and shut the Christians from the synagogue. We know now that they were mistaken. Christianity, starting within Judaism, was not an innovation to be dreaded; it was the finest flowering out that Judaism ever had. When the Master looked back across his heritage and said, "I am not come to destroy, but to fulfill," he perfectly described the situation. The Christian ideas of God, the Christian principles of life, the Christian hopes for the future, were all rooted in the Old Testament and grew up out of it, and the Master himself, who called the Jewish temple his Father's house, rejoiced in the glorious heritage of his people's prophets. Only he did believe in a living God. He did not think that God was dead, having finished his words and works with Malachi. Jesus had not simply a historic, but a contemporary God, speaking now, working now, leading his people now from partial into fuller truth. Jesus believed in the progressiveness of revelation, and these Jewish leaders did not understand that. Was this new gospel a real development that they might welcome, or was it an enemy to be cast out? And they called it an enemy and excluded it. One does wonder what might have happened had Gamaliel's wise tolerance been in control.

We, however, face today a situation too similar and too urgent and too much in need of Gamaliel's attitude to spend any time making guesses at supposititious history. Already all of us must have heard about the people who call themselves the fundamentalists. Their apparent intention is to drive out of the evangelical churches men and women of liberal opinions. I speak of them the more freely because there are no two denominations more affected by them than the Baptist and the Presbyterian. We should not identify the fundamentalists with the conservatives. All fundamentalists are conservatives, but not all conservatives are fundamentalists. The best conservatives can often give lessons to the liberals in true liberality of spirit, but the fundamentalist program is essentially illiberal and intolerant. The fundamentalists see, and they see truly, that in this last generation there have been strange new movements in Christian thought. A great mass of new knowledge has come into man's possession: new knowledge about the physical universe, its origin, its forces, its laws; new knowledge about human history and in particular about the ways in which the ancient peoples used to think in matters of religion and the methods by which they phrased and explained their spiritual experiences; and new knowledge, also, about other religions and the strangely similar ways in which men's faiths and religious practices have developed everywhere. Now, there are multitudes of reverent Christians who have been unable to keep this new knowledge in one compartment of their minds and the Christian faith in another. They have been sure that all truth comes from the one God and is his revelation. Not, therefore, from irreverence or caprice or destructive zeal, but for the sake of intellectual and spiritual integrity, that they might really love the Lord their God not only with all their heart and soul and strength, but with all their mind, they have been trying to see this new knowledge in terms of the Christian faith and to see the Christian faith in terms of this new knowledge. Doubtless they have made many mistakes. Doubtless there have been among them reckless radicals gifted with intellectual ingenuity but lacking spiritual depth. Yet the enterprise itself seems to them indispensable to the Christian church. The new knowledge and the old faith cannot be left antagonistic or even disparate, as though a man on Saturday could use one set of regulative ideas for his life and on Sunday could change gear to another altogether. We must be able to think our modern life clear through in Christian terms, and to do that we also must be able to think our Christian life clear through in modern terms.

There is nothing new about the situation. It has happened again and again in history, as, for example, when the stationary earth suddenly began to move, and the universe that had been centered in this planet was centered in the sun around which the planets whirled. Whenever such a situation has arisen, there has been only one way out: the new knowledge and the old faith had to be blended in a new combination. Now the people in this generation who are trying to do this are the liberals, and the fundamentalists are out on a campaign to shut against them the doors of the Christian fellowship. Shall they be allowed to succeed?

It is interesting to note where the fundamentalists are driving in their stakes to mark out the deadline of doctrine around the church, across which no one is to pass except on terms of agreement. They insist that we must all believe in the historicity of certain special miracles, preeminently the virgin birth of our Lord; that we must believe in a special theory of inspiration — that the original documents of the scripture, which of course we no longer possess, were inerrantly dictated to men a good deal as a man might dictate to a stenographer; that we must believe in a special theory of the atonement — that the blood of our Lord, shed in a substitutionary death, placates an alienated Deity and makes possible welcome for the returning sinner; and that we must believe in the second coming of our Lord upon the clouds of heaven to set up a millennium here, as the only way in which God can bring history to a worthy denouement. Such are some of the stakes that are being driven, to mark a deadline of doctrine around the church.

If a man is a genuine liberal, his primary protest is not against holding these opinions, although he may well protest against their being considered the fundamentals of Christianity. This is a free country, and anybody has a right to hold these opinions, or any others, if he is sincerely convinced of them. The question is: has anybody a right to deny the Christian name to those who differ with him on such points and to shut against them the doors of the Christian fellowship? The fundamentalists say that this must be done. In this country and on the foreign field they are trying to do it. They have actually endeavored to put on the statute books of a whole state binding laws against teaching modern biology. If they had their way, within the church, they would set up in Protestantism a doctrinal tribunal more rigid than the pope's. In such an hour, delicate and dangerous, when feelings are bound to run high, I plead this morning the cause of magnanimity and liberality and tolerance of spirit. I would, if I could reach their ears, say to the fundamentalists about the liberals what Gamaliel said to the Jews, "Refrain from these men, and let them alone: for if this counsel or this work be of men, it will come to nought: but if it be of God ye cannot overthrow it; lest haply ye be found even to fight against God."

That we may be entirely candid and concrete and may not lose ourselves in any fog of generalities, let us this morning take two or three of these fundamentalist items and see with reference to them what the situation is in the Christian churches. Too often we preachers have failed to talk frankly enough about the differences of opinion that exist among evangelical Christians, although everybody knows that they are there. Let us face this morning some of the differences of opinion with which somehow we must deal.

We may well begin with the vexed and mooted question of the virgin birth of our Lord. I know people in the Christian churches — ministers, missionaries, laymen, devoted lovers of the Lord and servants of the gospel — who, alike as they are in their personal devotion to the Master, hold quite different points of view about a matter like the virgin birth. Here, for example, is one point of view: that the virgin birth is to be accepted as historical fact; it actually happened; there was no other way for a personality like the Master to come into this world except by a special biological miracle. That is one point of view, and many are the gracious and beautiful souls who hold it. But side by side with them in the evangelical churches is a group of equally loyal and reverent people who would say that the virgin birth is not to be accepted as a historic fact. To believe in virgin birth as an explanation of great personality is one of the familiar ways in which the ancient world was accustomed to account for unusual superiority. Many people suppose that only once in history do we run across a record of supernatural birth. Upon the contrary, stories of miraculous generation are among the commonest traditions of antiquity. Especially is this true about the founders of great religions. According to the records of their faiths, Buddha and Zoroaster and Lao-Tzu and Mahavira were all supernaturally born. Moses, Confucius, and Mohammed are the only great founders of religions in history to whom miraculous birth is not attributed. That is to say, when a personality arose so high that men adored him, the ancient world attributed his superiority to some special divine influence in his generation, and they commonly phrased their faith in terms of miraculous birth. So Pythagoras was called virgin born, and Plato, and Augustus Caesar, and many more. Knowing this, there are within the evangelical churches large groups of people whose opinion about our Lord's coming would run as follows: those first disciples adored Jesus — as we do; when they thought about his coming they were sure that he came specially from God — as we are; this adoration and conviction they associated with God's special influence and intention in his birth — as we do; but they phrased it in terms of a biological miracle that our modern minds cannot use. So far from thinking that they have given up anything vital in the New Testament's attitude toward Jesus, these Christians remember that the two men who contributed most to the church's thought of the divine meaning of the Christ were Paul and John, who never even distantly allude to the virgin birth.

Here in the Christian churches are these two groups of people, and the question that the fundamentalists raise is this: shall one of them throw the other out? Has intolerance any contribution to make to this situation? Will it persuade anybody of anything? Is not the Christian church large enough to hold within her hospitable fellowship people who differ on points like this, and agree to differ until the fuller truth be manifested? The fundamentalists say not. They say that the liberals must go. Well, if the fundamentalists should succeed, then out of the Christian church would go some of the best Christian life and consecration of this generation — multitudes of men and women, devout and reverent Christians, who need the church and whom the church needs.

Consider another matter on which there is a sincere difference of opinion among evangelical Christians: the inspiration of the Bible. One point of view is that the original documents of the scripture were inerrantly dictated by God to men. Whether we deal with the story of creation or the list of the dukes of Edom or the narratives of Solomon's reign or the Sermon on the Mount or the thirteenth chapter of First Corinthians, they all came in the same way and they all came as no other book ever came. They were inerrantly dictated; everything there — scientific opinions, medical theories, historical judgments, as well as spiritual insight — is infallible. That is one idea of the Bible's inspiration. But side by side with those who hold it, lovers of the Book as much as they, are multitudes of people who never think about the Bible so. Indeed, that static and mechanical theory of inspiration seems to them a positive peril to the spiritual life. The Koran similarly has been regarded by Mohammedans as having been infallibly written in heaven before it came to earth. But the Koran enshrines the theological and ethical ideas of Arabia at the time when it was written. God an Oriental monarch, fatalistic submission to his will as man's chief duty, the use of force on unbelievers, polygamy, slavery — they are all in the Koran. When it was written, the Koran was ahead of the day, but, petrified by an artificial idea of inspiration, it has become a millstone about the neck of Mohammedanism. When one turns from the Koran to the Bible, he finds this interesting situation. All of these ideas, which we dislike in the Koran, are somewhere in the Bible. Conceptions from which we now send missionaries to convert Mohammedans are to be found in the Bible. There one can find God thought of as an Oriental monarch; there too are patriarchal polygamy, and slave systems, and the use of force on unbelievers. Only in the Bible these elements are not final; they are always being superseded; revelation is progressive. The thought of God moves out from Oriental kingship to compassionate fatherhood; treatment of unbelievers moves out from the use of force to the appeals of love; polygamy gives way to monogamy; slavery, never explicitly condemned before the New Testament closes, is nevertheless being undermined by ideas that in the end, like dynamite, will blast its foundations to pieces. Repeatedly one runs on verses like this: "It was said to them of old time . . . but I say unto you"; "God, having of old time spoken unto the fathers in the prophets by divers portions and in divers manners, hath at the end of these days spoken unto us in his Son"; "The times of ignorance therefore God overlooked; but now he commandeth men that they should all everywhere repent"; and over the doorway of the New Testament into the Christian world stand the words of Jesus: "When he, the Spirit of truth, is come, he will guide you into all truth." That is to say, finality in the Koran is behind; finality in the Bible is ahead. We have not reached it. We cannot yet compass all of it. God is leading us out toward it. There are multitudes of Christians, then, who think, and rejoice as they think, of the Bible as the record of the progressive unfolding of the character of God to his people from early primitive days until the great unveiling in Christ; to them the Book is more inspired and more inspiring than ever it was before. To go back to a mechanical and static theory of inspiration would mean to them the loss of some of the most vital elements in their spiritual experience and in their appreciation of the Book.

Here in the Christian church today are these two groups, and the question the fundamentalists have raised is this: shall one of them drive the other out? Do we think the cause of Jesus Christ will be furthered by that? If he should walk through the ranks of this congregation this morning, can we imagine him claiming as his own those who hold one idea of inspiration, and sending from him into outer darkness those who hold another? You cannot fit the Lord Christ into that fundamentalist mold. The church would better judge his judgment. For in the Middle West the fundamentalists have had their way in some communities, and a Christian minister tells us the consequence. He says that the educated people are looking for their religion outside the churches.

Consider another matter upon which there is a serious and sincere difference of opinion between evangelical Christians: the second coming of our Lord. The second coming was the early Christian phrasing of hope. No one in the ancient world had ever thought, as we do, of development, progress, gradual change, as God's way of working out his will in human life and institutions. They thought of human history as a series of ages succeeding one another with abrupt suddenness. The Greco-Roman world gave the names of metals to the ages — gold, silver, bronze, iron. The Hebrews had their ages too — the original Paradise in which man began, the cursed world in which man now lives, the blessed Messianic Kingdom someday suddenly to appear on the clouds of heaven. It was the Hebrew way of expressing hope for the victory of God and righteousness. When the Christians came they took over that phrasing of expectancy, and the New Testament is aglow with it. The preaching of the apostles thrills with the glad announcement, "Christ is coming!"

In the evangelical churches today there are differing views of this matter. One view is that Christ is literally coming, externally on the clouds of heaven, to set up his kingdom here. I never heard that teaching in my youth at all. It has always had a new resurrection when desperate circumstances came and man's only hope seemed to lie in divine intervention. It is not strange, then, that during these chaotic, catastrophic years there has been a fresh rebirth of this old phrasing of expectancy. "Christ is coming!" seems to many Christians the central message of the gospel. In the strength of it some of them are doing great service for the world. But, unhappily, many so overemphasize it that they outdo anything the ancient Hebrews or the ancient Christians ever did. They sit still and do nothing and expect the world to grow worse and worse until he comes.

Side by side with these to whom the second coming is a literal expectation, another group exists in the evangelical churches. They, too, say, "Christ is coming!" They say it with all their hearts; but they are not thinking of an external arrival on the clouds. They have assimilated as part of the divine revelation the exhilarating insight that these recent generations have given to us, that development is God's way of working out his will. They see that the most desirable elements in human life have come through the method of development. Man's music has developed from the rhythmic noise of beaten sticks until we have in melody and harmony possibilities once undreamed. Man's painting has developed from the crude outlines of the cavemen until in line and color we have achieved unforeseen results and possess latent beauties yet unfolded. Man's architecture has developed from the crude huts of primitive men until our cathedrals and business buildings reveal alike an incalculable advance and an unimaginable future. Development does seem to be the way in which God works. And these Christians, when they say that Christ is coming, mean that, slowly it may be, but surely, his will and principles will be worked out by God's grace in human life and institutions, until "he shall see of the travail of his soul, and shall be satisfied."

These two groups exist in the Christian churches, and the question raised by the fundamentalists is: shall one of them drive the other out? Will that get us anywhere? Multitudes of young men and women at this season of the year are graduating from our schools of learning, thousands of them Christians who may make us older ones ashamed by the sincerity of their devotion to God's will on earth. They are not thinking in ancient terms that leave ideas of progress out. They cannot think in those terms. There could be no greater tragedy than that the fundamentalists should shut the door of the Christian fellowship against such.

I do not believe for one moment that the fundamentalists are going to succeed. Nobody's intolerance can contribute anything to the solution of the situation we have described. If, then, the fundamentalists have no solution of the problem, where may we expect to find it? In two concluding comments let us consider our reply to that inquiry.

The first element that is necessary is a spirit of tolerance and Christian liberty. When will the world learn that intolerance solves no problems? This is not a lesson that the fundamentalists alone need to learn; the liberals also need to learn it. Speaking, as I do, from the viewpoint of liberal opinions, let me say that if some young, fresh mind here this morning is holding new ideas, has fought his way through, it may be by intellectual and spiritual struggle, to novel positions, and is tempted to be intolerant about old opinions, offensively to condescend to those who hold them and to be harsh in judgment on them, he may well remember that people who held those old opinions have given the world some of the noblest character and the most rememberable service that it ever has been blessed with, and that we of the younger generation will prove our case best, not by controversial intolerance, but by producing, with our new opinions, something of the depth and strength, nobility and beauty of character that in other times were associated with other thoughts. It was a wise liberal, the most adventurous man of his day — Paul the apostle — who said, "'Knowledge' puffs up. but love builds up."

Nevertheless, it is true that just now the fundamentalists are giving us one of the worst exhibitions of bitter intolerance that the churches of this country have ever seen. As one watches them and listens to them, he remembers the remark of General Armstrong of Hampton Institute: "Cantankerousness is worse than heterodoxy." There are many opinions in the field of modern controversy concerning which I am not sure whether they are right or wrong, but there is one thing I am sure of: courtesy and kindliness and tolerance and humility and fairness are right. Opinions may be mistaken; love never is.

As I plead thus for an intellectually hospitable, tolerant, liberty-loving church, I am of course thinking primarily about this new generation. We have boys and girls growing up in our homes and schools, and because we love them we may well wonder about the church that will be waiting to receive them. Now the worst kind of church that can possibly be offered to the allegiance of the new generation is an intolerant church. Ministers often bewail the fact that young people turn from religion to science for the regulative ideas of their lives. But this is easily explicable. Science treats a young man's mind as though it were really important. A scientist says to a young man: "Here is the universe challenging our investigation. Here are the truths we have seen, so far. Come, study with us! See what we already have seen and then look further to see more, for science is an intellectual adventure for the truth." Can you imagine any man who is worthwhile turning from that call to the church if the church seems to him to say, "Come, and we will feed you opinions from a spoon. No thinking is allowed here except such as brings you to certain specified, predetermined conclusions. These prescribed opinions we will give you in advance of your thinking; now think, but only so as to reach these results." My friends, nothing in all the world is so much worth thinking of as God, Christ, the Bible, sin and salvation, the divine purposes for humankind, life everlasting. But you cannot challenge the dedicated thinking of this generation to these sublime themes upon any such terms as are laid down by an intolerant church.

The second element that is needed, if we are to reach a happy solution of this problem, is a clear insight into the main issues of modern Christianity and a sense of penitent shame that the Christian church should be quarreling over little matters when the world is dying of great needs. If, during the war, when the nations were wrestling upon the very brink of hell and at times all seemed lost, you chanced to hear two men in an altercation about some minor matter of sectarian denominationalism, could you restrain your indignation? You said, "What can you do with folks like this who, in the face of colossal issues, play with the tiddledywinks and peccadillos of religion?" So now, when from the terrific questions of this generation one is called away by the noise of this fundamentalist controversy, he thinks it almost unforgivable that men should tithe mint and anise and cumin, and quarrel over them, when the world is perishing for the lack of the weightier matters of the law, justice, and mercy, and faith. These last weeks, in the minister's confessional, I have heard stories from the depths of human lives where men and women were wrestling with the elemental problems of misery and sin — stories that put upon a man's heart a burden of vicarious sorrow, even though he does but listen to them. Here was real human need crying out after the living God revealed in Christ. Consider all the multitudes of men who so need God, and then think of Christian churches making of themselves a cockpit of controversy when there is not a single thing at stake in the controversy on which depends the salvation of human souls. That is the trouble with this whole business. So much of it does not matter! And there is one thing that does matter — more than anything else in all the world —

that men in their personal lives and in their social relationships should know Jesus Christ.

Just a week ago I received a letter from a friend in Asia Minor. He says that they are killing the Armenians yet; that the Turkish deportations still are going on; that lately they crowded Christian men, women, and children into a conventicle of worship and burned them together in the house where they had prayed to their Father and to ours. During the war, when it was good propaganda to stir up our bitter hatred against the enemy, we heard of such atrocities, but not now! Two weeks ago Great Britain, shocked and stirred by what is going on in Armenia, did ask the government of the United States to join her in investigating the atrocities and trying to help. Our government said that it was not any of our business at all. The present world situation smells to heaven! And now in the presence of colossal problems, which must be solved in Christ's name and for Christ's sake, the fundamentalists propose to drive out from the Christian churches all the consecrated souls who do not agree with their theory of inspiration. What immeasurable folly!

Well, they are not going to do it; certainly not in this vicinity. I do not even know in this congregation whether anybody has been tempted to be a fundamentalist. Never in this church have I caught one accent of intolerance. God keep us always so and ever increasing areas of the Christian fellowship: intellectually hospitable, open-minded, liberty-loving, fair, tolerant, not with the tolerance of indifference as though we did not care about the faith, but because always our major emphasis is upon the weightier matters of the law.

FRIEDRICH SCHLEIERMACHER

Sermon at Nathanael's Grave

In this moving, sorrowful sermon, the "father of theological liberalism" speaks as the father of a dead son. He speaks as a parent — grieving, hurt beyond expectation, shaken to his roots. He speaks as a Christian believer — rich in love, and in hope, and in childlike submission. He speaks as a generous and thoughtful human being — not letting his grief cut the nerve of love or respect for his wife and his other children, not missing an opportunity to thank Nathanael's teachers and playmates or to bring to their open hearts a "well-meant gift of Christian admonition."

Tender, strong, remarkable in the riches of its faith and wisdom, Friedrich Schleiermacher's sermon speaks to strangers, generations later, with the same pathos it brought to Nathanael's grave.

Friedrich Schleiermacher, "Sermon at Nathanael's Grave," *Journal of Religion* 57, 1 (1978): 72-75. Reprinted by permission of the University of Chicago Press.

Sermon at Nathanael's Grave

My dear friends, come here to grieve with this stooped father at the grave of his beloved child, I know you are not come with the intention of seeing a reed shaken by the wind.[1] But what you find is in truth only an old stalk, which yet does not break even from this gust of wind that has suddenly struck him from on high, out of the blue. Thus it is! For a happy household, cared for and spared by Heaven for twenty years, I have God to thank; for a much longer pursuit of my vocation, accompanied by undeserved blessings; for a great abundance of joys and sorrows, which, in my calling and as a sympathetic friend, I have lived through with others. Many a heavy cloud has passed over my life; yet what has come from without, faith has surmounted, and what from within, love has recompensed. But now, this one blow, the first of its kind, has shaken my life to its roots.

Ah, children are not only dear pledges entrusted to us from God, for whom we must give account; not only inexhaustible subjects of concern and duty, of love and prayer: they are also an immediate blessing upon the house; they give easily as much as they receive; they freshen life and gladden the heart. Just such a blessing was this boy for our house. As the Redeemer said that the angels of the little ones see the face of this Father in Heaven,[2] so with this child it appeared to us as if such an angel beamed out from his countenance the kindness of our God. When God gave him to me, my first prayer was that fatherly love would never mislead me to expect more of the boy than was right; and I believe the Lord has granted me this. I know very well that there are children far more outstanding in gifts of mind, in eager alertness, and upon whom far greater expectations concerning what they will accomplish in the world could be raised, and I would rejoice should there be many of them. When I gave him the name he bore, not only did I want thereby to greet him as a precious and welcome gift of

1. Matt. 11:7.
2. Matt. 18:10.

God.[3] I wanted at the same time to express my earnest wish that he might become like his biblical namesake, a soul in which there is no falsehood; and this too the Lord has granted me. Honest and frank as our boy was, he looked everyone in the eye full of trust, doing only good to all, and we have never found anything false in him. And for this reason, my dear children whom I see around me here — because he was truthful — he also remained free from many sorrows which otherwise come even upon those of your age. A selfish nature was also something far from him, and he bore love and goodwill for all humanity. So he lived among us as the joy of the whole house. And when the time was come that it seemed necessary to transplant him to a larger community of young people and a wider circle of education, there too he began to acclimate himself and to thrive, and even the deserved and well-meant reprimands of his teachers fell on good soil.

Thus I had thought to follow him with fatherly eye still further, and I quietly waited to see to what degree his intellectual powers would further develop and to which area of human activity his inclination would turn. If I often said to myself — though in a sense wholly other than that which has now come to pass — that it would not be granted me to complete his upbringing, I was nonetheless of good courage. I regarded it as one more beautiful blessing of my calling that, in days to come, he would never fail to find faithful fatherly advice and strong support on my account, though I hoped he would not fail to find it on his own account as well.

This charge, important above all others for the remainder of my life, to which my heart clung full of love, is now ineradicably stricken through; the friendly, refreshing picture of life is suddenly destroyed; and all the hopes that rested upon him lie here and shall be buried with this coffin! What should I say?

There is one consolation, with which many faithful Christians soothe themselves in such a case, which already many beloved, friendly voices here have spoken to me in these days, and which is not to be simply dismissed, for it grows out of a correct assessment of

3. Nathanael derives from the Hebrew, "gift of God."

human weakness. Namely, it is the consolation that children who are taken away young are in fact delivered from all of the dangers and temptations of this life and are early rescued into the sure Haven. And this boy would certainly not have been spared these dangers. But, in fact, this consolation does not want to take with me, I being the way I am. Regarding this world as I always do, as a world that is glorified through the life of the Redeemer and hallowed through the efficacy of his Spirit to an unending development of all that is good and Godly; wishing, as I always have, to be nothing but a servant of this divine Word in a joyful spirit and sense; why then should I not have believed that the blessings of the Christian community would be confirmed in my child as well, and that through Christian upbringing, an imperishable seed would have been planted in him? Why should I not have hoped in the merciful preservation of God for him also, even if he stumbled? Why should I not have trusted securely that nothing would be able to tear him out of the hand of the Lord and Savior to whom he was dedicated, and whom he had already begun to love with his childlike heart — for one of his last rational responses in the days of his sickness was a warm affirmation to the question of his mother, whether he loved his Savior rightly. And this love, even if it was not fully developed, even if it had undergone fluctuations in him, why should I not indeed have believed that it would never be extinguished for him, that it someday would have possessed him wholly? And as I would have had the courage to live through all this with him — to admonish him, to comfort, to lead — therefore this way of thinking is not as consoling to me as it is to many others.

Still others who grieve generate their consolation in another way, out of an abundance of attractive images in which they represent the everlasting community of those who have gone on before and those who as yet remain behind; and the more these images fill the soul, the more all the pains connected with death are stilled. But for the man who is too greatly accustomed to the rigors and cutting edges of thinking, these images leave behind a thousand unanswered questions and thereby lose much, much of their consoling power.

Thus I stand here, then, with my comfort and my hope alone in the Word of Scripture, modest and yet so rich, "It doth not yet appear what we shall be; but when it shall appear, we shall see Him as He is,"[4] and in the powerful prayer of the Lord, "Father, I would that where I am, they also may be whom Thou hast given me."[5] Supported by these strong beliefs, then, and borne along by a childlike submission, I say from my heart, the Lord has given him: the name of the Lord be praised,[6] that he gave him to me; that he granted to this child a life, which, even though short, was yet glad and bright and warmed by the loving breath of his grace; that he has so truly watched over and guided him that now with his cherished remembrance nothing bitter is mixed. On the contrary, we must acknowledge that we have been richly blessed through this beloved child. The Lord has taken him: His name be praised, that although he has taken him, yet he has left us, and that this child remains with us here also in inextinguishable memories, a dear and imperishable individual.

Ah, I cannot part from the remains of this dear little form, ordained for decay, without now, after I have praised the Lord, expressing the most moving thanks of my heart: before all, to the dear half of my life through whom God gave me the gift of this child, for all the motherly love and trust which she bestowed on him from his first breath to his last, expired in her faithful arms; and to all my beloved older children, for the love with which they were devoted to this youngest and which made it easier for him to go his way, bright and happy, in the straight path of order and obedience; and to all the beloved friends who have rejoiced in him with us, and with us have cared for him; but especially to you, dear teachers, who made it your pleasure to take an active part in the development of his soul; and to you, dear playmates and schoolmates, who were devoted to him in childlike friendship, to whom he was indebted for so many of his happier hours, and who also mourn for him, since you would have liked to go forward with him still farther on the common way. And to all of those who have made this hour of parting more beautiful and celebrative for me, my thanks.

4. 1 John 3:2.
5. John 17:24.
6. Job 1:21.

But with thanks it is always good that some gift be joined in return; and so, all of you, accept as a remembrance of this moment, so painfully significant for me, a well-meant gift of Christian admonition. My wife and I have both loved this child tenderly and with all our hearts, and what is more, amiability and gentleness are the ruling tone of our household. And yet, here and there, there steals through our memories of our life with this beloved child a soft tone of reproach. And so I believe that perhaps no one passes on, concerning whom those who lived most closely with him are completely satisfied when they examine themselves before God — even if the allotment of life has been as short as this one. Therefore let us all truly love one another as persons who could soon — alas, how soon! — be snatched away. I say this to you children; and you may believe me that this advice, if you follow it, will tarnish no innocent joys for you; rather it will surely protect you from many errors, even though they may be small. I say this to you parents; for even if you do not share my experience, you will enjoy even more unspoiled the fruits of this word. I say it with my sincerest thanks to you teachers; for even if you have to do with young people in numbers too great to allow you to develop a special relation with each individual, yet all the more must those things which you do to keep order and good discipline be infused with the right spirit of holy Christian love. Ah yes, let us all love one another as persons who could soon be separated!

Now, thou God who art love, let me not only resign myself to thy omnipotence, not only submit to thy impenetrable wisdom, but also know thy fatherly love! Make even this grievous trial a new blessing for me in my vocation! For me and all of mine let this communal pain become wherever possible a new bond of still more intimate love, and let it issue in a new apprehension of thy Spirit in all my household! Grant that even this grave hour may become a blessing for all who are gathered here. Let us all more and more mature to that wisdom which, looking beyond the void, sees and loves only the eternal in all things earthly and perishable, and in all thy decrees finds thy peace as well, and eternal life, to which through faith we are delivered out of death. Amen.

WILLIAM SLOANE COFFIN

Alex's Death

From its first remarkable sentence on, this sermon commands the hearer. Courageous, intimate, sometimes raw, always candid, "Alex's Death" leads us through a welter of emotions and convictions. Its preacher has lost a son, and the wound is open. Nothing — not rage or tenderness, not grief or hope, not bitterness or tenacious faith — can separate the preacher from Alex's death. The truth is that a parent's heart has been broken.

But when the sermon finally turns from lament toward consolation, and even doxology, another truth takes hold. This is a truth we can listen to, and perhaps accept, because the preacher has painfully won the right to recommend it.

Alex's Death

Texts: Psalm 34:1-9; Romans 8:38-39

As almost all of you know, a week ago last Monday night, driving in a terrible storm, my son Alexander — who to his friends was a real day-brightener, and to his family "Fair as a star when only one is shining in the sky" — my twenty-four-year-old Alexander, who enjoyed beating his old man at every game and in every race, beat his father to the grave.

Among the healing flood of letters that followed his death was one carrying this wonderful quote from the end of Hemingway's *Farewell to Arms:* "The world breaks everyone, then some become strong at the broken places." My own broken heart is mending, and largely thanks to so many of you, my dear parishioners; for if in the last week I have relearned one lesson, it is that love not only begets love, it transmits strength.

Because so many of you have cared so deeply and because obviously I've been able to think of little else, I want this morning to talk of Alex's death, I hope in a way helpful to all.

When a person dies, there are many things that can be said, and there is at least one thing that should never be said. The night after Alex died I was sitting in the living room of my sister's house outside of Boston, when the front door opened and in came a nice-looking middle-aged woman, carrying about eighteen quiches. When she saw me she shook her head, then headed for the kitchen, saying sadly over her shoulder, "I just don't understand the will of God." Instantly I was up and in hot pursuit, swarming all over her. "I'll say you don't, lady!" I said. (I knew the anger would do me good, and the instruction to her was long overdue.) I continued, "Do you think it was the will of God that Alex never fixed that lousy windshield wiper of his, that he was probably driving too fast in such a storm, that he probably had had a couple of 'frosties' too many? Do you think it is God's will that there are no streetlights along that stretch of road, and no guard rail separating the road and Boston Harbor?"

For some reason, nothing so infuriates me as the incapacity

of seemingly intelligent people to get it through their heads that
God doesn't go around this world with his finger on triggers, his
fist around knives, his hands on steering wheels. God is dead set
against all unnatural deaths. And Christ spent an inordinate amount
of time delivering people from paralysis, insanity, leprosy, and muteness. Which is not to say that there are no nature-caused deaths (I
can think of many right here in this parish in the five years I've
been here), deaths that are untimely and slow and pain-ridden,
which for that reason raise unanswerable questions, and even the
specter of a Cosmic Sadist — yes, even an Eternal Vivisector. But
violent deaths, such as the one Alex died — to understand those is
a piece of cake. As his younger brother put it simply, standing at
the head of the casket at the Boston funeral, "You blew it, buddy.
You blew it." The one thing that should never be said when
someone dies is "It is the will of God." Never do we know enough
to say that. My own consolation lies in knowing that it was *not* the
will of God that Alex die; that when the waves closed over the
sinking car, God's heart was the first of all our hearts to break.

I mentioned the healing flood of letters. Some of the very
best, and easily the worst, came from fellow reverends, a few of
whom proved they knew their Bibles better than the human condition. I know all the "right" biblical passages, including "Blessed
are those who mourn," and my faith is no house of cards; these
passages are true, I know. But the point is this: While the words
of the Bible are true, grief renders them unreal. The reality of grief
is the absence of God — "My God, my God, why hast thou forsaken me?" The reality of grief is the solitude of pain, the feeling
that your heart is in pieces, your mind's a blank, that "there is no
joy the world can give like that it takes away" (Lord Byron).

That's why immediately after such a tragedy people must come
to your rescue, people who only want to hold your hand, not to quote
anybody or even say anything, people who simply bring food and
flowers — the basics of beauty and life — people who sign letters
simply, "Your broken-hearted sister." In other words, in my intense
grief I felt some of my fellow reverends — not many, and none of
you, thank God — were using comforting words of Scripture for
self-protection, to pretty up a situation whose bleakness they simply

couldn't face. But like God herself, Scripture is not around for anyone's protection, just for everyone's unending support.

And that's what hundreds of you understood so beautifully. You gave me what God gives all of us — minimum protection, maximum support. I swear to you, I wouldn't be standing here were I not upheld.

After the death of his wife, C. S. Lewis wrote, "They say, 'the coward dies many times'; so does the beloved. Didn't the eagle find a fresh liver to tear in Prometheus every time it dined?"

When parents die, as did my mother last month, they take with them a large portion of the past. But when children die, they take away the future as well. That is what makes the valley of the shadow of death seem so incredibly dark and unending. In a prideful way it would be easier to walk the valley alone, nobly, head high, instead of — as we must — marching as the latest recruit in the world's army of the bereaved.

Still there is much by way of consolation. Because there are no rankling unanswered questions, and because Alex and I simply adored each other, the wound for me is deep, but clean. I know how lucky I am! I also know that this day-brightener of a son wouldn't wish to be held close by grief (nor, for that matter, would any but the meanest of our beloved departed), and that, interestingly enough, when I mourn Alex least I see him best.

Another consolation, of course, will be the learning — which better be good, given the price. But it's a fact: few of us are naturally profound; we have to be forced down. So while trite, it's true:

> I walked a mile with Pleasure,
>   She chattered all the way;
> But left me none the wiser
>   For all she had to say.

> I walked a mile with Sorrow
>   And ne'er a word said she;
> But oh, the things I learned from her
>   When sorrow walked with me.
>   Robert Browning Hamilton

Or, in Emily Dickinson's verse,

> By a departing light
> we see acuter quite
> Than by a wick that stays.
> There's something in the flight
> That clarifies the sight
> And decks the rays.

And of course I know, even when pain is deep, that God is good. "My God, my God, why hast thou forsaken me?" Yes, but at least, "My God, my God"; and the psalm only begins that way, it doesn't end that way. As the grief that once seemed unbearable begins to turn now to bearable sorrow, the truths in the "right" biblical passages are beginning, once again, to take hold: "Cast thy burden upon the Lord and He shall strengthen thee"; "Weeping may endure for a night, but joy cometh in the morning"; "Lord, by thy favor thou hast made my mountain to stand strong"; "for thou hast delivered my soul from death, mine eyes from tears, and my feet from falling." "In this world ye shall have tribulation, but be of good cheer; I have overcome the world." "The light shines in the darkness, and the darkness has not overcome it."

And finally I know that when Alex beat me to the grave, the finish line was not Boston Harbor in the middle of the night. If a week ago last Monday a lamp went out, it was because, for him at least, the Dawn had come.

So I shall — so let us all — seek consolation in that love which never dies, and find peace in the dazzling grace that always is.

JOANNA ADAMS

The Only Question

What can we say? A thirty-one-year-old man, suffering for nearly a decade from schizophrenia, stops taking his medicine, refuses to see his psychiatrist, and becomes dangerous. His sixty-five-year-old father, a church officer, watches these developments with growing alarm. What if his son should hurt someone? Panicked, the father slays his son and then himself.

What can we say? Who has the right words for an event that is never in season? Eloquently aware that she must speak when no one can speak, Joanna Adams, the family's pastor, rose to preach the gospel into circumstances that seemed to mock its goodness.

The words of her sermon are shaped not only by the sorrow of the moment, and not only by the pastor's keen compassion, but also by the cross at the center of the Christian faith. Pastors refer people to the cross, not to explain suffering that is inexplicable, but rather to let us see that God is a co-sufferer and can therefore be trusted.

Joanna Adams, "The Only Question," reprinted by permission of the *Journal for Preachers*, P.O. Box 520, Decatur, GA 30031-0520.

The Only Question

The Reformed theologian Karl Barth said that people come to church on the Sabbath with only one question in their minds: Is it true? The providence of God, the saving power of Jesus Christ, the comforting presence of the Holy Spirit, the resurrection from the dead, the forgiveness of sin: Is it true? When we come to church at 2:00 p.m. on a Monday afternoon for a memorial service for two people who died untimely deaths, the question is even more compelling: Is it true? Can God be trusted on a day like today?

There are other questions, of course: *Why* did it happen? *Why* did Mark get so sick? *Why* did Jim sink into such despair? They are the questions one asks late at night when sleep won't come, and our psyches are demanding an explanation. We are only human after all, seeing through a glass dimly, trying to figure things out, wanting to know why bad things happen to good people who didn't do a thing to deserve the hand life dealt them. We want to know why.

Do you remember Rabbi Harold Kushner's best-selling book a few years ago? Most people thought the title was *Why Bad Things Happen to Good People;* it was *When Bad Things Happen to Good People*. The Christian faith begins at the same place as the rabbi's book. Faith doesn't spend a great deal of time explaining *why* bad things happen to good people. In a world that fell from grace a long time ago, brokenness, illness, tragic endings are facts of life — inevitable, universal, unavoidable.

Because we are human, we want to know why; because we are only human, we cannot know why. The Scripture promises that someday we will know why, but that day is not today. God knows what we need today is not an explanation; what we need today is faith. What we need is reassurance that the resurrection is real. God knows that beneath all our why's is the only question that matters: Can God be trusted with the deaths of those we love? We can live without an explanation, but we cannot live without knowing if it is true that God can be trusted.

In answer to our question, God says, "Yes, it is true." Christ died and was raised so that Jim and Mark could live again. Eternal life is true. Even when fear and sorrow beat their restless wings close around us, it is true. It is true that God will lead us through the worst life can do. When the shadow seems so thick there can never be light again, it is still true: The comfort of God will seek us out and gradually, gently subdue our grief and restore our spirits.

"How have you endured all of this?" I asked Carolyn (Jim's widow and Mark's mother) on Saturday. "God and the angels," Carolyn said. You see, we are not dealing today with a God who comes around only when things are rosy and the birds are singing. There is a cross up there! The God we know in Jesus Christ knows about suffering. The God we know in Jesus Christ gets to the valley of death, of loss and grief, before we get there, so that he can get ready to catch us when we stumble blindly in, so that he can guide us through the dark. As Carolyn put it, "all the way through the valley, Joanna. *Through* the valley." It is true that God can be trusted.

It is also true that bad, even unbelievably bad things happen to good people. Look at Mark. He could no more help his illness than someone helps having cerebral palsy or Hodgkin's disease. In a way you could say Mark died more than his share. Bad things happen to good people.

Look at Jim — a man of God who would have any day given up his life for his son, and did, in the end. A helplessness overcame him for which he was no match. It is also true that none of it was God's will. Don't you know that God's heart was the first of all hearts to break last Friday morning?[1] Where is God in all this? Grieving with us, weeping for us, but more than that — drying tears, creating life out of death, hope out of despair, forgiving sin, restoring wholeness.

God is so relentlessly committed to being the God of life that God can use even the worst that can happen, in ways we cannot fathom, for God's good purposes. The question is not *why* bad things happen, but: Can God be trusted when they do? Should we hope again? Can we live again, and if so, how?

---

1. See William Sloane Coffin, "Alex's Death" (pp. 263-66 in this volume).

The gospel is so exquisitely clear and simple at this point: "Abide in Christ," it says. "Stay close to me," Jesus says. "Bring your brokenness to me." Cut off from him, how could any live? But abiding in him, staying close to his body, the church, we can endure.

I met somebody yesterday I had not met before. Her name is Lauren. She is three years old, Jim and Carolyn's granddaughter, a bright and happy blond-headed little girl. She wore a bib with a duck on it, and a ready smile on her face as she sat on Carolyn's knee and met the preacher. "Tell Joanna what you say before you have your supper," Carolyn said. Lauren looked at me, a perfect stranger, and spoke as if she was sharing with me the most wonderful news you could imagine: "God is great," Lauren said. "God is good," she said, and suddenly I could not wait to come to church today, so that I could tell you what Lauren said and what the Scripture promises and what faith knows even when the pain is piercing and the shadows fall. God is still great. God is still good. It is true!

AUSTIN FARRER

Holy Angels

Austin Farrer was as unpretentious and nonfashionable in his preaching as in his considerable scholarship. In both, he had what Basil Mitchell has called "the natural expression of a unified intellectual and spiritual vision." With modesty and acuity, Farrer went his own way. He never hesitated to address subjects so unpopular as to be almost rakish.

In this sermon for the celebration of the Eucharist, Farrer expresses his vision of a realm often neglected by modern Christians, except, perhaps, for a small fluttering of wings around Christmas. The world is too much with us, Farrer is saying, and angels too little. For they reflect the light and glory of God. To celebrate the Eucharist is to celebrate the communion of saints and angels, the whole cloud of witnesses in heaven and on earth — the ones that, altogether too often, we either ignore or else entertain unwittingly.

Austin Farrer, "Holy Angels," reprinted by permission of the Trustees of the Farrer Estate.

Holy Angels

Fear not, for they that be with us are more than they
that be with them.

2 Kings 6:16, KJV

Do you ever read or hear the experiences of people who explore
caves underground? Through the dark they go by the light of their
torches, and then, maybe, they see a suspicion of light round the
next bend of the tunnel they are following. They push on, and
suddenly the roof goes up and up, and in the top there is a crack
like a chimney. They cannot see through it, but that doesn't stop
a long thin ray of light falling from it, and scattering itself in the
vast cave, lighting up the dripping walls. Up at the top there are
even a few ferns growing. Daylight! The explorers are suddenly
reminded of the open-air world above. They think, if a mere trickle
of sunlight can make the huge cave visible, what must be the power
of the sun up there where he has free scope and nothing stands in
his way? They remember the floods of golden glory pouring on
land and sea, and looking at the pale green ferns in the roof, think
of the flowers of every color that drink life from sunlight in the
fields and gardens of the world. What mugs we are, they may think,
ever to have taken on this exploration down here in the dark.

Well now, there's a parable for you, and I dare say you've
guessed the point of it already, knowing as you do the sort of
groove that sermons follow. You'll have guessed that the cave in
my story means the world, and that we ourselves are the explorers.
We try to find our way about through this life by the light of our
own torches, which are our natural wits and abilities; but then we
meet traces of a light fully from above — the grace and the glory
of God.

I wonder whether you have read the book by C. S. Lewis in
which he describes his own early life, very much as a pilgrimage
through a dark tunnel. He calls the book an odd name, *Surprised*

by Joy — surprised by joy, because of the surprising gleams of glory that came down on his path from time to time, and which he traced at last to their origin, and found they came from God. So he became a Christian — he was an atheist before. If you and I began swapping stories about our own life, and especially our early life, no doubt we could tell one another about gleams of glory here and there, not only occasional glimpses of natural beauty that have taken our breath away — for instance, the sun going down over the sea and making a path of gold on the waves — not only glory like that, but occasional encounters with divine goodness in other men. Of all the luck I ever had, none was better than this — knowing a man who was, I believe, something of a saint; a man who did not *try* to love God, on and off, as you and I do, he just loved him, as young men love their wives or mothers their children, and he never thought about himself at all. Well, I tell about him freely to you, because he is dead, he threw his life away for his friends, as such men like to do. It is really stupid of me to talk to you about a man you didn't know, but I do it to remind you of the gleams of glory you may yourselves have seen in the world of men.

Now those people in the cave, with whom I started — their thoughts ran up the ray of light as though it were a golden ladder, into the world above; and so I, remembering my friend now dead, may run up in thought to the God who made him, and whose glory he reflected. For God has made every one of us in his own image, after his own likeness, even though, alas, the eyes of God do not look out through our eyes as they look out through the eyes of the saints. But when I think of this man, who was my friend, it is easy for me to see the ray of glory there, and to trace it up to God.

Why the glory of God shines so dimly in this world of men is a question we might discuss for a great while. Some of us know well enough why his glory shines so faintly on our own faces, because we each of us know our own vices. But we will not talk of that now. Let's take it for granted that this world is a strange mixture of the bright and the dark, as St. John says on the first page of his gospel, "The Light shineth in the darkness, and the darkness comprehended it not."

Here the light shines in darkness, a ray through the roof of our cave; but somewhere above, the Light shines in Light, and fills a world of Light. Somewhere above, the goodness of God just overflows like water from a fountain and meets no obstacle. There, all his creating, making power pours out in splendid creatures, unspoilt beings, worthy of the God who makes them: they, like God himself, are light, and in them is no darkness at all. We call them the holy angels.

Why do we believe in the holy angels? What's the point of it? Well, obviously we believe in them on the word of Jesus Christ, on the testimony of saints and of the holy church, and because it was an angel brought the tidings to Mary when she conceived by the Holy Ghost. But if you ask what is the principal part of the belief — why we are to suppose that God created angels — I shall reply that the puzzle isn't why God created angels, but why he ever created anything else. It does not puzzle me that the sun in the sky surrounds himself with light, for it's his nature to shine in all directions; so why should it puzzle me that God surrounds himself with glorious angels, in whom his creative goodness is displayed? The sun shoots the same quality of light in all directions, up, down, and round, but on this point the sun differs from God, who never sends out two rays of glory that are alike. His power is so various that each of his creatures expresses it differently: Michael, Gabriel, Raphael, thousands on thousands of shining spirits, each serve and love God in their own unique way and reflect a different aspect of his infinite glory.

Why do we believe in angels? We start from what we can see, the glory of God in this mixed world of bright and dark. We say, this world of ours isn't the home of glory, glory comes from above; it descends, as St. James says, from the Father of lights, in whom is no change nor shadow of alteration. We trace glory up to its home and ask how that home is furnished and populated. We reply, it is peopled with angels.

When the enemies of Jesus came to take him at Gethsemane, when Judas kissed him, when Peter drew his sword, "Put back thy sword again into its sheath," said Jesus. "Thinkest thou I could not, if I wished, entreat my Father, and he send me even now more than twelve regiments of angels?" When Jesus used these words, Peter understood exactly what he meant, for Peter, like any Jewish child, knew the story of Elisha; the story to which, in speaking thus, Jesus was plainly alluding. For Elisha, once, had been looked for by armed enemies, as Jesus then was; and Elisha's disciple had been as troubled as were the disciples of Jesus in Gethsemane, when he saw the flash of swords. "Alas, my master," said he, "what are we to do?" "Fear not," said Elisha, "for they that be with us are more than they that be with them." Then Elisha prayed, and said, "Lord, I pray thee, open his eyes, that he may see." So (we read) the Lord opened the eyes of the young man, and he saw; and behold the mountain was full of horses and chariots of fire round about Elisha. These were the hosts of God, these were the holy angels made for the moment visible to that disciple's mind, so he might understand what Elisha had told him: they that be with us are more than they that be with them.

They that be with us are more than they that be with them: the forces of God, the allies of the church, far outbalance the enemies of the church, the forces of Satan; even though it doesn't look like it to our beclouded eyes. How weak, how few we are! and how much we're up against! How much you are up against, in the parishes where your homes are. You're a mere handful, aren't you, compared with the masses of indifference and unbelief. Well, but remember, we only see what's in the cave, and if we get into rocket ships and go whizzing to the moon or even as far as Mars, we shall still only be flitting about like bats inside the great cave of the world. The heaven of angels is God's open air, and it is far greater than the world of men. The forces of God are overwhelmingly strong, the balance of power in his creation is all on the diviner side; and how could it be otherwise, since God is God? They that are for us are more, many, many times more, than they that are against us. We see a contrast between the disciple of Elisha in the Old Testament and the disciples of Jesus in the New. Elisha's disciple saw the regiments of angels, standing by to rescue his master; and they did rescue him. The disciples of Jesus did not see any twelve legions of angels, for their divine master refused to summon them: he would not be rescued, he went to his death. Yet by that very death Jesus opened the eyes of his disciples to see the angels, for whom in his greatest need he had refused to pray. The women went to his sepulchre on the third day, and there the angels were, one at the head, one at the feet, of the place where Jesus had lain. It was by dying that Jesus set open forever a door between earth and heaven: his sepulchre is a piece of heaven, a place of angels. Where Jesus lies sacrificed for us, heaven is opened, a great shaft of light falls from above, and the angels of God are seen ascending and descending upon the Son of Man.

For the act of love that makes the Son of God die for us brings all the angels down. Those pure spirits, those brave and flaming hearts have been loving the Lord their God ever since they were created, with all their mind and soul and strength: but they have never been able to make him such an offering as they see Jesus make, when he gives himself to die for us men and for our salvation. So the air is thick with wings, wherever a Christian priest, by Christ's command, brings back upon the altar the sacrifice of Christ; and whenever we offer the Holy Sacrament we are bidden to join our weak praises with the whole choir and company of heaven, with angels and archangels lauding and magnifying the only Glorious Name, and crying Holy, Holy, to him with whose glory heaven and earth are filled.

See, then, with whom we unite, and whose supplicating voices support our prayers here: certainly when we gather before the altar we know that they who are with us are more than they who are with our enemies.

One Sunday it happened that St. John could not be at church with his friends, for like Elisha, like Jesus, he was taken by the armed men and held in prison. But God consoled him with a vision: he saw the Christian sacrament that morning not as men see it, but as it is seen in heaven. His spirit went up; he saw the throne of glory, and the four cherubim full of eyes in every part, who sleep not, saying Holy, Holy, Holy. And he saw the sacrifice, the Lamb of God: a Lamb standing as though slaughtered; a Lamb alone worthy to open for mankind the blessed promises of God. He saw the Lamb, and then the angels. I saw, he says, and heard the voice of many angels round about the Throne, the number of them ten thousand times ten thousand, and thousands of thousands: saying with a loud voice, Worthy is the Lamb who was slain to receive the power and riches and wisdom and might and honor and glory and blessing.

That is the Christian Eucharist. Certainly when we gather here, those that are with us are more than those who stand upon the opposing side. For all heaven is one with us, when once we lift our hearts up to the Lord, and praise the everlasting Love, the One God in three Persons, Father, Son, and Holy Ghost; to whom be ascribed, as is most justly due, all might, dominion, majesty, and power, henceforth and forever.

JOHN TIMMER

Owning Up to Baptism

In a sermon that appears at first to center in the concerns of biblical feminism, one of the preeminent preachers of a conservative Reformed denomination explores the politics of baptism — of *baptism,* as he insists, not of the ordination of women. After all, most Christians do not ordain women, and even many of those who do still treat women as an underclass.

But all baptize, and most have underestimated the significance of baptism. In straight, deft strokes, Timmer hammers out some of the meaning of union with Christ and of the sacrament that expresses and strengthens it. To get *in Christ* means, among other things, to drown ancient tyrannies and exclusions and to be resurrected into a whole new world in which the old subordinations have been rendered antique.

This is a sermon for the celebration of the sacrament of holy baptism and, especially, for reminding us of its force.

John Timmer, "Owning Up to Baptism," from *The Reformed Journal* 39 (May-June 1990), pp. 12-14. Used with permission.

Owning Up to Baptism

For as many of you as were baptized into Christ have put on Christ. There is neither Jew nor Greek, there is neither slave nor free, there is neither male nor female; for you are all one in Christ Jesus.

Galatians 3:27-28

Each year I spend a couple of weeks at Princeton Seminary and while there spend many an hour in the bookstore, looking over new publications. While doing so again last summer, something struck me. It struck me how little most bookstore sections grow. Only three sections grow markedly: black theology, liberation theology, and feminist theology. Here, each year, I come across a lot of new titles. Black theology, liberation theology, feminist theology — what these three theologies have in common is

- that they are born out of pain;
- that they are forged in conversations rather than in lectures;
- that their spokespersons are the oppressed.

Here are the growing edges of theology. The theologians I studied during my student days were all of them male, white, and European: Augustine, Aquinas, Luther, Calvin, Bavinck, Kuyper, Berkouwer, Ridderbos, Berkhof. All were professors holding important teaching posts. These men taught us how to think about God and how to talk about God. We students thought *they* had all the answers — only to discover, years later, how parochial their vision of God really was; how conditioned by the time and place in which they lived.

Today much theology is written by a different breed of people. Today many voices speaking about God are those of the "wretched of the earth" — the poor, the marginalized, the victims. There are blacks . . . Asians . . . and Latin Americans. There are also women.

We call them feminists, but must do so with great care, for there are different kinds of feminists. Some feminists are so radical that they find Christianity hopelessly irredeemable. These radical feminists urge women to leave Christianity behind and to adopt a purely feminist spirituality. There are also fundamentalist "feminists." They discourage women from assuming fully adult roles in church and in society. They encourage women to find total womanhood in subjecting themselves to their husbands.

But there are also feminists whose agenda is deeply biblical, whose focus is the basic theme of the gospel, whose inspiration is Jesus Christ himself.

The main item on the agenda of these feminists is the meaning of their baptism. They say: Everything that divides Christians has been drowned in the water of baptism. They say: Everything that reduces women to second-class Christians has been drowned in the water of baptism. Baptism is the gateway to the new age. Baptism is the sacrament that says, Having died with Christ in the water of baptism, we have also risen with him from this water to a new life. The old divisions that tear community apart, that place men above women, that keep women in a subordinate position — all these are left behind. Everything is fresh and new. For men and women are *equal* now.

That, as I understand it, is the main item of the agenda of biblical feminism: that the church should own up to the implications of baptism. In the death and resurrection of Jesus, all men and women are equally redeemed. In the sending of the Holy Spirit all are joined in a communion where the social distinctions of class, race, and sex are overcome. Baptism entitles women to serve as fully in the church as men do. Therefore baptism and not ordination is the main item on the agenda of biblical feminism. Ordination is a large item on its agenda, but not the main item. It is a large item because of what ordination symbolizes. Ordination symbolizes the lack of equality in the church; it symbolizes women's exclusion from all significant decision making. However, the *main* item on the biblical feminist agenda is larger than ordination. For even in churches where women *are* ordained, they continue to be treated as second-class members.

Biblical feminism draws its inspiration primarily from Jesus. So revolutionary was Jesus' attitude toward women, so radically different from that of his contemporaries, that it has taken 2,000 years for this particular time bomb to explode in our part of the world. Jesus treated women as fully human, as equal to men. He did this, not so much by what he said, as by how he related to women, how he treated them. Jesus was remarkably open to women. He closely associated with women in all phases of his ministry. Some of his closest friends were women: Mary Magdalene, and the sisters Mary and Martha. Jesus broke powerful ancient taboos when he spoke with the Samaritan woman and the Syrophoenician woman. He chose a woman — Mary — as the first witness of his resurrection.

Much of Jesus' attitude toward women spilled over into the early church, where women were active as disciples, prophets, teachers, and missionaries. Jesus' attitude toward women, however, was too radical, too countercultural. So, as it became apparent that the return of Christ was not going to happen immediately, and as the church accommodated itself increasingly to the surrounding male-dominated culture, the church forgot, or ignored, the equality of women.

To a church, however, that constantly listens to the Word of God, that periodically reflects on the meaning of baptism, forgetting the equality of women must, sooner or later, become impossible and intolerable. And we are experiencing this in our day. Now, biblical feminism's main mission is to make sure that the church won't forget the equality of men and women; it is to remind the church of the meaning and implications of baptism; it is to remind the church of such baptismal passages as Galatians 3:27-28: "For as many of you as were baptized into Christ have put on Christ. There is neither Jew nor Greek, there is neither slave nor free, there is neither male nor female; for you are all one in Christ Jesus."

All this flows out of baptism. All equality before God flows out of baptism. To those who are baptized into Christ, all dividing lines should cease to exist; all segregation and discrimination should cease to exist.

When we are baptized, we enter upon the new age. And this new age runs on a different set of values than does the old age to which those people belong who have *not* been baptized, who have *not* died and been raised with Christ.

So we must remember that. We must remember that biblical feminism basically wants one thing: it wants the church to live up to what it teaches about baptism; it wants the church to own up to the implications of baptism.

In Paul's letter to the Galatians, circumcision represents the old age. Circumcision, says Paul, is pre-Christian. Why? Because it discriminates and does not liberate. Circumcision is bad news, not good news. Why? Because it does not equalize but divides. It divides male from female. It divides Jew from Gentile. It is exclusive, not inclusive, the way baptism is. That's why Paul lashes out against those Jewish Christians who want to hang on to circumcision. Christ redeemed us from circumcision and all the divisions it promoted, Paul proclaims. Don't you move back now from the new age to the old age, from baptism and its freedom to circumcision and its bondage!

In the old age, the Jews had religious advantages over the Greeks. In the old age, the free had social advantages over the slaves. In the old age, the men had religious and social advantages over the women. That situation is now at an end, says Paul. That advantage went out with baptism.

When you were baptized, you drowned to your old advantages. When you were baptized, you rose to the kind of life in which no one has advantage over another. When you were baptized, the whole business of privileged status went by the board. All racial, social, and sexual distinctions were deprived of their advantage.

Our problem, then, is this: We don't understand baptism very well. We have an underdeveloped understanding of baptism. I can tell from my annual interviews with eleventh and twelfth graders. I always ask them: What does your baptism mean to you? What if you had *not* been baptized? What difference would that make?

Then I sit back and watch them agonize over an answer. They agonize over it because they never gave it much thought. They never gave it much thought because their parents evidently never gave it much thought either. The fact that they were baptized as infants does not help any.

Baptism just isn't part of their living experience. They never stepped down into a river. They never went down under water and came up again, as a symbol of their dying and rising with Christ. Baptism simply is not part of their living experience. All the more reason for parents to discuss the meaning of baptism with their children. "For as many of you as were baptized into Christ have put on Christ. There is neither Jew nor Greek, there is neither slave nor free, there is neither male nor female; for you are all one in Christ Jesus."

The words of our text are a baptismal formula; they were spoken when new Christians were baptized. As these new Christians went down under water, as they drowned to their old, pagan way of life, as they drowned to the old age in which they once lived, all the divisions that marked their old way of life drowned along with them; all the twisted and perverted social relationships drowned along with them. At least they did so symbolically, for, as Frederick Buechner reminds us, the old Adam and the old Eve are mighty good swimmers.

Then, as these new Christians rose from the baptismal waters as new creatures in Christ, their social relationships rose along with them. For these too had been baptized into Christ. These too had been raised with Christ.

Being baptized into Christ, so Paul is saying, has profound *social* implications. It leads to a breakdown of racial, social, and sexual barriers. It has a healing effect on all human relationships, especially on the relationship between Jew and Gentile, between slave and free, between male and female.

Now . . . Paul didn't just grab these three relationships out of a bag. He chose them very carefully, very deliberately. The society of Paul's day was split three ways. It was split according to race, social class, and sex.

Deeper divisions than these did not exist, not in the Greco-Roman world and not in the Jewish world. We know this from an ancient prayer that every Jewish male had to pray daily:

Blessed art thou,
  O Lord our God,
  king of the universe,
  who hast not made me a gentile.
Blessed art thou,
  O Lord our God,
  king of the universe,
  who hast not made me a slave.
Blessed art thou,
  O Lord our God,
  king of the universe,
  who hast not made me a woman.

Race, social class, and sex: these were the Berlin Walls of the
Jewish world. Poor you, if you were a Gentile. Poor you, if you
were a slave. Poor you, if you were a woman.

Not anymore! says Paul. For Christ has changed all that. When
you were baptized, you joined a community of people who had
left these divisions behind . . . in the water of baptism.

Paul did not fully implement his own words. He did not fully
implement the equality of men and women — one reason being
that he didn't have time for it. But he did take the initial steps. He
did point the church in a definite direction. He left it up to the
church that came after to take bigger and bolder steps.

Unfortunately, this is not what happened. Unfortunately, the
church succumbed too much to the spirit of the old age. Martin
Luther, for example, can say all he wants about the priesthood of
all believers — the priesthood of all male and female believers —
but he did nothing to reform the domination of men over women.
What he declared was: "Women are on earth to bear children. If
they die in child-bearing, it matters not; that is all they are here to
do."

And even in our own day, and even with the secular world
prodding us, we as a church are very slow and reluctant in allowing
women to play roles that are rightfully theirs by virtue of their
baptism.

In our text, Paul lays down the basic principle. In Christ there is neither male nor female. In Christ woman is restored to her full equality with man. IN CHRIST! Note these two words.

Through Christ's death and resurrection that equality of men and women has already been created. Our responsibility is to implement that equality. Our responsibility is to make that equality visible, so that everyone who has eyes can see that in the church of Christ there are no first- and second-class members, but only men and women who, in Christ, are equally free.

GARDNER C. TAYLOR

His Own Clothes

In a sobering sermon for Good Friday, Gardner C. Taylor ponders one of the most appalling dimensions of Jesus' suffering. The mockery of Jesus by bored Roman soldiers is, like all mockery, a vandalism of the human spirit. Mockery always strips and violates. What is so appalling about it, as Thomas Macaulay once observed in a related connection, is not merely that it causes the victim so much pain, but also that it causes the spectators so much pleasure.

More appalling still, according to Taylor, the burlesque of Jesus Christ has never stopped. The one who "bears our griefs and carries our sorrows" in the biblical text must endure them still — that is, until we behold him clothed with the gospel.

In Taylor's strong and compassionate treatment, a single biblical image expands into an emblem of all that is wicked and all that is graceful in the human response to Jesus Christ.

Gardner C. Taylor, "His Own Clothes," in *Outstanding Black Sermons,* vol. 3, edited by Milton E. Owens, Jr., pp. 63-68, published by Judson Press, copyright © 1982. Used by permission of Judson Press.

His Own Clothes

And when they had mocked him, they took off the purple
from him, and put his own clothes on him, and led him
out to crucify him.

Mark 15:20, KJV

Short of the cross itself and the betrayal by Judas, what the soldiers
did to Jesus may well have been the most humiliating part of our
Lord's suffering and death for you and me. We may be greatly
wronged and deeply hurt, but we want to be able to hold on to
our human dignity, the feeling that we are a part of the family of
mankind. Great suffering may be visited upon us, but there can be
a certain nobility, a mark of grandeur, in the way people hold their
heads high and bear bravely whatever it is they must go through.

There is something uniquely cruel in being laughed at and
made the target of ugly jibes, cruel comment, and cutting laughter.
One of the most painful and sinister weapons used historically
against black people in this country was mockery and ridicule.
Physical features were caricatured and exaggerated, and so the large,
white-lipped, wide-eyed blackened faces in minstrel shows became
the notion of the way black people looked and acted. I am not far
enough from the experience of that mockery to be able to see the
art in this kind of thing, no matter what the occasion may be. The
purpose of the foot-shuffling, head-scratching, wide-grinning,
ghost-frightened darky was to ridicule, scorn, and humiliate. Every
southern town once had its village idiot whom children would
shamefully taunt. Children who are different know how cruel such
horseplay can be.

Far crueler than our own experience was the kind of scorn
and ridicule that the soldiers heaped upon our Lord on the night
of his crucifixion. While it may be true that the sport these members
of the Praetorian guard, Pilate's military escort, made of Jesus had
little venom in it, still it chills the spirit to think of the Son of God,

the Savior of the world, the blessed Redeemer, being the object of the rude jokes and the broad barracks' humor of these rough and dull-witted soldiers.

The Master moved toward his death on our behalf over a road that grew constantly more steep and more terrifying. This was followed by betrayal, after which the chains were put on Jesus as a common criminal. Later that night they blindfolded our Lord and then struck him a stinging slap in the face taunting, "Prophesy. Who is it that smote thee?" Then they did spit in his face to add to the outrage. Each new assault seemed designed to outdo the last.

Following all these things, they scourged the Lord. This painful humiliation probably took place on the platform where the trial had been held and in sight of all. The victim was stripped down to the waist and was stretched against a pillar with hands tied. The instrument of torture was a long leathern strip, studded with pieces of lead and bits of bone. The whip left lashes, and the lead and bone tore out chunks of flesh. Some died under the lash, and others emerged from the torture raving mad. Through all of these things Jesus passed in the interest of all of our souls.

All of these things, as horrible and as appalling as they are, were but preliminary and secondary to the supreme sacrifice of Calvary. So we read that after our Lord was scourged with the lash, sentence was pronounced, and it was the sentence of death by crucifixion, the most awful and painful of the Roman methods of execution. Cicero declared that it was "the most cruel and horrifying death." (William Barclay thought that the Romans picked up this method of execution from the Persians, who believed the earth was sacred and wished to avoid defiling it with an evildoer.) Lifted on a cross, the condemned slowly died, and the vultures and carrion crows would dispose of the body.

The Roman ritual of condemnation and execution was fixed. Sentence was pronounced, "Illum duci ad crucem placet." The sentence was that this man should be hung on a cross. Then the judge turned to the guard and said, "I, miles, expedi crucem." Go, soldier, and prepare the cross. It was at this point that Jesus our Lord was turned over to the soldiers who formed the personal guard of Pilate as governor.

These men were hard-bitten professional soldiers who chafed at their unpleasant assignment in such a hot, fly-ridden place as Palestine and among all of those strange and offensive people. They took their pastime and sport when and where they could find them. One of their pleasures was to taunt and torture convicted criminals, who cringed before them like cornered and helpless animals. The Son of God was turned over to them, and they went to work with their cruel jibes.

The whole detachment gathered in their barracks with the Savior of the world before them and, as they thought, in their hands. They stripped him of his clothes. Having picked up some thread of the charge that Jesus claimed to be a king, they jammed a reed in his hand to mock a scepter, plaited a crown made out of a thorn bush for his brow, and flung around the Lord's shoulder an old, faded red tunic, the scarlet cloak that was part of the parade uniform of the Roman soldier. All this was done to mock him as king, and so they bowed down in ridicule as if to honor and worship him. "We will be your devotees and subjects, King Jesus. Look at us kneeling before you," and then their loud, uncouth laughter rang and echoed through the barracks.

There are still many who put cloaks of imitation honor and false respect on the Lord Jesus as surely as those soldiers put their old scarlet robe on the Savior. Such do not mean their patronizing words of respect about the Lord Jesus. You can hear them now and again. One says, "I respect and honor Jesus. His golden rule is enough religion for anyone to live by. I admire his life and believe it to be a thing of beauty. His ethics are splendid principles of conduct and human relations."

As to his church and all of that, these smart people are very lofty. "It is all right for those who need it, but I do not go to church. I do not feel the need of it, really." And so saying, they feel they have delivered themselves of something very profound and, if not profound, then chic and fashionable. Well, I had a dog, a Doberman pinscher, who never went to church either. I feel like answering such glib dismissal of the church for which Christ died by saying, "My dog did not go to church either. He never felt the need of it because he was a dog. Now, what is your reason?"

There are still others who put garments of mock royalty on the Lord and who call his name but who feel no deep loyalty to him, no crowning and controlling love for the Lord who has done so much for us. You may see them now and then in church, now and then among the people of Christ. They throw their leftovers at the Lord, who made us all, as a man would toss scraps to a pet dog. They are neither hot nor cold, and to such the word of the Revelation applies, "I will spew thee out of my mouth" (Rev. 3:16).

There is a lot of sham religion in this country, people going through the motions for whom Christ is not a living, determining presence. Again and again people ask, "What is wrong with us as a nation?" One word is the answer: godlessness. Never mind the churches and synagogues and mosques; godlessness is what is wrong with us. Never mind the public prayers and taking of oaths on the Bible. Godlessness is what is wrong with America. How does it come out? In the swagger of a gun lobby and money that stops congressmen from passing a gun law. In greed and bigotry and the attitude "anything goes." In lies and deceit in a nation that has no room for worship or things of the spirit.

You ask what is wrong with us as a people. Listen to any national telecast. See how all of our national interest is built around what some self-serving people in Washington do: crime, scams, confusion. See how little of the heart and mind, how little room for things of the spirit there is in our national telecasts. Godlessness! And until we turn to the Lord, it will not get better; it will get worse. And yes, one thing after another will go wrong.

Have I put fake garments on the Lord Jesus? Have I cloaked the Savior of the world in scarlet robes of pretense, claiming that I honor him as Lord while my heart is far from him? Do I take my faith in the Lord Jesus seriously? Am I willing, as George Eliot put it, to sacrifice anything as long as the result is not unpleasant?

And then we read that when the soldiers had tired of their ugly game of ridicule and making sport of the Son of God, they took off the old scarlet tunic and put his own clothes back on him. This was the final preparation for crucifixion. They put on our Lord his own clothes. And "his own clothes" says worlds to us. We need to see him as he is, "in his own clothes," not mocked and ridiculed by false respect and pious hypocrisy. When we see the Lord "in his own clothes," in his true character and force, we see someone who makes us cry out for forgiveness and for his good favor and approval. Looking at Jesus as he is, we see ourselves as we are.

When our Christ is not mocked by false garments of respectable sneer or false enthusiasm, when we see him in his own clothes as he is, we want to do better. Dr. Donald Shelby, the California United Methodist preacher, has told of a terrible storm on Lake Michigan in which a ship was wrecked near the shore. A Northwestern University student, Edmond Spenser, went into the raging water again and again and single-handedly rescued seventeen people. When friends carried him to his room, nearly exhausted and faint, he kept asking them, "Did I do my best?" In the presence of Christ we ask, "Lord, did I do my best?" I am a preacher, and each time I preach I must ask, "Lord, did I do my best?" Officer, choir member, usher, did you do your best?

Jesus in his own clothes going to Calvary did his best. His garments on that lonely hill were rolled in blood, making understandable the old cry of Isaiah, "Who is this that cometh from Edom, with dyed garments from Bozrah? this that is glorious in his apparel, travelling in the greatness of his strength?" (Isa. 63:1). We ask, "Wherefore art thou red in thine apparel, and thy garments [thy clothes] like him that treadeth in the winefat?" (Isa. 63:2). And he answers, "I have trodden the winepress alone. . . . For the day of vengeance is in mine heart, and the year of my redeemed is come" (Isa. 63:3-4).

In his own clothes he went to Calvary and made everything all right, not temporarily all right but for always. At Calvary Christ was at his best. Nothing had been left undone. On no other day does Jesus have to go back to finish his work at Calvary. This he did once. "Now once in the end of the world hath he appeared to put away sin by the sacrifice of himself. . . . So Christ was once offered to bear the sins of many" (see Heb. 9:26-28). He died in his own clothes as Savior and Redeemer. Once for all. It is all right now. The crooked way has been made straight; we may arise and shine, for our light is come. It is all right now.

We shall see him yet in other clothes. Ellen White, the prophetess of Seventh Day Adventism, pictures that day when Christ shall appear with an old, faded red cloak around his shoulders, no longer mocked by soldiers, no longer wearing simple garments of this earth. Every eye shall see him. We will see him as heaven's king, victor over death, hell, and the grave, the admired of angels. Every eye shall see him. Ten thousand times ten thousand and thousands and thousands of angels and the triumphant sons and daughters of God will escort him. His raiment will outshine the sun. And on his vesture, his garment, a name will be written, "King of Kings and Lord of Lords." Shall we not shout his name who has lifted us to heights sublime and made us his own people forever?

FREDERICK BUECHNER

The End Is Life

Not everyone can get Rembrandt to paint for him, but in this memorable Easter sermon Frederick Buechner pulls it off. Buechner commissions a chiaroscuro rendering of that Matthean moment in which chief priests and Pharisees gather at Pilate's doorstep to ask for reinforcements in the area of Jesus' tomb. They do have a valid concern: what if the disciples should stage a "resurrection"?

Pilate's reply, perhaps only a dismissive and bureaucratic little burble, turns deliciously ironic in Buechner's Rembrandt painting. Pilate replies, "You have a guard of soldiers; go, make it as secure as you can." And the petitioners turn to each other with questioning looks that only a master can paint: How secure is that?

"You are not sure whether to laugh or cry," says Buechner of these devout men, earnestly trying to secure the world against its central miracle. And what of contemporary Easter preachers who try their best to seal the tomb against some terrible outbreak of the Son of God? We might as well try to stop the wind with a machine gun, says Buechner. We might as well try to stop the sun from rising.

Frederick Buechner, "The End Is Life," from *The Magnificent Defeat* by Frederick Buechner, pp. 74-81. Copyright 1966 by Frederick Buechner. Reprinted by permission of HarperCollins, Publishers, Inc.

The End Is Life

Next day, that is, after the day of Preparation, the chief priests and the Pharisees gathered before Pilate and said, "Sir, we remember how that impostor said, while he was still alive, 'After three days I will rise again.' Therefore order the sepulchre to be made secure until the third day, lest his disciples go and steal him away, and tell the people, 'He has risen from the dead,' and the last fraud will be worse than the first." Pilate said to them, "You have a guard of soldiers; go, make it as secure as you can." So they went and made the sepulchre secure by sealing the stone and setting a guard.

Matthew 27:62-66

To begin with, let us first consider the words of the governor — the ones that he spoke to the delegation when they confronted him with their darkest fears and suspicions and asked for his help. To be more accurate, one should say "*almost* their darkest fears and suspicions," because there was one even darker still, which for good reason they left unspoken. Let us consider the words of Pontius Pilate, that apprehensive, puzzled, somehow doomed Roman patrician who had at least the virtue of great patience. Heaven knows they had put him through plenty already: forcing him to take official cognizance of an incident that he would certainly have preferred to overlook; insisting that he try the man for offenses against Jewish piety when as far as he was concerned Jewish piety could not have mattered less; and finally threatening to inform against him to his patron and emperor, Tiberius Caesar, if he did not yield to their pressure and have the man executed, which, of course, he finally did, although not before announcing first that as far as he was concerned the man was innocent, and then publicly washing his hands to symbolize his wish to disassociate himself personally from the whole dirty business. Let it be on the heads of the barbarians.

And then, on the day after the sentence had been carried out, when he might very reasonably have believed that at last the case could be considered closed for good, there they were back at him again — the same crowd of chief priests and Pharisees, still clamoring at him with their complaints and petitions. It is to Pilate's credit as both a Roman and a civil servant, I think, that he seems to have kept his words entirely free from any trace of irritation when with great economy he answered them by saying simply, "You have a guard of soldiers; go, make it as secure as you can." These are the words to consider.

Of all the great painters of the world, the one that I would choose to paint this scene is Rembrandt. I would want it done in chiaroscuro, in terms of light and shade, with the chamber where Pilate receives the delegation almost entirely in shadow and with the light coming mainly from the faces themselves, especially the bearded faces of the Jewish elders, the creased faces of these pious old men as they lean a little too intensely forward to hear the Roman's answer. What will he say? Then the helpless, old-man look when they are not quite sure that they have heard correctly as Pilate tells them in effect to do whatever they want to do. They have their own Temple guard, after all. "Make it as secure as you can," he tells them. This is precisely the moment for Rembrandt to paint: the venerable old men turning toward each other now, their faded old eyes wide with bewilderment, their mouths hanging loose — the kind of dazed, tremulous fear of old men suddenly called upon to do a young man's job. You are not sure whether to laugh or to cry. "As secure as you can," the Procurator of Judea tells them. But how secure is that? Their lips move, but no sound comes. God knows they have good reason to be afraid.

God knows. I think that we can say they have two reasons for being afraid, although they mentioned only one to Pilate, namely, that the dead man's disciples may, in the words of Matthew, "go and steal him away and tell the people, 'He has risen from the dead,'" in which case, they explain, "the last fraud will be worse than the first" — the first being the man's claim to have been the Messiah, the *Christos,* Christ. So their spoken fear is just that — the fear of a religious hoax. But as fears go, that is not such a terrible one, really, because in the not-so-long run religious hoaxes always tend to burn themselves out, as the chief priests and the Pharisees had good reason to know, living as they did in an age when would-be Messiahs were a dime a dozen, so much so that you had a hard time remembering even their names, let alone the wild rumors of miracle that circulated about them for a little while.

So, even if the disciples were successful in their theft of the body, and even if for a time their claim of resurrection flourished, it could not really flourish long without something more substantial than merely rumor to feed upon. The Jewish elders must have been perfectly aware of this, of course, yet they gave all the signs of being really very afraid anyway. In other words, beneath the fear that they spoke about to Pilate lay another fear that they had not spoken about to anyone probably, not even to each other. This was the fear which I doubt very much if any one of them had had the courage to face more than fleetingly even within the secrecy of his own heart — the fear that the man whom they had crucified would *really* come alive again as he had promised, that the body which now lay dead in its tomb, disfigured by the mutilations of the cross, that this body or some new and terrible version of it would start to breathe again, stand up in its grave clothes and move toward them with unspeakable power. To the extent that deep within themselves the Jewish elders feared this as a real possibility, their being told by Pilate to make things as secure as they could was to have the very earth pulled out from under them. How does an old man keep the sun from rising? How do soldiers secure the world against miracle?

Yet maybe it is not as hard as they feared. I suspect that many of us could have greatly reassured them. I suspect that many of us could tell them that all in all there is a lot one can do in defense against miracle, and, unless I badly miss my guess, there are thousands upon thousands of ministers doing precisely that at any given instant — making it as secure as they can, that is, which is really quite secure indeed. The technique of the chief priests and the Pharisees was to seal the tomb with a boulder and then to post a troop of guards to keep watch over it; but even for its time that was crude. The point is not to try to prevent the thing from happening — like trying to stop the wind with a machine gun — but, every time it happens, somehow to explain it away, to deflect it, defuse it, in one way or another to dispose of it. And there are at least as many ways of doing this as there are sermons preached on Easter Sunday.

We can say that the story of the resurrection means simply that the teachings of Jesus are immortal like the plays of Shakespeare or the music of Beethoven and that their wisdom and truth will live on forever. Or we can say that the resurrection means that the spirit of Jesus is undying, that he himself lives on among us, the way that Socrates does, for instance, in the good that he left behind him, in the lives of all who follow his great example. Or we can say that the language in which the Gospels describe the resurrection of Jesus is the language of poetry and that, as such, it is not to be taken literally but as pointing to a truth more profound than the literal. Very often, I think, this is the way that the Bible is written, and I would point to some of the stories about the birth of Jesus, for instance, as examples; but in the case of the resurrection, this simply does not apply because there really is no story about the resurrection in the New Testament. Except in the most fragmentary way, it is not described at all. There is no poetry about it. Instead, it is simply proclaimed as a fact. *Christ is risen!* In fact, the very existence of the New Testament itself proclaims it. Unless something very real indeed took place on that strange, confused morning, there would be no New Testament, no church, no Christianity.

Yet we try to reduce it to poetry anyway: the coming of spring with the return of life to the dead earth, the rebirth of hope in the despairing soul. We try to suggest that these are the miracles that the resurrection is all about, but they are not. In their way they are all miracles, but they are not this miracle, this central one to which the whole Christian faith points.

Unlike the chief priests and the Pharisees, who tried with soldiers and a great stone to make themselves as secure as they could against the terrible possibility of Christ's really rising again from the dead, we are considerably more subtle. We tend in our age to say, "Of course, it was bound to happen. Nothing could stop it." But when we are pressed to say what it was that actually did happen, what we are apt to come out with is something pretty meager: this "miracle" of truth that never dies, the "miracle" of a life so beautiful that two thousand years have left the memory of it undimmed, the "miracle" of doubt turning into faith, fear into hope. If I believed that this or something like this was all that the resurrection meant, then I would turn in my certificate of ordination and take up some other profession. Or at least I hope that I would have the courage to.

If I thought that when you strip it right down to the bone, this whole religion business is really just an affirmation of the human spirit, an affirmation of moral values, an affirmation of Jesus of Nazareth as the Great Exemplar of all time and no more, then like Pilate I would wash my hands of it. The human spirit just does not impress me that much, I am afraid. And I have never been able to get very excited one way or the other about moral values. And when I have the feeling that someone is trying to set me a good example, I start edging toward the door.

So what do I believe actually happened that morning on the third day after he died? When I was young, I would never have dreamed of asking a minister that question, not even if someone had offered to pay me; and I would have to know one quite well to ask now. Nobody has ever asked it of me, and I have been asked just about everything else. I do not mean some theological version of the question: what is the relevance of the resurrection to the doctrine of man or something. I mean the very straightforward, naked, somehow unmentionable thing itself: what do we think really happened? If you had been there yourself, what do you think you would really have seen?

One night I stood on the bridge of a small British freighter somewhere near the middle of the Atlantic. I was talking to a young junior officer with red hair who told me something that it is very useful to know. He had been looking around to see if he could spot the lights of any other ships on the horizon, and what he told me was this: the way to see lights on the horizon is not to look *at* the horizon but to look at the sky just above it. And I discovered that he was right. This is the way to do it. Since then I have learned that it is also the way to see other things.

I do not think that I would have looked straight at the tomb if I had been there, at the large boulder that they had rolled up to seal it with. I do not think that I could have even if I had wanted to, in that queer, seething light between night and daybreak when you cannot look long at anything before it begins to disappear. I would have looked just above it, or off to one side.

One of the guardsmen asleep on the ground, his helmet resting in the crook of one arm, his other arm flung out on the damp grass. He stirs in his sleep and murmurs something unintelligible. Then, lying there on his back in the dark, he suddenly opens his eyes: the fire of a billion stars.

Or the leaves of an olive tree, gray-green, unmoving in the still air. Nothing moves. Then, out of nowhere, a breeze comes up — stiff and fresh and smelling of the dawn: underneath, each olive leaf is the color of silver.

A voice is shouting, high and soft and from far away like the voice a child hears calling him home, at the end of a long summer dusk. The sound of running feet.

I cannot tell you anything more than this about what I think I would have seen if I had been there myself. No man can honestly. I do not believe that even the ones who actually were there could have told you more, if any were there and had stayed awake.

But I can tell you this: that what I believe happened and what in faith and with great joy I proclaim to you here is that he somehow *got up,* with life in him again, and the glory upon him. And I speak very plainly here, very unfancifully, even though I do not understand well my own language. I was not there to see it any more than I was awake to see the sun rise this morning, but I affirm it as surely as I do that by God's grace the sun did rise this morning because that is why the world is flooded with light.

He got up. He said, "Don't be afraid." Rich man, poor man, child; sick man, dying; man who cannot believe, scared sick man, lost one. Young man with your life ahead of you. "Don't be afraid."

He said, "Feed my sheep," which is why, like the chief priests and the Pharisees, we try to make that tomb as secure as we can. Because this is what he always says: "Feed my sheep . . . my lambs." And this is what we would make ourselves secure from, knowing the terrible needs of the lambs and our abundance, knowing our own terrible needs.

He said, "Lo, I am with you always, even unto the end of the world."

Anxiety and fear are what we know best in this fantastic century of ours. Wars and rumors of wars. From civilization itself to what seemed the most unalterable values of the past, everything is threatened or already in ruins. We have heard so much tragic news that when the news is good we cannot hear it.

But the proclamation of Easter Day is that all is well. And as a Christian, I say this not with the easy optimism of one who has never known a time when all was not well but as one who has faced the cross in all its obscenity as well as in all its glory, who has known one way or another what it is like to live separated from God. In the end, his will, not ours, is done. Love is the victor. Death is not the end. The end is life. His life and our lives through him, in him. Existence has greater depths of beauty, mystery, and benediction than the wildest visionary has ever dared to dream. Christ our Lord has risen.

For Further Reading

On the history of preaching, see Yngve Brilioth, *A Brief History of Preaching* (Philadelphia: Fortress, 1965); Dewitte T. Holland, *The Preaching Tradition: A Brief History* (Nashville: Abingdon, 1980); and Paul Scott Wilson, *A Concise History of Preaching* (Nashville: Abingdon, 1992).

For sermon collections, see the massive *20 Centuries of Great Preaching,* ed. Clyde E. Fant and William M. Pinson, 13 vols. (Waco, TX: Word, 1971), which contains sermons from the biblical period to Martin Luther King, Jr.

Andrew W. Blackwood's *The Protestant Pulpit: An Anthology of Master Sermons from the Reformation to Our Day* (Nashville: Abingdon-Cokesbury, 1947) offers classic examples of Protestant preaching through the centuries. For two helpful collections of contemporary sermons, see James Cox, ed., *The Twentieth Century Pulpit* (Nashville: Abingdon, 1978) and *The Twentieth Century Pulpit,* vol. 2 (Nashville: Abingdon, 1981).

J. Alfred Smith, Walter B. Hoard, and Milton E. Owens, eds., have collected African-American sermons in *Outstanding Black Sermons,* 3 vols. (Valley Forge, PA: Judson, 1976-1982). Another anthology of excellent African-American sermons is Samuel D. Proctor and William D. Watley [authors], *Sermons from the Black Pulpit* (Valley Forge, PA: Judson, 1984).

Outstanding sermons by women are collected in David A. Farmer and Edwina Hunter, eds., *And Blessed Is She: Sermons by Women* (San Francisco: Harper & Row, 1990), and Ellen Pearson Mitchell, ed., *Those Preachin' Women: Sermons by Black Women Preachers* (Valley Forge, PA: Judson, 1985).

Contributors

ELIZABETH RICE ACHTEMEIER is Adjunct Professor of Homiletics at Union Theological Seminary in Virginia. She has written many books and articles in the areas of preaching and Old Testament studies, including *Creative Preaching* and *Preaching as Theology and Art*.

JOANNA M. ADAMS is Senior Pastor of the Trinity Presbyterian Church in Atlanta. The author of a number of published articles and sermons, she is also a community activist for children's welfare.

KARL BARTH (1886-1968), perhaps the major theologian of the twentieth century, wrote the monumental *Church Dogmatics* and a great many other works. His lectures on preaching are gathered under the title *Homiletics*.

ALLAN A. BOESAK, a South African preacher and political activist, is a former president of the World Alliance of Reformed Churches, and a persistent leader in the fight for racial equality. He is author of *The Finger of God: Sermons on Faith and Socio-Political Responsibility; Comfort and Protest; If This Is Treason, I Am Guilty;* and other works.

FREDERICK BUECHNER is a Presbyterian minister and writer known both for his published sermons and also for his awardwinning essays and novels. Some of Buechner's sermons evolved from his chapel talks at Phillips Exeter Academy, where for a number of years he held the position of minister and teacher. Among his many books are *The Hungering Dark, The Magnificent Defeat, Godric, The Faces of Jesus, The Book of Bebb,* and *The Clown in the Belfrey*.

WALTER J. BURGHARDT, S.J., is Theologian-in-Residence at Georgetown University and Professor of Theology, Emeritus, at Catholic University of America in Washington. Besides several collections of homilies, he has published a homiletics textbook entitled *Preaching: The Art and the Craft*.

DAVID G. BUTTRICK is Professor of Homiletics and Liturgics at the Divinity School, Vanderbilt University. His books include *Homiletic: Moves and Structures, Preaching Jesus Christ*, and *The Mystery and the Passion: A Homiletic Reading of the Biblical Traditions*.

GEORGE A. BUTTRICK (1892-1980), a native of England, served as pastor of the Madison Avenue Presbyterian Church in New York City and as Minister to the University at Harvard. He also taught preaching at Union Theological Seminary in New York and at the Southern Baptist Theological Seminary in Louisville, Kentucky. Buttrick is the author of *Prayer, The Parables of Jesus*, and *Sermons Preached in a University Church*.

ERNEST T. CAMPBELL was pastor of the First Presbyterian Church of Ann Arbor, Michigan, and, from 1968 to 1976, of the Riverside Church in New York City. He has also held positions in the homiletics departments of Princeton Theological Seminary and Garrett–Evangelical Seminary. Campbell is the author of a number of books and articles, including a collection of his sermons, *Locked in a Room with Open Doors*.

JOHN R. CLAYPOOL, formerly a Southern Baptist minister, is now Rector of St. Luke's Episcopal Church in Birmingham, Alabama. Claypool is the author of *Tracks of a Fellow Struggler, The Preaching Event*, and *With Glad and Generous Hearts*.

WILLIAM SLOANE COFFIN, Presbyterian minister and social activist, served as chaplain at Yale University during the Vietnam war and succeeded Ernest Campbell as minister of the Riverside Church. Among Coffin's published works are the sermon collections *The Courage to Love* and *Living the Truth in a World of Illusions*.

FRED B. CRADDOCK was, until his retirement in 1993, the Bandy Professor of New Testament and Preaching at the Candler School of Theology, Emory University, Atlanta. He is the author of well-known works in the field of preaching, especially *As One Without Authority, Overhearing the Gospel*, and *Preaching*.

HERBERT O. EDWARDS, SR., has been minister of five Baptist churches and has taught at the University of Hartford, Harvard Divinity School, and Duke Divinity School. He is currently Acting Director of the Morgan Christian Center, and Professor of Religious Studies at Morgan State University in Baltimore.

AUSTIN FARRER (1904-1968) was Chaplain and Fellow of Trinity College, Oxford, and Warden of Keble College. He wrote prolifically in philosophy and theology and published several volumes of sermons, among them *The End of Man* and *A Celebration of Faith.*

ANNA CARTER FLORENCE is a doctoral student in homiletics at Princeton Theological Seminary. She has served as Associate Pastor of Westminster Presbyterian Church, Minneapolis, and has written *At the River's Edge.* Her sermons have appeared in *Sacred Strands* and in *Best Sermons 5.*

HARRY EMERSON FOSDICK (1878-1969), for more than forty years minister of the Riverside Church in New York, was during this period one of the best-known Protestant ministers in America. As preacher and as homiletics teacher at Union Theological Seminary, Fosdick influenced two generations of American preachers. Among the collections of his sermons are *Living Under Tension* and *A Great Time to Be Alive: Sermons on Christianity in Wartime.*

JOHN R. FRY, retired Presbyterian minister, author, and civil rights leader, has pastored churches in New York, Cincinnati, and Chicago; has held editorial positions with *Crossroads, Presbyterian Life,* and *Frying Pan;* and has published a number of sermons, articles, and books, including *The Trivialization of the Presbyterian Church* and *The Great Apostolic Blunder Machine.*

C. S. LEWIS (1898-1963) was a literary scholar at Oxford and Cambridge Universities who became famous for his children's works, especially the Chronicles of Narnia, for his space trilogy, and for his Christian theology and apologetics. Examples of the latter include *Mere Christianity, The Screwtape Letters, Surprised by Joy,* and *The Great Divorce.*

JÜRGEN MOLTMANN is Professor of Systematic Theology at the University of Tübingen, Germany. A significant voice in contemporary theology, Moltmann has published, among other works, *Theology of Hope, The Crucified God, The Trinity and the Kingdom,* and *God in Creation,* Moltmann's Gifford Lectures for 1984-85.

WILLIAM MUEHL, theologian, attorney, and politician, was for years the Clement Professor of Christian Methods at Yale Divinity School. He has written *The Road to Persuasion, All the Damned Angels,* and *Why Preach? Why Listen?,* his Beecher Lectures at Yale.

DOUGLAS E. NELSON (1913-1989) served Presbyterian pastorates in Pennsylvania and Texas before moving to New Haven, Connecticut, in 1954. From that time until he retired twenty-three years later, Nelson was minister of the First Presbyterian Church of New Haven, a congregation that always included a sizeable contingent of Yale University students. A number of Nelson's sermons are collected in *Is There Any Word from the Lord?*

EUGENE H. PETERSON served for more than twenty years as pastor of Christ Our King Presbyterian Church in Bel Air, Maryland, and is currently the James M. Houston Professor of Spiritual Theology at Regent College in Vancouver, British Columbia. Peterson has written a number of theological books, groups of sermons, and biblical commentaries, including *A Long Obedience in the Same Direction, Working the Angles,* and *Reversed Thunder.*

CHARLES L. RICE is Professor of Homiletics at the Theological and Graduate Schools of Drew University. Among his homiletical works are *Interpretation and Imagination: The Preacher and Contemporary Literature; The Embodied Word: Preaching as Art and Liturgy;* and the pioneering textbook *Preaching the Story* (with Edmund Steimle and Morris J. Niedenthal).

FRIEDRICH SCHLEIERMACHER (1768-1834), often judged to be the greatest theologian between the Reformation and the twentieth century, was a translator of Plato, a pastor as well as a theologian, and the author, among other works, of *The Christian Faith* and *Religion: Speeches to Its Cultured Despisers.*

LEWIS B. SMEDES, a minister of the Christian Reformed Church in North America, was Professor of Religion and Theology at Calvin College and an editor of *The Reformed Journal.* Now Professor of Integrative Studies in the Graduate School of Psychology at Fuller Theological Seminary, Smedes is the author of such books as *All Things Made New, Mere Morality, Love Within Limits, Forgive and Forget,* and *A Pretty Good Person.*

EDMUND A. STEIMLE (1907-1988) was a Lutheran minister and, for many years, Brown Professor of Homiletics at Union Theological Seminary in New York. He was especially well known for his radio sermons on the Lutheran Series of "The Protestant Hour." Among his books are *Disturbed by Joy, God the Stranger,* and *Preaching the Story* (with Charles Rice and Morris Niedenthal).

BARBARA BROWN TAYLOR is Rector of Grace-Calvary Episcopal Church in Clarkesville, Georgia. She received the Polly Bond Award for Excellence in Broadcasting in 1990 for her Episcopal Series of radio sermons on "The Protestant Hour." She is the author of *Mixed Blessings, The Seeds of Heaven*, and *The Preaching Life*.

GARDNER C. TAYLOR, pastor of the Concord Baptist Church in Brooklyn for more than forty years, is now Adjunct Professor of Preaching at Princeton Theological Seminary. In 1975, Taylor delivered the Beecher Lectures in Preaching at Yale Divinity School, subsequently published as *How Shall They Preach?*

SUSAN PLOCHER THOMAS is pastor of University Lutheran Church, Cambridge, Massachusetts, and coauthor of *Excellent Words*, a worship resource.

PAUL TILLICH (1886-1965), the other giant theologian of the twentieth century (with Karl Barth), was dismissed from his German university post in 1933 for his opposition to Hitler. The same year, Tillich moved to the United States and began a distinguished sequence of theological professorships at Union Theological Seminary in New York, Harvard University, and the University of Chicago. His works include the classic three-volume *Systematic Theology* and several collections of sermons, including *The Shaking of the Foundations, The New Being*, and *The Eternal Now*.

JOHN TIMMER, a minister of the Christian Reformed Church in North America, has been a Christian missionary in Japan and pastor of churches in New Jersey and Michigan. Now senior minister of Woodlawn Christian Reformed Church, Grand Rapids, Timmer is the author of a number of articles and of such books as *God of Weakness* and *Once Upon a Time*.

JOHN VANNORSDALL, a Lutheran minister and the former president of Lutheran Theological Seminary, Philadelphia, has also been chaplain at Yale University and preacher on the Lutheran Series of "The Protestant Hour" radio program. Vannorsdall is the author of *Dimly Burning Wicks: Reflections on the Gospel After a Time Away*.

WILLIAM H. WILLIMON, former pastor of several Methodist congregations, is Dean of the Chapel and Professor of Christian Ministry at Duke University. Willimon is the author of *Sighing for Eden, Worship as Pastoral Care*, and (with Stanley Hauerwas) *Resident Aliens*, as well as of numerous essays and published sermons.